THE MOON LOOKS ON THEM ALL

All rights reserved. No part of this work covered by the copyright herein may be reproduced or used in any means – graphic, electronic, or mechanical, including copying, recording, taping, or information storage and retrieval systems – without written permission of the publisher.

Printed by ImprintDigital
Upton Pyne, Exeter
www.imprintdigital.com

Typesetting and cover design by The Book Typesetters
hello@thebooktypesetters.com
07422 598 168
www.thebooktypesetters.com

Published by Greenwich Exchange

First published 2024
© Copyright: John Lucas
© Cover image: Pauline Lucas

The moral right of the author has been asserted.

ISBN 978-1-910996-83-6

THE MOON LOOKS ON THEM ALL
of friends and friendship

JOHN LUCAS

> Ye are the salt of the earth.
> – *The Gospel according to St. Matthew, ch. 6, v. 13*

> Now north and south and east and west
> Those I love lie down to rest;
>   The moon looks on them all,
> The healers and the brilliant talkers,
> The eccentrics and the silent walkers,
>   The dumpy and the tall.
>   – *W.H. Auden*, 'A Summer Night'

To the memory of Nigel Lucas

CONTENTS

Preface   11

THE MOON LOOKS ON THEM ALL

Anne	17
Ted	44
The Death of "Sheffield Tommy" Burton	63
Bas	66
Barry	89
Our Cat	115
A Wish	123
Letting Go	124
Arnold	126
Olive	169
Cloughie	193
What Holds Them	218
An Irregular Ode on the Retirement of Derek Randall, Cricketer	219
Lol	221
As a Rule	248
Letters of Introduction: Matt and Gael	250
Paul	270
E.M. Forster: An Enabling Modesty	284
Acknowledgements	314

Preface

THE TITLE FOR THE FOLLOWING COLLECTION of essays was prompted in the course of a conversation I had with my friend, the poet and publisher, Anthony Rudolf, in London during the summer of 2022. What was I working on at the moment, Tony asked. I told him that I was considering whether I might put together some pieces on people who during my life have meant much to me, not because they are or were ever famous, although two certainly were, but because in their different ways I thought and still think of them as men and women who embodied or testified to qualities that made them worth cherishing, made them memorable for all the right reasons. Good people.

'Oh, you mean salters,' Tony said.

For a mad moment I thought he was referring to psalters. But I wasn't planning to write any kind of sacred book. 'Salt of the earth,' Tony added, perhaps wanting to clear up any confusion. 'Yes,' I said, 'that's it, although I don't suppose anyone still uses the phrase.' And I found coming into my head a remark of E.M. Forster's, one he uses in his essay, 'What I Believe'. Throughout my life, at all events since I first read *A Room With A View*, Forster has been a kind of touchstone for me. That wispy, apparently inconsequential championing of the private spirit, that refusal to be grand or to adopt a public stance; and yet the implacable belief in the worth of individuality, the refusal to bend the knee to public avowal, to grand utterance. At a late moment in 'What I Believe', which I first encountered at the very beginning of the 1960s when he recorded it as one side of an Argo LP, Forster speaks up for what he calls the aristocracy of the 'plucky, the considerate, and the sensitive'. The what? The words seemed absurd, an at best whimsical, fey tribute to values which, given that the essay was written in 1938 and then, with slight alterations, made into a BBC broadcast the following year when Hitler's Germany was threatening Europe and beyond, were surely beside the point, almost ridiculous. Oppose Fascism with pluck and sensitivity? As Larkin might have said, 'In a pig's arse, friend'.

But still. Forster's voice, and his use of a vocabulary which draws on the chatty, the knowingly unofficial, speaking as it does of the need not to be 'rattled', is also one that speaks up for values which are close to or in sympathy with those of 'salters'. Not that, at all events as far as I know, Forster himself ever used the word. But as Tony and I talked over lunch and a glass of wine, and recalling 'What I Believe', it occurred to me to imagine that Forster, or his Shade, might not mind my attaching the term 'Salters' to the kind of people he values and whom, he says, you can find 'knocking about' in all areas of society. Why, given enough of them, you might even find yourself welcoming into existence the kind of society Forster most values, and which he refers to as 'Love, the beloved Republic'.

In my end is my beginning. I am a democratic socialist, whereas Forster called himself a Liberal. But for all that, he has always meant much to me. This is why the final essay in the present collection, focussing on what I call Forster's 'enabling modesty', reprints a talk given at a Conference held at the University of Birmingham, the papers from which were gathered together as 'Revolving Commitments: France and Britain 1929-1950' in 2008. (Cambridge Scholars Publishing) If I'd thought of it at the time I was writing the essay, I might even have called it 'In Praise of Salters', which, for a while, I thought of giving to the present collection. In the end, however, I decided to settle for a different title, *The Moon Looks On Them All*, which comes from Auden's 'A Summer Night', a poem celebrating friends and friendship, lines from which provide one of the collection's two epigraphs. The other is, inevitably, from the King James' version of the New Testament of the Gospel of St. Matthew.

The Moon Looks On Them All

Anne

THE FOLLOWING ESSAY, '"MAKING POETRY": THE Exemplary Anne Stevenson', was written for a collection called *Critical Essays on Anne Stevenson*, edited by Angela Leighton, and published in 2010 by Liverpool University Press. Seven years earlier, and with help from Peter Lucas and Matt Simpson, I had put together a festschrift to celebrate the poet's seventieth birthday. *How You Say The World* (Shoestring Press, 2003). Earlier still, in the pages of the *TLS*, I had laid into a collection of essays offering to report on the more important poets to emerge in the 1960s and 1970s in which there was no mention of either Anne or of Derek Mahon, even though the latter's 'A Disused Shed in Co. Wexford' had already appeared; and if *that* isn't a poem to define our age then I don't know what is.

When I wrote the *TLS* review essay, I wasn't personally acquainted with either poet, but as it happened I met both not long afterward, Mahon in London, Anne at Loughborough where I'd invited her to read her poems to the University's Literary Society. She arrived by car, having been driven down from Durham by the man with whom she was then living, a gentle soul obviously in awe of her and certainly not destined for a long-term partnership with a poet I soon came to realise was, for all her appearance of trim containment, fiery-souled and inclined to restlessness. By the time she came to Loughborough, Anne had already left two marriages; and in addition there had, I learned, been several liaisons, including a stormy affair with the poet, Philip Hobsbaum, during the brief time she lived in Glasgow. I've forgotten how she came to be there – a Poetry Fellowship, perhaps? – but I do know that she had previously lived in London, Cambridge, and Oxford, and that after Glasgow she was for some years helping to run the poetry bookshop at Hay-on-Wye, where her then partner was also a poet. A bad idea, that, for two poets to marry each other.

Her Loughborough reading was a fine occasion. Her voice was clear, each word exactly pronounced and at the same time resonant with an unmistakable musical inflection that must, I suppose, have owed something to her early years of studying to become a cellist, though by the time I came to know her well those years were long behind her, and signs of deafness had begun to plague her. But she was, as she always remained, a vivid conversationalist, one who delighted in stirring the pot of controversy.

She was lucky in finding in Peter Lucas – no relation – a good man who loved her, esteemed her, and acted as an unfailingly soothing spirit when, as so often, she was stirred to at least momentary fury by what she took to be unearned praise for poets W or X, or the scanting of work by poets Y Z. At such times, especially if a group of us were gathered at dinner round a table, she would clench her fists, lean forward, and deliver a scornful denunciation of whoever had had the temerity to over- or under-valuate whichever poet's work was being discussed. And she would then look around her, attending to each of us in turn, chin jutting forward, eyes gleaming with a kind of fiery joy.

For a while she took to sending me drafts of poems she was working on, asking for my comments. But any suggestion that a word or phrase be amended, no matter how tentatively offered, was met with an explosive response, and though the next day's post would bring a conciliatory letter, even an acknowledgement that perhaps one or two of my suggestions were worth considering, it was all a bit fraught. I suggested to Matt Simpson, a poet I had introduced to Anne, and one who had become a friend of hers, that he might be better at coping with her pieces of paper gelignite, and Matt said that he'd be happy to look at drafts of any poems she might like to send him. Anne having agreed to this proposal, drafts of poems were despatched from Durham to Liverpool, Matt read and returned them with his comments, and a few days later phoned me to say that he was thinking of buying a tin hat to protect him from the flaming arrows from the north that had been aimed at his head. But of course arrows were followed by salves, so Matt stuck to his task.

The fact is that for all her occasional furious outbursts, Anne was quick to make amends, and to insist that friendship with those she valued wasn't, she hoped, at stake. Nor was it. I loved her, as did Matt. And at her home in Durham, as well as at the cottage in North Wales which Peter had inherited from his mother and where he was a reliably calming, reassuring presence, she took pleasure in her flair for rustling up excellent meals and in bringing guests together to eat, drink, and talk.

Ah, Peter. They had, I think, met, probably through mutual friends in Cambridge, where Anne, whose first husband had connections, would go to meet other poets and literary figures, and where Peter, who had been born into the family which included F.L. Lucas, whose nephew he was, became from early years fascinated by, and then deeply knowledgeable about, 19th-century evolutionary science and especially the life and work of Charles Darwin. With his large blue eyes, tousled hair, slightly unkempt appearance and customarily baggy corduroys, Peter sometimes gave the impression of being not so much a mad as an unworldly scientist; but his unruffled, calming manner and steady, mellifluous voice acted as ideal counterpoint for Anne's air and fire. He was the steadying presence *par excellence*, and they seemed to go everywhere together, by train, by aeroplane, and by motor vehicle, which in his case was a four-wheel drive which he steered with a not-to-be-flustered authority around the rough terrain of North Wales where his cottage stood.

Peter loved Anne, was devoted to her, dazzled a little, as we all were, by her mercurial brilliance, and when she died I suspect he could see no great merit in life without her. At all events, I know that I wasn't greatly surprised to learn that a few months after Anne's death, in mid-September 2020, Peter, too, had died. I was out of the country at the times of their deaths, but their presences are with me still.

'"Making Poetry": The Exemplary Anne Stevenson'

> Lying awake in a provincial town
> I think about poets. They are mostly
> men or Irish, turn out old yellow
> photographs, may use four-letter words,
> stick pigs or marry twice, and edit
> most of the books and magazines.[1]

THIS, THE OPENING STANZA OF ELIZABETH Bartlett's poem, 'Stretchmarks', comes from her collection *The Czar Is Dead*, published in 1986, which seems a bit late to be complaining. In the bibliography at the back of *Consorting with Angels: Essays on Modern Women Poets*, Deryn Rees-Jones lists nearly 150 'collections of poetry by women which appeared during the 1980s, and although a few were editions of dead poets, and some neither lived nor

---

[1] Elizabeth Bartlett, 'Stretchmarks', in *The Czar Is Dead* (London: Rivelin Grapheme Press, 1986), quoted in *Modern Women Poets: A Companion Anthology*, ed. Deryn Rees-Jones (Tarset: Bloodaxe Books, 2005), p. 121.

worked in the UK, they were all published here.'[2] Two decades earlier matters were very different. A. Alvarez notoriously excluded women from the twenty poets featured in his 1962 anthology, *The New Poetry*.[3] True, he added Sylvia Plath to the revised and enlarged second edition, because her late poems, not published when he first went to press, fitted in with his prescription for the new seriousness, whereas her first collection, *The Colossus*, published in 1959, did not. But Rees-Jones' persuasive account of the title poem of that collection implicitly shows not only how inadequate Alvarez' response was, but why it was likely to be so. 'As a poem that enacts mourning,' Rees-Jones writes, '"The Colossus" deals with the loss of a literally small pre-adolescent self and both the loss of the father and the phallus, a necessary act if self-integration is to be achieved.'[4] The new seriousness Alvarez wanted to promote was indifferent to such matters. Even when he praises Plath's first collection, as he does in the piece he wrote by way of introducing her last poems to *The Review*, he claims that 'Throughout *The Colossus* she is using her art to keep the disturbance, out of which she made her verse, at a distance … The *real* poems began in

---

[2] Deryn Rees-Jones, *Consorting with Angels: Essays on Modern Women Poets* (Tarset: Bloodaxe Books, 2005), pp. 271–76.

[3] A. Alvarez (ed.), *The New Poetry* (Harmondsworth: Penguin, 1962).

[4] Rees-Jones, *Consorting with Angels*, p. 276.

1960, after the birth of her daughter, Frieda.'⁵

Nobody would deny that the poems that make up *Ariel* are greater than those in the earlier collection, but to rule *The Colossus* out of consideration for an anthology that includes work by at least half-a-dozen obviously inferior poets seems perverse. In the first place, and as Rees-Jones argues, Plath was *not* keeping disturbance at a distance. In the second, Alvarez is asking for a kind of programmatic engagement with violence and suffering the prescriptiveness of which comes close to dangerous simplification, not least in its scanting of 'mere' craft.

All this is familiar enough, and I draw attention to it only because the evidence suggests that English women poets, especially younger ones, at the time felt themselves to be trapped by the seeming alternatives of 'craft' versus 'disturbance', to put it crudely. Hence, the following passage from Mairi MacInnes' memoir, *Clearances*, where she records her experience of meeting John Wain, either early in the 1950s or at the tail end of the 1940s, and of reading his poems:

> [there were no] poems of feeling, except elegies for feeling. There were poems in tight form, tightly controlled, the resonance kept within bounds. He wasn't describing emotion, like me, nor the events that produced emotion ... The sell in the poems was the presentation, the intricate rhymes. He knew what he was doing, which I did not, when I thought about

---

⁵ *The Review*, no. 9 (October 1963), p. 21.

it. If I didn't think about it, sometimes I came near poetry ... I was looking for the very essence of poetry, he was not, he was after the craft ... What drove him to poetry? The desire for fame, mostly, and the belief that he was extremely clever at poetry, and the desire to reform the present state of letters, wrecked by the excesses of Dylan Thomas. He admired William Empson's knotty poems and the slight, graceful efforts of Robert Graves.[6]

To be fair to Wain, he was not by any means as hostile to Thomas as were Kingsley Amis and others who made contributions to Robert Conquest's anthology, *New Lines* (1956); and to be fair to Graves, his best poems, while certainly 'graceful', cannot be dismissed as 'slight'. But that said, MacInnes' charge is pretty well on the button. Wain in 1950 had written the first, and perhaps still the best, essay on Empson's poetry: 'Ambiguous Gifts' appeared in the last issue of Penguin New Writing. His own first full collection, published in 1956, takes its title, *Word Carved on a Sill*, from Graves' poem 'End of Play': 'Yet love survives, the word carved on a sill/Under the antique dread of the headsman's axe'. As Alvarez was one of those who for a while had been under Wain's considerable influence, *The New Poetry* has to be seen as, at least in part, his public renunciation of that influence. Hence the comparison he

---

[6] Mairi MacInnes, *Clearances: A Memoir* (Nottingham: Shoestring Press, 2007), p. 106. The book was first published in the USA by Pantheon Books, 2002.

famously makes in his Introduction between Larkin's 'At Grass' and Ted Hughes' 'A Dream of Horses', the one beautiful but, damningly, 'unpretentious' (for which read unambitious), the other an attempt to deal with 'a powerful complex of emotions and sensations'.[7]

A year after *The New Poetry* was published, two collections of poetry by young women poets appeared, which between them exemplify the terms of the debate between what, for the sake of shorthand convenience, I will call 'craft' and 'essence'. (The only other collection by a British woman poet to appear in 1963 was the fifty-one-year-old Anne Ridler's *Who Is My Neighbour; and How Bitter the Bread*.) Patricia Beer's *The Survivors* is Gravesian, while the impulse behind Rosemary Tonks' *Notes on Cafés and Bedrooms* is apparent from her introductory words: 'My ethos is a great European metropolis; I want to show human passion at work and to give eternal forces their contemporary dimension in this landscape.' It is difficult to read this credo, printed on the fly leaf of Tonks' handsomely produced hardback, without thinking that she is either heavily under the influence of the Introduction to *The New Poetry*, or at all events wants her readers to think that she is. Beer is the more skilful writer by far. On the other hand, I certainly think, *mutatis mutandis*, that you could apply to *The Survivors* the words Alvarez used of *The Colossus*: it uses art to keep disturbance at a distance.

Take, for example, 'New Year', which begins 'Now I am

---

[7] Alvarez, *The New Poetry*, pp. 26–27.

got with child in this raw weather', and ends with:

> But this set of facts makes me a true rarity,
> Proud as a leper with my unique disease. Wild
> In the Winter solstice rages the delicate child
> Entrusted to the new year, and to my charity.[8]

The cool web of the poem's language does not so much wind us in as spread a foreboding shroud across any possible entry. Both in mode (the teasing fable) and its almost marmoreal, chiselled metrics, it is a very Gravesian exercise. The child is presumably a metaphor for the making of poetry – a process that cannot be disclosed, though it is to be celebrated. 'Proud as a leper with my unique disease' – I doubt that any leper was proud of his disease but, following Edmund Wilson's famous interpretation of Philoctetes and his suppurating wound as a myth of the poet cast out from, but necessary to, and so recalled by society, you could hardly turn a corner in 1960s England without bumping into someone claiming to be a writer and therefore keen to show you his wound.

Under its modest, unrufflable surface, Beer's poem is making a large claim. This duckling is in fact a flying swan. But, skill in handling the stanza aside – and I certainly don't want to belittle that – there is little to make you feel that the claim is justified. When in the title poem of the same collection Beer writes that she will praise the women

---

[8] Patricia Beer, *The Survivors* (London: Longmans, 1963), p. 31.

who do not die as tragic heroines, but who 'sucked blood from dust,/Not for the joy but for the habit of life,/Sanctified, the survivors',[9] I want to protest that the terms are overloaded and the praise little more than an empty gesture. The poem stops where it should start. Who *are* these survivors? Why not tell us something about them? The answer, I suspect, is that the poem's moral is to be affirmed, not within the poem itself, but by an implicit appeal to those arbiters of taste whom Beer is anxious to appease or be approved by: the Gravesians.

Tonks is more open in her claims, and more ambitious. Here are the first and last stanzas of 'The Flâneur and the Apocalypse':

For his inebriated tread, the whole of Europe
With its great streets full of air and shade,
Its students and cocottes,
And traffic, roughly caked with blood …

…

Is not mysterious enough for his infatuated tread!
The Furies are modern, they don't drive you they entice
With cafés, lovers, dusty streets … with the Apocalypse
Not this one – but the *next*,' they hiss.[10]

---

[9] Beer, *The Survivors*, p. 1.
[10] Rosemary Tonks, *Notes on Cafés and Bedrooms* (London: Putnam, 1963), p. 14.

Confronted with this, most readers are likely to be thankful that *Notes on Cafés and Bedrooms* runs to no more than twenty-five pages. Yet a glance at the Acknowledgements shows that Tonks' work appeared in the pages of a number of prestigious journals, including the *Transatlantic Review*, the *London Magazine*, the *Times Literary Supplement*, the *New Statesman* and *Encounter*, and her book gained a Poetry Recommendation. Tonks was clearly thought to be doing something right. In a charitable introductory note to the three poems included in *Modern Women Poets*, Rees-Jones quotes Tonks as follows:

> 'Ideally, whatever is heightened should be justified both by art and by life; while the poet remains vulnerable to those moments when a poem suddenly makes its own terms – and with an overwhelming force that is self-justifying … Telling the truth about feeling requires prodigious integrity … Some poets do manage to converge on their inner life by generating emotion from an inspired visual imagery.'[11]

There is no reason to doubt Tonks' sincerity. She really *did* want to converge on her inner life, and her later decision to embrace Evangelical Christianity; which entailed a repudiation of all her writing – she had published novels as well as poetry – was a decision to live by faith, the light of which inevitably exposed 'what a lying lot the

---

[11] Rees-Jones, *Modern Women Poets*, p. 171.

writers are'. As Peter Porter puts it in the poem which bears that title, 'people make metaphysics out of this' – 'this' being not merely the gap between life and art but the endless speculation about the possibilities of bridging it. Tonks hoped that poetry, her poetry, might be such a bridge, but, harried by Alvarez' imperatives and supplied with a charivari of borrowings from Edith Sitwell, Dylan Thomas and French symbolists, she got very little way beyond some arresting phrases and lines, which was hardly enough to realise the ambitious project she had in mind.

***

Meanwhile, in 1961, a young American woman poet, new to England, was writing a poem that might at first reading be thought to warrant a title very similar to *Notes on Cafés and Bedrooms*, although it is not about 'a great European metropolis' but about the American town, where she had for some time lived. Anne Stevenson's 'Ann Arbor' contains within parentheses its subtitle '(A Profile)', which teasingly suggests both a sideways glance and a biographical sketch or character study. That 'Profile' is at once a disclaimer – only an outline – and a more assertive suggestion of proffered insights. The poem begins:

> Neither city nor town, its location,
> even, is ambiguous.
> of North and East and Middlewest it is
> and is not; in every sense,

a hopeless candidate for the picturesque.
Trees and a few grand accidentally preserved
eyesores save it from total suburbanisation,
give it the mildly authentic complexion
of secondhand furniture.[12]

To say that much of Stevenson's poetry is made out of her being never entirely at home in any one location is a commonplace. But then this is a characteristic of many modern and contemporary poets, for whom the big words like 'displacement' and 'alienation', with their emotional under-swell of anger, contempt and, of course, yearning for the lost great good place, are regularly recruited. Such words won't at all do in trying to account for the unique tone Stevenson brings to this poem, which is far more quizzical, amused, and largely tolerant, as well as engaged, though the engagement is for the most part that of the active mind fed by the eager, speculative eye. ('Speculative' here has to be cleansed of its connection to abstract theory: it is what the *OED* defines as 'looking, gazing, inspecting closely'.) You could, perhaps, complain that there is something a bit condescending about the stance towards the place in 'Ann Arbor':

Love is frequently experienced over
jugs of California claret, politics are important,

---

[12] Anne Stevenson, *Poems 1955–2005* (Tarset: Bloodaxe Books, 2005), pp. 32–33. Henceforth cited in the text.

and culture so cheap and convenient
that every evening you expect thin strains of Mozart
to issue from half a dozen windows.

(p. 33)

Happy the place, I say, where culture is cheap and convenient, if that means ready access to books, paintings and music; and why should such convenience render Mozart strains as 'thin'?

But leaving that aside, the point to make about this poem is that it is so much more adroit than anything to be found in either Beer or Tonks, even though its guise of modest informality, of not making a fuss about poetry, allows Stevenson not to capitalise the initial letters of her lines and apparently to produce a mere sketch, a profile. But 'Ann Arbor' has a rhythmic sure-footedness as well as a flexibility which are incomparably superior to those English poets, so that although the poem seems 'mere' notation, it is formally adroit in a manner they are not, Beer because she is constrained by top-table manners, Tonks because she mistakes letting fly for flexibility. By contrast, Stevenson is not bothered by the choices the English poets thought open to them; she is not playing to an audience. Hence, the unpatterned but detectable near-rhymes – more, perhaps, a matter of consonance (location/suburbanisation/complexion, important/convenient); hence, the internal sound links, and hence, too, the wit. This is not merely a matter of phrasing, but of line breaks used to undercut or qualify apparently, unguarded statements: 'a few grand accidentally preserved/eyesores', or, most tellingly, 'Of North and East and Middlewest it is/and is not'. 'A serious house on serious earth it is' – I have no idea whether Larkin's affirmative pentameter was somewhere in Stevenson's mind when she was at work on her poem, but the effect of her enjambment is wittily to undo the claim to authority her iambics have set up. The result is that an attentive reader can take delight in the care with which this poem is being made. It is not pleading with the reader to notice its affiliations with any fashion or prevailing orthodoxy. Its attention is instead fixed on being answerable to one thing alone: the making of the poem itself.

In this context Stevenson's use of polysyllabic words deserves some mention. In spite of Pope's warning against slavish obedience to monosyllabic utterance – 'And ten low words oft creep in one dull line' – there was in 1950s and '60s England an orthodoxy, as for that matter there still is, according to which the English language, being basically monosyllabic, requires that in the interests of strength and authority as many words as possible should be crammed into a single line, especially an iambic line. Pope himself seemed on occasions unsure about the advisability of permitting polysyllabic words much space. In his Second Epistle, 'Of the Characters of Women', which begins with the statement, 'Nothing so true as what you once let fall,/ Most women have no characters at all' (one trisyallable, two disyllables, thirteen monosyllables), he writes 'Ladies, like variegated Tulips, show,/'Tis to their Changes that their charms they owe'. '[V]ariegated Tulips' dominate the hemi-distich with their seven lovely, buoyant syllables. But order is restored in the next line with the judgement on flowers that alter their colours season by season. No character there.

It is impossible to read early Stevenson without sensing that her use of polysyllabic words involves a rejection, or at any rate a discounting, of metric exactitude, of regular and repeated stress patterns; and in this respect, as in others, her reading of Elizabeth Bishop must have been wonderfully enabling. One can, of course, feel Bishop's presence behind 'Ann Arbor', as one can feel it behind many poems by Stevenson, although this is not to imply that such poems are derivative – just as to say that Larkin took a good deal from Louis MacNeice is not to make 'Large Cool Store' derivative of such poems as 'Birmingham' or 'Sunday Morning'. It is more that in each case the senior poet sprang a latch which freed the younger one to explore new territory.

However, there is one important respect in which Bishop could not help. 'A woman's life is her own/until it is taken away/by a first particular cry' (p. 124), Stevenson writes in 'Poem for a Daughter', a recollection of childbirth which is explored in detail in 'The Spirit Is Too Blunt an Instrument' (p. 122). This early masterpiece about becoming a mother is also a declaration about being a poet, of achieving poetry. Of course, these things could be said about several key poems in *Ariel*, but Stevenson is very different. The poem's twenty-seven lines are made of such 'intricate/exacting particulars' that fully to account for them would, I sometimes think, take a whole book:

> The spirit is too blunt an instrument
> to have made this baby.
> Nothing so unskilful as human passions
> could have managed the intricate
> exacting particulars: the tiny
> blind bones with their manipulating tendons,
> the knee and the knucklebones, the resilient
> fine meshings of ganglia and vertebrae,
> the chain of the difficult spine.
>
> Observe the distinct eyelashes and sharp crescent
> fingernails, the shell-like complexity
> of the ear, with its firm involutions
> concentric in miniature to minute
> ossicles. Imagine the
> infinitesimal capillaries, the flawless connections
> of the lungs, the invisible neural filaments
> through which the completed body
> already answers to the brain.
>
> Then name any passion or sentiment
> possessed of the simplest accuracy.
> No, no desire or affection could have done
> with practice what habit
> has done perfectly, indifferently,
> through the body's ignorant precision.

It is left to the vagaries of the mind to invent
love and despair and anxiety
and their pain.

There is a tangled complex of responses here, of love and, in the first verse paragraph especially, of apprehension. The particulars are, after all, not so much 'exact' as 'exacting', hence the deep, searching puns on 'manipulating tendons' and 'difficult spine', and these are connected to the exploratory mapping of a body, one that through awkward, even rebarbative consonants – made, managed, manipulating, meshings – acknowledges the irreducible, stubborn reality of this separate being: its blind bones – a wonderful moment of synaesthesia – knee and knucklebones, ganglia and vertebrae. These near-paratactic phrases almost bizarrely establish links between disconnected parts of the body, and they also suggest or perform a troubled apprehension which displaces any simple feeling of delight, let alone wonderment. This is unsettling, but necessarily so. In its absolute attentiveness to what might be called the to-fro movement of an observing, experiencing consciousness, the opening paragraph makes clear that it will not evade the complex of feelings through which that consciousness discovers itself.

In the middle verse paragraph there is a shift. The command to 'Observe' is far less an invocation to the reader than a call to attention to the mother who is also the poet. Accurate, detailed observation is a quality Stevenson brings to her many bird poems, and this guarantees their unsentimental regard for the natural world – as in, to take one example, the tart, comic but unflinty *'Phoenicurus phoenicurus'*, which ends *'Phu-eet,* a more and more panicky piping, *phu-eett!/*And not meaning anything I mean. In the grammar of *tweet/*why did we ever say birds should sound *sweet, sweet?'* (p. 73). No anthropomorphism here. If the poem has all the attentiveness to its subject that John Clare could wish, its refusal to accommodate the natural to the human is nevertheless in accord with Darwin's reporting, for instance, on the habits of the pepsis wasp. But in 'The Spirit…' there is necessarily a closing gap between observer and observed, given the intimate and therefore complicating link between them; and this is further complicated by the fact that the observer is a poet as well as a mother. Both are required to take careful note of the phenomena which make up a separate life. There is a Darwinian scrupulousness about this engagement, this seeing-as-recording-as-knowing, which, while it is in some ways reminiscent of Bishop and, behind her, Marianne Moore, has its own musicality, its own signature. One can hear it in the linked sounds in which the stubborn consonants of the first paragraph are replaced by the short 'i' that threads together the words – distinct, involutions, concentric, miniature, imagine, infinitesimal capillaries, invisible, filaments; and the 'f' in fingernails, firm, infinitesimal, filaments, is altogether lighter, breathes more easily, than anything in the preceding paragraph. As a result, 'the completed body/already answers to the brain' achieves its effectiveness as statement because of the intricately woven strands of sound that precede this requirement to observe.

The challenge thrown out at the beginning of the third paragraph is, however, not wholly turned inwards. It is more a rebuke to, an impatience with, conventional pieties. The body's 'ignorant precision' has made this baby, though the 'vagaries of the mind' will certainly invent things of the spirit: those comparatively blunt, imprecise emotions by which we live and which, now, are directed by the mother to the child her body has created. The rebuke, the voiced impatience, is audible in the repeated plosives: passion, possessed, practice, perfectly, precision and, at the very last, pain. But 'pain', ending the poem's final short line, reverses the rebuke; or rather, it accepts human consciousness as equally a way of making. '[L]ove and despair and anxiety/and their pain' acknowledges with an exquisite adjustment of tone, one that hovers between the plaintive and the wry, that the burden a mother carries is not, cannot be, merely of the body. If it were, there could be no poem. And although I do not want to be precious about this, it is worth noting that 'burden' means both a physical weight and the under-song of a melody. By the end of this extraordinary poem the baby's presence has, then, become known through a double act of making.

Stevenson is justly praised for her sceptical, questioning, teasing ruminations on the mind-body dualities, and 'The Spirit is Too Blunt an Instrument', its witty title at once raising questions and, who knows, hackles, is perhaps the earliest example, of just how intelligently this poet engages with the issues such dualities prompt. But this is to risk making her sound aridly cerebral, whereas her poems delight in the play of ideas. Take, for example, 'Trinity at Low Tide', which at first seems an innocuous enough anecdote about walking along the seashore, 'Sole to sole with your reflection/on the glassy beach,/your shadow gliding beside you' (p. 273).[13] But 'sole' is at once a pun and yet a renunciation of the word with which it puns aurally. The end of the second, last stanza, deepens the tone: 'All blame is packed into that black, featureless/third trick of light that copies you/and cancels you'. Just as the poem's title refuses to have any truck with the three-in-one God, so this last line rejects the mystery of Emmaus. Such an ending, seemingly casual, sardonic, abruptly snapping off the 'trick of light', shows what poetry *as poetry* can do.

As for 'The Spirit Is Too Blunt an Instrument', its precise, informed vocabulary demonstrates a remarkable ability to link words on threads of sound that are the more alluring because they are not dependent on a boot-heavy metric thump. And this has much to do with the number of polysyllabic terms the poem uses, terms that float on the ear rather than invade it with leaden insistence. Most trisyllabic words are either dactyl or amphibrach, and no matter where they occur in a line this means that they end

---

[13] Anne Stevenson, 'Trinity at Low Tide', *Voyages Over Voices*, ed. Angela Leighton (Liverpool: Liverpool University Press, 2010), pp. 20–22.

on a light syllable and do not therefore drag on or impede the line's forward momentum. As for even longer words, these can be mobilised either to take or to elide the stresses they require in prose utterance. This, which snatches a grace beyond the means of art, gives them a cadence free of regular emphasis, and allows a kind of hovering stress, even a *rubato*, which is intrinsic to their meaning. (Anyone who has heard Stevenson read will, I think, acknowledge this to be so.) 'Infinitesimal capillaries' is a perfect decasyllabic, five-stress line, though if you read it as belonging to the line the poet provides, you pass over certain stresses so lightly that, with the addition of 'the flawless connections', you have a line perfectly calibrated to act, to my ear at least, as a septenary. Not that it matters. What does, is the line's rhythmic aplomb. To take the measure of this poem is to understand the prescience of Edward Thomas' claim, made at the very beginning of the last century, that 'Increasing complexity of thought and emotion will find no such outlet as the myriad-minded lyric, with its intricacies of form.'[14]

'Intricacies of form' – Stevenson seems always to have understood the need for a poem to find its own shape, so that although she is a poet of great formal accomplishment, form in her case does not so much impose on the subject as enable it to discover itself. She is perhaps less

---

[14] *Edward Thomas: The Annotated Poems*, ed. Edna Longley (Tarset: Bloodaxe Books, 2008), p. 16. Thomas' article originally appeared in the News Chronicle, 27 August 1901.

showy than such acknowledged American masters of formal intricacy as Richard Wilbur and Anthony Hecht, and, more recently, Brad Leithauser, but actually this allows her to learn by going where she had to go (to borrow a line from Theodore Roethke's villanelle), whereas with them you often feel that a poem has to submit to being 'plumped up', a bit like a sagging cushion being banged into shape. Rhyme and metre are not so much recruited as dragooned into service.

It seems appropriate, then, to draw attention to a passage in Stevenson's essay, 'The Melting Metaphor', in which she notes that she does not see herself as called on to defend a wholly 'formalist' approach to poetry. Her rejection of such an approach is a constant, and goes with a confidence, or at least a readiness, to be entirely serious about her chosen profession – something her English counterparts in the early 1960s lacked. Of course she is far more talented than they are, but she also works harder at poetry than they do, is more dedicated, more ambitious, more daring, though emphatically not more attention seeking. Behind her, naturally, were great names: Bishop, Moore, Dickinson.

Stevenson's lovely, witty 'Making Poetry' appeared in her 1985 collection *The Fiction Makers*, and the nature of its concerns with poetry is a constant in her work. It begins with a statement that is offered as though *ex cathedra*: '"You have to inhabit poetry/if you want to make it."' This prompts the question: 'And what's "to inhabit"?' along with its answer:

> To be in the habit of, to wear
> words, sitting in the plainest light,
> in the silk of morning, in the shoe of night;
> a feeling bare and frondish in surprising air;
> familiar ... rare.

Trying to scan this by conventional means is almost impossible, and yet, speaking it one can, without difficulty, hear that the first three lines take four stresses, the fourth, despite its twelve syllables, takes five stresses, and the last takes two or three, depending on whether the third syllable of 'familiar' is elided. The stresses do not, however, settle into any dominant rhythm, let alone metre. The verse's surprising air is all in its lilting variety with equal aplomb. Hopkins? But he has often to indicate where a stress goes, *contra natura*. Marianne Moore? But her verse machines, delightful though they may be, can look like the unlikely amalgamation of some surrealist's *objets introuvables*, or the tesserae of a Gothic craftsman who's taken rather too many pulls on the wineskin. Ingenious as they are, their arbitrary patterning inhibits the poet from structuring syntax in accordance with the line. Reading a Moore poem, you have either to come to an abrupt stop at the line break, as though struck by momentary aphasia, or else you must read on as though the line break isn't there, which is how, as recordings make plain, she herself read her poems. But in 'Making Poetry', as in Stevenson's other poems, the line is an integral unit, as well as being integral to the stanza to which it belongs. This is why, in the almost miraculously assured stanza above, the 'surprising air' rides on both internal and end rhymes, as well as on the chime of assonance, while sustaining the wit of 'shoe of night' and the 'feeling bare and frondish', where 'frondish' plays with the idea of a frond-like upstarting of life – hinting, too, perhaps at the seventeenth-century French usage, of a malcontent, one who will not conform. Rare indeed, such writing, and therefore deserving of the pause preceding the stanza's last word.

The last verse, which confronts the triple-headed question, 'why inhabit, make, inherit poetry', answers:

> Oh, it's the shared comedy of the worst
> blessed; the sound leading the hand;
> a wordlife running from mind to mind
> through the washed rooms of the simple senses;
> one of those haunted, undependable, unpoetic
> crosses we have to find

This seems to be heading for self-pity, but avoids it by last word from the expected cliché 'bear' to 'find', voicing compulsion which is free from personal resentments. The 'wordlife running from mind to mind' cherishes and vitalises a poetic lineage in which running means encouragement.

There is a defiant gaiety about 'Making Poetry', a kind of buoyant indifference to the law-makers, which goes to the heart of Stevenson's best poetry, and which, to judge from *Poems 1955-2005*, seems as an ambition always to have been there. From the early 1960s she was producing poems which, in their accomplishment, act as an implicit rebuke to many of the poets around her, including those who have had prizes and praises heaped on them. One needs a certain ferocity of spirit to resist the blandishments of fashion, to learn by going where you have to go. Form, for Stevenson, is not a matter of rule. Skill is not a matter of something learned, once and for all. Discoveries have repeatedly to be made; new styles of architecture are always required. Hence the fact that, even within a single poem, stanza shapes and line numbers may vary, stress is not in any way metronomic, rhythm and line length alter, internal and end rhymes flicker in and out, threads and chains of assonance and alliteration gleam and disappear as the poem's needs require. The overall effect is therefore of work which, at its truest, finds itself in the act of making.

Ted

IN THE SUMMER OF 1957, AT the end of my first year as a student of Philosophy and English Literature at Reading University, I worked for the best part of two months as a general labourer. My employer, Gamblins, was a building firm in Sunbury, a small town in Middlesex. The town centre was locally famous for a clock tower – Sunbury Cross – and two miles beyond the town the road curved down to run beside the Thames before joining a wider, more important road that led to Hampton where, between 1948 and 1955, I would leave the bus to walk a mile to Hampton Grammar School. The school, a single-sex institution, was reputedly of an educational status superior to any of the nearby county grammar schools, though you could have fooled me. And given that it was six miles from Ashford, the town where my parents had come to live, I was in a minority of outsiders attending the school, because most pupils lived in Hampton itself, or, failing that, Twickenham or Teddington. They knew about places I'd never heard of: Pope's Grotto, Teddington Lock, the ice rink at Richmond.

All I could offer was Kempton Park Racecourse. Our

bus ran beside the racecourse after turning away from the Thames, and I would study its green curves with some interest, because it was rumoured that fortunes were made and more frequently lost at the course, and that those whose lives were ruined by incautious bets sometimes ended up by killing themselves. Their bodies were retrieved from the Thames or from the long grass that bordered the bevelled green where horse and rider sped. Perhaps they did, although I never saw any evidence of dead bodies. There was nothing, as guide books used to say, to detain the curious traveller.

There was certainly nothing out of the ordinary about Gamblins. It was little more than a narrow builder's yard with, halfway along, a single-storey brick-built office, no more than 30 feet in length, with, in front and beyond it, waste ground where building materials were stored: brick stacks, bags of cement, some scaffolding poles, tiles, tarpaulins, at least one flat-bed lorry, and a Bedford van – the usual impedimenta and appurtenances of such a place.

I have written about my experience of working for Gamblins before, in *Next Year Will Be Better: A Memoir of England in the 1950s*, and there is no need to repeat what I then said. The work was for the most part tedious, exhausting, and as a general labourer I learnt little apart from how to heft bricks on a hod, prepare and carry buckets of cement, and, when required, mix mortar. Skinned shoulders, badly-blistered hands, aching thigh and calf muscles still throbbed when I returned to university for my second year. I remember those aches, alright, or fancy I can. But I also remember the men with whom I worked, in whose company I took considerable pleasure, and from whom I learnt much. The two brickies, Harry and Hector, the carpenter, Nogger Newman, a morose-looking, manually adroit man of few words, whose sniff was more eloquent than any voiced rebuke, Len, decorator and part-time trouble maker, 'Spikey Bill', a Teddy Boy of about my age, like myself a general labourer, as well as a genial companion who taught me something about the skills and dedication required for night fishing, and the gaffer, Malcolm, aka Sparks, an electrician who saw himself as above the others.

He undoubtedly thought himself a better man than Ted. Ted, Malcolm implied, may even have said, was riff-raff. Well, no, Ted wasn't. I worked with him on some pretty mucky jobs, especially the one that required us to clean out a grimed, putrescent warehouse which had once housed a variety of better-not-thought-about industrial cast-offs, plus the corpses of dead rats, slimed tiles, of pigeons heaving with maggots, of sacking we tried not to disturb because, when toe-ended, it released a soup of smells guaranteed, as Ted remarked, to put you off food for the rest of your life. Each evening, at the end of our nine-hour working day – start at 8 am, finish at 5, an hour off for mid-day mealtime, Ted and I would spend a good half-hour scraping ourselves down, banging filth out of our overalls, combing – and combing and combing – our hair, trying to rid ourselves of the scrim of showerings that fell from our heads and spread like a fine network across the floor. After which we'd wait for Malcolm to drive up in his Bedford van so as to return us to Gamblins headquarters, from where we'd bicycle back home, through the still warm evenings of that summer.

Malcolm would supervise our entry to and exit from the van, almost hysterically determined to preserve its appearance. We were never allowed to open or shut the doors. He did that. Layers of newspaper were spread across the green leather upholstery before we were allowed to perch on the back seat. 'Don't lean back, please, I've only just cleaned the inside.' 'No, we won't, Malcolm, promise.' 'And keep your feet off the carpeting.' 'Yes, Malcolm, we will, Malcolm.'

And so, winking and smirking pretend disapproval at each other, we'd ride like propped-up wooden marionettes back to the yard, mount our bikes, and from there, having shouted 'See you tomorrow', 'If I last that long', we'd begin our separate journeys back home, me cycling six miles to Staines, to which my parents had now moved from Ashford, Ted going the far shorter distance to a row of terraced houses not far from Sunbury Cross, in one of which he lived with the wife and two small children he adored.

* * *

I knew about Ted's family because some days – though not when we were working in the Pit of Gomorrah, as I began to call it – he'd ask me back to his house where his wife would prepare a midday meal for him and I could eat my sandwiches, sitting at table with them or in an easy chair which Ted would draw up beside him and where, he said, 'We can have a bit of a chin wag.' At first, Sally – he never called her 'Sal' – tried to get me to share in the food she prepared, but I wouldn't. I didn't really like eating in the middle of the day, and anyway I was chary of taking food from their mouths. But being with them gave me the chance to realise how devoted a couple they were, and how Ted not merely loved but revered her.

So, after we'd banged as much of the morning's work dirt as we could out of our clothes, and having taken off our shoes, I'd follow him into the front room where Sally, who'd cycled back from her assistant's work at a local pharmacy, would have laid the table for the two children and the 'menfolk', as she called us.

I once wondered aloud whether the children would have preferred school meals, but Sally made plain that she liked to know what they were being fed. 'And it's good for them to see their father. He sometimes doesn't get home at evening before they're ready for their beds.' It wasn't that Ted stopped off for an evening pint, as Harry and Hector did; but if extra work was available, or required, he'd be the one Malcolm could turn to. Like Barkis, Ted was willin'. After all, each hour of extra work paid time and a half. 'Keeps the kiddies in shoes,' he said to me. 'Anyway, keeps 'em in laces.' And he'd laugh his smoke-tangled laugh.

'Careful how much you smoke,' I said to him on one occasion when he was bent double over a coughing fit. The previous year a mobile X-Ray van had come to Reading and we were all encouraged to have our lungs examined, not merely for signs of TB but because, perhaps for the first time, smoking was being associated with lung cancer.

'Nah,' Ted said. 'Cough it all out, that's what I do.'

In those years that was what many others believed would keep lung cancer at bay. The great jazz clarinet maestro, Sandy Brown, giving a friend of mine a lift back to London after the Brown-Fairweather Band had been in session at Eel Pie Island, reassured his passenger that no clarinet player would contract the disease. 'Not if you blow hard and blow often.' When Brown died at the age of forty-four he was suffering from an undiagnosed disease linked to his heart; but it's difficult not to think that the amount he smoked contributed to his early death. If the right one don't get you, the left one will. Lung cancer, heart disease: between them they accounted for a growing number of early deaths among men, and, increasingly, women, in the generation ahead of mine.

By contrast, what you ate and drank wasn't thought to be much of a problem. It certainly didn't trouble Ted's household. In the nineteen-fifties a 'fine figure of a man' was still reckoned to be one with an evident stomach and clothes that hinted at muscle verging on flab. Not that Ted was inclined to either. He was one of what my mother called 'Jacob's lean kine', and in this he was aided by his wife's cooking. Sally always prepared nutritious meals in which greens regularly featured. 'I want our kids to grow up straight-boned,' she once told me when cutting short their grizzlings about the helpings of sprouts she insisted they 'got down them' – Ted's interjection, that – before they were allowed slices of jam roly-poly. By then, rickets, that dreadful bone disease which had affected earlier generations of working-class children, thanks to the coming of the NHS and the national supply of milk, together with concentrated orange juice and other free offerings to children such as malt extract and cod liver oil, was no longer a major worry. Vitamin D deficiency was on the way out.

The nation was fitter in those post-war years than it had ever been, obesity, especially child obesity, not yet a problem. Many working men cycled to work, or they went by bus and walked at either end, or they used 'Shanks's pony'; and for those who were labourers, physical labour kept them, if not slim, then well within the bounds of acceptable weight. They could handle three square meals a day because of the nature of their work, both inside and outside factory walls. Most of Ted's work, even in the winter months was, so he told me, outside. He could do tiling, he knew how to paint and decorate exteriors; and although not a carpenter of Nogger's expertise, he could hang doors and fix window frames. He could also if required turn his hand to bricklaying. Like Harry and Hector, he had the unerring knack of breaking a brick into a part required to fill any gap that was spotted along a wall. Take a brick in one hand, your trowel in the other, measure with your eye the size of gap to be filled – an inch, two-and-a-half inches, say – bring the edge of the trowel smartly down on the brick, scoop a slather of mortar onto the piece left in your hand, and you had exactly the amount of brick needed to fill the gap. How each of them could do this without ever miscalculating was a wonder to me, but to them it was an accomplishment they took for granted. 'Unskilled labour?' Forget it.

* * *

Ted was, he liked to say, 'fighting fit'. He told me a good deal about his life while we worked together, most especially, perhaps, during the days when we cleared the filthy warehouse to prepare it for its putative future as a packaging plant. He was agile, lean, and though short – not much more I guessed than five feet – gave off an air, as the phrase went, of being well able to look after himself. His berry-brown skin and dark eyes suggested gypsy origins, though I never asked him about this. I did, though, wonder aloud about the absence of most of his front teeth. Had he suffered from botched dental attention?

'Nah,' Ted said, laughing. 'Left 'em in the ring.' And grinning in response to my puzzled expression, he explained that, after he'd completed his national service some years earlier, still at that time of eighteen months' duration rather than the two years to which it was soon raised, he tried to make a living as a fairground scrapper. During his time in uniform, he'd had some success as a regimental flyweight, had even won a medal or two, and after his discharge and with no plans as to what he might do now he was free of the army, various pals had suggested he could do worse than turn up at fairgrounds where one of the more popular attractions lay in inviting any likely lad to challenge the management's professional bruiser to three rounds in 'the ring'.

'Ever seen one?' he asked, and I nodded. 'Yes,' I said, knowing what he was referring to.

Go to a travelling fair and you'd often find that a boxing ring would have been set up in a large marquee, where the entrance fee for those who crowded in guaranteed a hefty return for the promoter as well as a decent purse for the pro. And, for any challenger, there was the chance to gain a financial reward. I think the going rate for lasting the distance was £5, a whole £10 if you knocked the pro down.

For some months Ted was on to an earner. In the immediate post-war years and for well into the 1950s, touring fairs frequently pitched themselves on village or town greens or football fields in summer, and, in winter, cricket grounds. All-the-year-round entertainment. Boxing rings a regular feature. Earning yourself a fiver for one Saturday night's work was good money at a time when miners' weekly wages were still pegged to less.

'Sally and me had been childhood sweethearts, but she wanted to make me respectable,' Ted told me, 'didn't fancy being married to a grifter.'

'So that put an end to your career in the ring.'

Ted laughed. 'Worse than that. What stopped me was a left hook. Never saw it coming. Flat on my back, counting stars until a couple of mates dragged me out. That was the end, that was, I quit, got regular work, and me and Sally got married. I said I'd get the gnashers fixed, but she said not to bother. She'd take me as I was.'

He paused, looked at me, grinning. 'Taught me a lesson, though. Never get into the ring with a bloke who don't look all that much bigger than you. See, most of them pros were old uns', heavyweight, a bit punch drunk, you know, slow on the turn; they'd had plenty of batterings, so if you were smart you kept out of their way. No point in going toe-to-toe. But this one, he was on the bill at some fair near Oxford. Had his name announced before the fight started, but it meant nothing to me. I was "Battling Brian", that was the moniker I travelled under.'

'And what was he called, the one who ended your ring days. Ding-Dong Dave?'

Ted looked sideways at me. 'He was called Randolph Turpin.'

'You're kidding.'

But Ted wasn't.

As I write these words getting on for seventy years later, I wonder how many readers will recall Randolph Turpin. A few, a very few, perhaps. But for a while in the nineteen fifties Turpin was a national hero. He was the boxer from Leamington (I think) who briefly held the title of World Middleweight Champion, and his nearly handsome, hawk-like profile regularly appeared in the sports pages of newspapers and sometimes on front pages, too, especially after his successful fight in London against the then reigning world champion, Sugar Ray Robinson. And for weeks afterward, key moments from the fight which had been 'captured' for film newsreels brought queues to cinemas across the nation.

Even after his defeat in the return match in America – 'fixed' for Robinson so the British press hinted by Turpin's being lured into drinking clubs and vice dens – he was still held in affectionate awe, the colour of his skin – I think he was of 'mixed blood' – part of his allure. Equally famous were Bruce Woodcock and Freddie Mills. The former was a genuinely skilled boxer who once fought on though his jaw had been broken in an early round against a New Yorker called, I think, Jo Baksi, while Freddie was for some years featured in 'B' films as a hard man, his incompetence as an actor unique even for those days of cheapo black-and-white second features, and especially evident when he was required to speak a few words.

Football had Billy Wright and Wilf Mannion, while Denis Compton's handsome face with its carefully combed, brylcreemed hair, sometimes with a packed Lord's behind it, gazed in profile from thousands of billboard posters. (Len Hutton, England's first professional cricket captain, also posed for Brylcreem.) And for a brief period of glory Randolph Turpin seemed about to join them.

But the glory days didn't last for long, especially for boxers. There was Jack Gardner, a heavyweight who came soon after Turpin, had a 'classic' upright stance – front foot well forward, front fist out ahead, rigid as a ramrod – who was known for the words he spoke into the BBC microphone after he gained the British 'crown' – 'Mother,

Gracie, we got that'; there was Jack Bodell, a pig farmer from Claycross, of whom it was once cruelly said that his pigs tried to teach him to speak but he got no further than 'oink'; and there was Don Cockell, British champion for a very short time and then taken to America to be 'matched' against Rocky Marciano, who after the fight was over – and to be fair, Cockell went the fifteen-round distance, probably because he couldn't move fast enough to avoid Marciano's fists – said to a BBC commentator (who may or may not have been Raymond Glendinning) – 'You sure have a fighter in Mister Don Cockell. [Emphasis on second syllable]. I kept hitting him but he would *not* go down.'

Turpin's success, brief though it was, became a cause for national pride. In 1957 his name was still one to be revered. And here was my mate, telling me that on his way to international fame the Leamington Lion (as I think he was sometimes known) had knocked Ted out. 'Can I carry your sandwich box,' I might have asked. But of course Ted went home for his meal. In fact it was as we were sipping the tea Sally had brewed for us before seeing the children out of the front door for their return to school – 'And work hard and pay attention' – that he told me about his three-rounder against Turpin. 'Nearly got to the final bell, too,' Ted said. 'But that hook did for me.'

Had Ted and Turpin exchanged post-fight pleasantries, I wondered. 'Not much hope of that,' Ted told me with a rueful grin. 'By the time I was back upright, he'd gone. Didn't even get his autograph. 'Course, it was before he was famous.'

'So you don't dine out on the story.'

It was a silly remark, but Ted understood. 'Nah. Don't ever talk about that. Sally knows all about it, of course, she said if she ever met Turpin she'd give him a piece of her mind, but that apart you're the first person I've mentioned it to in years.'

'I'm flattered,' I said and I meant it.

Next day when we reached his house, where his two children were already sitting at the front-room table waiting for their midday meal, I greeted them in what I hoped was a suitably friendly manner. I was wondering whether they knew about their father's ring encounter and whether I dared to mention it; but they weren't interested in me. As Ted, having washed himself at the kitchen sink, took his place at the head of the table, eight-year old Jimmy had a question ready for his father.

'What has four legs, two legs, and three legs?'

Ted looked mystified. 'What?'

'It's a riddle,' Jimmy said, shouted almost. 'We did it at school. Come on, Dad, tell us.'

By now Sally was putting food in front of the three of them. 'Don't shout,' she rebuked her son, 'and don't talk with your mouth full. Especially not in front of – of guests.'

She was smiling, a little awkwardly, and I sensed how keen she was to present her family as one to be proud of, and how much loving care went into her determination to dress the children well, keep the house as 'clean as a new pin', to use one of my mother's many expressions, and to provide nourishment for them all. She loved them, she adored Ted who plainly adored *her* – you could see that in the glances they exchanged as well as the number of times they found an opportunity to touch each other – but in her case love was inseparable from pride in all she'd achieved: her children, the house, even Ted. He, by comparison, was more inclined to take such achievements for granted.

Among these was his young son's progress at school. 'Keen as mustard,' he'd once said to me when he was telling me about both Jimmy and Jean, younger than her brother by two years, and, I thought, at least equally bright. It was Jean who now repeated the riddle to her father, giggling at Ted's look of bewilderment, his admission, 'Not a clue. Tell us, then, clever clogs.'

Jimmy turned to me. 'Do you know, Mister John?'

They were all looking at me now, Sally, with an arm round her daughter's shoulders, not so much smiling as challenging me. Go on, you're a university student, you tell us.

I said to Jimmy, 'It's the riddle of the Sphinx, isn't it, although you've learnt it before most people do. The answer is a man, any man. Crawling in infancy, then standing upright, then using a stick in old age.'

Nodding, but disappointed, Jimmy asked, 'Do *you* know any riddles?'

'I know a silly one.'

'Clear your plate first,' his mother told him, 'then perhaps John will tell you.'

Arm still round her daughter, she was looking at her

son, not me, her face, fringed by the light brown hair that was almost certainly set in what was then called a home perm, curled across the collar of her green cardigan. The cardigan, together with a green, pleated skirt, presumably acted as her shop uniform, and a lifetime later I can still see that moment, Sally, not conventionally pretty but with a plump-cheeked, unlined freshness of appearance and unwavering gaze (though I can't remember the colour of her eyes), the two children staring across the table at me, and Ted, his gap-toothed mouth half-open in a rictus of laughter, as I said, 'Here's the riddle, then. If it takes a week to walk a fortnight, how long does it take a beetle with clogs on to walk through a barrel of treacle?'

There was a pause, before Ted asked, 'Do you know the answer? Cos I'm bugg – I'm blessed if I do.'

'There *isn't* an answer,' Jimmy said scornfully. 'It doesn't make sense. It's rubbish.'

And before Sally could rebuke her son for blurting the words out, 'You're right, Jimmy,' I said. 'There's no answer. No explanation. It's a bit of fun.'

'What's the point of that, then?' Jean asked, looking at Jimmy, who returned her look of contemptuous wonder. Another daft adult, the look said.

And Ted, dear Ted, sparing my embarrassment, said to his children, 'See, John's giving you two tearaways time to finish your grub before you get back to school.'

* * *

One other moment comes back to me from that time, this one always with a keen pang of guilt. It was a Friday night. Ted and I had finished our work, not merely for the week but, in my case, for ever. My days at Gamblins had come to an end. The following week I'd be returning to university as a second-year student, the eight weeks of labour a world away from the routine of lectures, of seminars, tutorials, and of evening meals in hall where, gowned for formal supper, we'd be crammed together on hard benches as we tried – none too hard – to force down the vile, indigestible food put in front of us by the male 'servants' who in their white jackets came and went for mostly short periods of service. Came, went, reappeared.

But the food never varied. Stews that were all gristle and turnip, fish that had the consistency of starched linen and could barely be separated from ribs of steely, unbending bones, hard-boiled potatoes like cannonballs or which someone identified as mashed after they had been pounded into submission; and, to follow, sponge puddings that had given up the will to live long before they were interred in slatherings of cold, lumpy custard.

Afterward, some of us would head for evenings in the university library that usually ended with a scramble to get to one of the pubs which remained open until ten-thirty: *The Turk's Head*, *The County Arms*, or, if I got away earlier, *The Nob* (aka *The Queen's Head*), uphill from the library but promising Symonds' ale, not excellent but less noxious than the Double Diamond or George's of Bristol on sale at most other 'hostelries'.

And while we drank our beers we might compare notes about holiday work. Who had done what, for how long, with what financial reward? But I held back from telling friends about Ted and until I began to write this piece, I have hardly ever spoken or written about him. How could I – how *can* I explain my feelings for him. He and I weren't friends, and inevitably we had little in common. But I didn't want to forget him or his family. For some years I regularly sent them Christmas cards, though after a while I began to lapse from the custom, and memories of him faded.

One, though, has remained vivid. And troubling. That Friday night when I finished at Gamblins Malcolm was late arriving to pick us up, and when the Bedford van eventually swung onto the forecourt where Ted and I were waiting, he began some rigmarole I don't think either of us listened to with any degree of interest. The gist of it was that he'd spent longer than intended in having his estate van 'professionally gone over, inside and out'. He and his wife would be spending the weekend with cousins of hers 'in the country'. Ted and I risked exchanging a quizzical glance as Malcolm told us this. He then said that before we left he would need to look over our work, in order to satisfy himself that we'd made a creditable job of it all – 'one the firm can be proud of,' he added, as though the words held a threat – and he and Alan (he was on first name terms with Gamblin) wanted to be certain that the warehouse we'd been cleaning and 'titivating' was in fit condition to be handed over to its new owners.

As he levered himself out of the van and marched into

the building, I said, 'Do you reckon Malcolm's got titled connections?'

And Ted, joining in my laughter, said, 'Probably spending the weekend at Windsor. It's only a few miles down the road', and did a reasonable imitation of Malcolm's 'in the country'.

I had an uneaten apple in my pocket which I took out and lobbed at Ted.

He caught it and lobbed it back. Each time we threw the apple we threw harder, backing away from each other, and the distance between us rapidly increased. At last, I hurled the apple, pitcher-style at Ted, who was standing near Malcolm's van. It was a wild throw, well beyond the stretch of his arm, and it splattered on the windscreen.

And at that moment Malcolm reappeared. He was too late to see who was responsible for fouling his van, but Ted, moving swiftly, pulled out his handkerchief and began to wipe the windscreen, saying, as he did so, 'Sorry, Malcolm, my fault. I'm no cop at throwing.'

Pushing him aside, Malcolm reached into the van for a chamois cloth, began to clean and polish the windscreen and its surround, his face red, contorted with rage. 'You're muck, you are, Ted,' he shouted, 'pure muck. Not fit for decent people to be with.'

Behind his back, Ted winked at me, then pulled a face. 'Yeh, well, like I said, I can't throw for toff ...' and then, checking himself, he said, 'tuppence.'

'You're not *worth* tuppence,' Malcolm said, his voice calmer. Rage had become contempt.

I stood there, dumb. After what was far too long a moment, I opened my mouth to tell Malcolm that I was the one who'd thrown the apple, but Ted got in first. 'Sorry, Malcolm,' he said. 'Don't let it spoil your weekend.'

Without bothering to speak, Malcolm opened the van's rear door and gestured for us to get in. We drove in silence back to Gamblins yard where Malcolm stopped to let me out.

'Bye, Ted,' I said and Ted held up a hand in a salute.

'See you,' he said. And the van lurched away.

I watched it disappear beyond Sunbury Cross, then got on my bike and cycled back to Staines.

* * *

A few years later I learnt from my father, a friend of Alan Gamblin, that not long after my summer work at the Sunbury builder's yard, Ted had left to become a warehouseman at a nearby dairy. Though, to repeat, for some years I sent Christmas cards to him, and to Sally, and the children, I never saw him again, but from time to time I think of that incident when he chose to draw on himself Malcolm's unworthy rage and contempt, and always I feel chastened and, I know, humiliated by my moment of silence. Ted was a better man than me.

The Death of "Sheffield Tommy" Burton

'The Death of "Sheffield Tommy" Burton' is a true story. Tommy Burton, "Sheffield Tommy" as he was known in Beeston pubs and no doubt elsewhere, was employed as a dish-washer at Nottingham University. One Friday night in the late 1980s, he was followed by two young thugs as he left the Royal Oak, in Villa Street. Having set on him, knocked him down, kicked and knifed him, and stolen the 52 pence which was all he had on him, they left him dying near his lodgings at Hyson Green.

Dish-washing chores ended at six that night,
Friday, pay day. A quick glance in the mirror
To tip his hat brim just so. "Debs Delight?

I think not, Thomas, but no horror, either.
Right, old lad, a quick march up the High Street
To where the Prince awaits us, there drop anchor

While one or two are sunk, then point the feet
Towards the Royal Oak, its Shipstone's Ale
The reason why so many of us meet

In Snug or Lounge or Public, to regale
Each other with True Tales of the Last War
While their good ladies stand by to inhale

The odour of their menfolk's grit, that rare Good
Comrade scent which put the Teds* to flight
And had old Adolf shedding half his hair."

He talked like that. But we all loved his light
Cantabile, sweet tone, pitch holding true
As he ran through his favourites, "Silent Night",

"Roses of Picardy", "The Moon is Blue",
And for an encore no one ever asked for
But always got, "I'll be Seeing You".

Head back, eyes watering, he'd bump ashore
From vasty depths of pure, salt-water grief
As though the troopship where he'd been once more

In waking dreams was realer than the brief
Scattered applause that greeted his last note.
Cairo was what he saw and the relief

When Monty came to right the yawing boat
Of empire, followed by Churchill. "He said 'Burton
That food you cook is a right antidote

To Rommel's bastard tricks. This war'd be won
Inside a week if others coped as well
In *their* field kitchens. Burton, a grateful nation

Will thank you when we're through this desert hell.'
Yes, Churchill knew my worth." But he was stopped
From more by cries of "TIME". Chris thwacked the bell

And out into the Beeston night we trooped.
Most left in pairs, and while some steered a route
To bedsit land, others slowly re-grouped

As wives and husbands. Tommy's last cheroot
Led him, flambeau-like, down Heroes' Parade
Where he marched anticipating the crowd's salute

But not the blow that dropped him, nor the blade,
Nor boot that smashed into his dreaming head,
Nor that, for the 52 pence they looted,

Two yobs would leave him bleeding and soon dead.

---

* "Tedesco", the Italian word for German was inevitably shortened to "Teds" by British soldiers who took part in the Italian campaign in WWII.

Bas

OUR FIRST MEETING, ON A CHEERLESS damp Wednesday afternoon in May, 1965, could hardly have been less propitious. And the venue itself, a wooden pavilion at the back of a factory in Loughborough which manufactured cranes and smelt of scorched metal, seemed as glum as the weather. Changing into cricket gear, I asked the man who stood beside me, naked apart from a pair of sandals under ribbed grey socks, whether he thought there'd be much chance of our actually playing a game that afternoon.

He looked at me as if I was daft. 'Shouldn't think so,' he finally said.

'So it's not worth getting changed?'

'Shouldn't think so.'

As he seemed disinclined to say any more, I turned elsewhere. The man opposite, already in his whites, said, 'Take no notice of old misery guts. He never expects to play. Give him a hot day in August and he'll complain of heat stroke.'

So I went on with my preparations, and some half-an-hour later, a new recruit to Nottingham University Staff XI, I stood with others in the damp outfield, waiting the arrival at the crease of the opposition's openers. And that was how my friendship with Bas began.

* * *

But the groundwork had been laid earlier. Soon after Pauline and I and our two small children arrived in Nottingham in the late summer of 1964 I found an opportunity to enquire whether the University which had appointed me to a lectureship in the English Department ran to a Staff cricket team. It did, although the season had now ended. 'We start again next May,' the senior lecturer in Chemistry to whom I'd been directed told me. 'Why was I enquiring? Did I myself play cricket?' Yes, I said, I did. And as he plainly required further enlightenment, I added that I'd played regularly for a variety of teams in the Reading area, most especially one called 'Mr Fletcher's Particulars', though I didn't go so far as to explain that although including experienced and genuinely talented cricketers, the Particulars was often made up of a gallimaufry of improbable characters known to the club's captain, Ian Fletcher.

Ought I to have said more? I decided against. A poet and wonderfully louche Man of Letters, Ian was a lecturer in Reading University's English department, to which he had been appointed by the great, eccentric Departmental head, D.J. Gordon, Renaissance scholar and man of genuine erudition who waved away protests that Ian not only had no degree but that he had never been a university student. 'He knows rather more than most of *you*,' Gordon would reply, which was undoubtedly so. Ian remains one of the most learned men I've ever known, and universities are lesser places now that such wandering scholars as he have vanished from their corridors.

In his earlier years as a freelance writer, Ian, who, despite chronic short-sightedness and lack of any observable athleticism, loved cricket, was the proud possessor of a cover drive which he claimed was modelled on that of Walter Hammond's. He also claimed to have 'turned out' for a variety of teams in and around greater London, including one associated with regular contributors to the BBC's Third Programme. In its brief heyday, 1961-1964, Mr Fletcher's Particulars not infrequently included radio actors, producers, script writers, and even the occasional poet, although the team was mainly reliant on lecturers and students, most of whom were good club cricketers, all of them content to appear at a variety of grounds ranging from minor county level to small Berkshire village greens. It was at Pangbourne's pleasant ground beside the Thames, that in June, 1964, I returned my best ever bowling figures: 13.2 overs, 7 maidens, 23 runs, 10 wickets. (I still have the score card.)

Getting on for a year after my Pangbourne triumph, and now in the damp Midlands, I made my first appearance for Nottingham's Staff Team. The opposition, I learned, went under the club name of Loughborough Tradesmen, the match would be played at the Tradesmen's ground, and I could be assured that although the outfield might in places prove 'a bit rough', the wicket itself would be in excellent condition. In those days of mid-week early closing, Tradesmen's teams across the Midlands and the North played their most serious cricket on Wednesdays or Thursdays – Saturdays and Sundays tended to be recreational and allowed space for club members of no great ability to be included in the chosen eleven. It was taken for granted that wives and girlfriends would be in attendance with plates of sandwiches and freshly baked cakes. The teas for mid-week matches were by comparison poor things, the cricket itself far keener. Saturday's dropped catch was easily forgiven. 'Sorry, skip, sun in my eyes.' (Even when the sky was leaden with impending rain.) 'Forget it, Charles. Could have happened to anyone.' But Wednesday's missed run-out, say, was met with sullen reproach. You did not risk offering an apology, and in the silence that followed your gaffe you could hear the imagined comments. 'Prat'. 'Wall-eyed git'. 'Gormless wonder'.

The mood could be especially tense when Ilkeston Tradesmen were the opposition. For their home games the Tradesmen were granted the town's Council ground. Because it was where Derbyshire played some county games, as well as Sunday matches, the ground was always kept in good condition, and the table itself was superb. A Tradesmen Eleven might well include county players returning to fitness after injury. I once had a recuperative Alan Ward, who in those days was probably England's fastest bowler, pinging the ball round my ears, though the Tradesmen's wicket keeper, a plump, cheerful newsagent called 'Broody' Webster, assured me that 'there's nowt to fear, lad, he'll keep t'ball up', which to be fair Ward did.

Loughborough Tradesmen were no slouches, either. That first game I was asked to come on as first change after the home team had won the toss and chosen to bat. I marked out my run-up and as I did so noticed that our wicket keeper, a short, fresh-faced man with disconcertingly steel-grey hair, gauntleted hands on hips, was staring up the pitch at me, presumably wanting to know whether he should stand up or back. I waved him back. He did as required, and, as I ran up and he crouched, he seemed to be snarling. The ball, a loosener, passed the batsman, the keeper took my delivery with almost disdainful ease, lobbed it to first slip – I'd been given two slips and a gully – and by the end of the over had made evident that he saw no great need to be positioned as far behind the stumps as I'd directed.

Between overs I asked him whether he was prepared to risk coming closer.

He shrugged. 'Up to you,' he said. Then, 'There's nothing in the strip.' A pause. 'Might as well stand up,' he said.

No quick bowler relishes the suggestion that he isn't *that* much of a speedster. Next over, still with the suggestion of a snarl, he stood up to the stumps, as though he was taking to a spinner. I bent my back, as the saying goes, tried for full speed, and was part-pleased, part mortified when, in the middle of the over, the keeper whipped off the bails of Loughborough's opening batsman, and the umpire raised his finger. My first wicket for the club. I congratulated the keeper, and he allowed himself the briefest of nods. 'Like a pudding, this strip,' he said.

I bowled a further four overs, without success but also without conceding more than a couple of runs, then made way for spin. Several hours later on that cold, bleak day, the game meandered to a close without either side distinguishing itself. Most of the participants, now changed from whites into their daily dress, trooped into the nearby Railway Tavern. I found myself standing beside our keeper, whose first name I now knew to be Basil and whose surname he gave as 'Haynes. Lecturer in Animal Husbandry.'

'He chases sheep,' someone informed me, and another said, 'When he's not after the pigs.' I introduced myself and we chatted inconsequentially until I risked trying to make a joke about what I took to be the snarl he directed at me as I ran up to bowl. Did he do that to all bowlers? Was it some sort of warning?

He looked at me quizzically. 'I was concentrating,' he said. And one of the other cricketers, leaning in, said, 'You should be flattered he took you seriously.'

* * *

What the remark meant, as I soon came to realise, was that Bas, for all the disproportion of his physical appearance which had become apparent when we changed after the match – long body, short legs – was a quite outstandingly good wicket keeper, one who could have played at the highest level. He was nimble, he had extraordinary eye-hand co-ordination, he was rarely off-balance, and he had very fast reflexes. That early May evening, as we stood chatting in the bar, I learnt that some years previously, after graduating from Nottingham and while a research student at Liverpool, he had played cricket for Nelson in the Lancashire League, as well as minding the net for Notts at hockey. (I think he'd also been called up on more than one occasion as reserve for the England hockey team.) What I also soon began to realise was how much I liked him. By the time we said goodbye to each other that evening I think we both knew that we were to become close friends, though I don't imagine that either of us sensed that the friendship would deepen over the years until I could fairly regard him as one of my closest mates.

* * *

It was soon obvious to me that the disproportion between body and legs was of use to Bas the wicket-keeper. But in other respects it proved a disadvantage. He suffered from a bad back which in time became so severe that he needed an operation to fuse bones in his spine that would bring relief from the constant pain he endured as he crouched behind the stumps. He rarely complained about this, but if we were travelling any distance to away games he preferred to lie supine on the back seat of my car in order to ward off the worst effects of the journey. And for match days he took to wearing a corset complete with suspenders. Inevitably this provoked ribald comment but it was a help and meant he was able to bat as well as keep cricket. Because he was so keen-eyed, he coped with a batting technique that relied almost exclusively on two strokes. One was an elaborate forward defensive prod. The other was a back foot cross-batted swish with which, given his reflexes and timing, he could send the ball to most parts of the ground. With these two strokes, such as they were, in good working order, he once scored 87 against Notts Unity to the disbelief of Unity bowlers, several of whom were on Notts' books. (Unity was a 'feeder' club for the County.) The following week, I had reached 80 against Ilkeston Tradesmen in a home fixture when Bas, captain for the day, inexplicably declared. In the pavilion, as I removed my pads, I asked, 'Why the declaration? I'd have got to my hundred in a few more overs.'

Bas smiled his evil smile. (His front teeth were discoloured and oddly malformed, and he enjoyed parting his lips so as to discompose anyone facing him.) 'Exactly,' he said. He raised his hands as though to explain a simple matter to an unusually stupid student. 'And I'm not having you score more runs than me.'

By then he was married to his second wife, Judy. He and his first wife, Enid, had parted amicably a few years after a too-early marriage, their divorce being finalised while Bas was away for a year in America, where he had been offered a visiting lectureship at Houston, Texas. That was in 1967-8, the year that Pauline and I and our two very young children were in Washington DC, where I had a Fulbright Fellowship to go with a visiting Professorship at the University of Maryland. Bas stayed with us for a couple of nights on his way south and I remember taking him to a bar in Georgetown where he sampled, and greatly enjoyed, a bowl of clam chowder. (He could be nervous about tasting food new to him but even so was always prepared to try an unfamiliar dish. It was part of his dauntless curiosity about the world.)

After our lunch I took him to the airport where he was to catch a flight to Houston. 'Nervous?' I asked him.

'Nervous of what?'

'It's a long way from home.' I knew by then that he'd been born into a working-class family near Peterborough and that his father was a jobbing builder, a bit like Ted, perhaps. As he got out of my car – an American Rambler, vast by my reckoning though about the cheapest automobile on the market – Bas said, 'If you're not scared of driving this old heap of scrap metal, I'll be OK in Texas.'

I saw little of him for the rest of the year, although he sent occasional postcards from points of travel – New Orleans, Atlanta, even Jamaica, where he had flown for a couple of days to watch a Test match in which the English tourists were being trounced by the Windies and where he fell asleep in the sun and woke to find his feet so badly burnt that he had to be carried aboard the aeroplane for his return journey. And at Easter time he paid us a brief visit during which he told me that he was involved in an affair with a married woman with whom he had travelled to various parts of the Deep South. 'Her husband doesn't seem bothered,' he told me. 'A nice enough bloke but he prefers golf. We've played a few rounds together.'

How to take life as you find it. Typical Bas.

But also typical Bas in that he stopped the golf rounds once he became aware of the man's casual, disgusting racism. This had shown itself when, as the pair of them drove past a field in the heat of the day where black men were at work, Bas said he thought nobody should be labouring in such heat. 'Too hot for horses,' the driver agreed, and laughed. 'OK for the n*****s though.'

* * *

Once he was back in England, Bas bought himself a house – more of a country-style cottage – in a village called Willoughby-on-the-Wolds, near to the university's Agricultural College where he was a lecturer in Animal Husbandry. He'd taken an undergraduate course in Chemistry, had done well enough to be offered a postgraduate degree at Liverpool – hence his playing cricket for Nelson – and had then gone onto post-doctoral work at Aberdeen University. While there, he had seen that Nottingham were advertising for a lecturer in organic chemistry, applied, was interviewed, and then became a lecturer in Animal Husbandry at Sutton Bonington.

He told me this over a post-match pint in Beeston. 'But what's the connection between Chemistry and Agriculture,' I wondered. 'And anyway, you weren't being interviewed for a post at Sutton Bonington.' Bas, whom I sometimes thought could be surprised by little, if anything, said, 'But the chair of the interviewing committee was one of the big white chiefs in agriculture, and he offered me more money, so I accepted.' I didn't really follow, but it helped me understand something important about Bas, his readiness to say 'welcome to life' in a manner of which Walt Whitman would have approved.

I had further evidence of this not long afterward. A warm day in July. We were playing Notts Schoolmasters at the University ground when we became aware of a flying display above our heads. Tiger Moths and other antiquated aircraft were fussing about the sky, flares plumed from their tails, clumsy dives sent the planes down and then up in the air, and from some of them parachutes blossomed and began slowly to descend. In its way it had an improbable charm and the game paused awhile as we all watched the black figures come down through the blue.

'I wonder what that would be like,' I said to Bas, 'falling to earth from middle air.'

'Not bad,' Bas said.

He'd tried some parachute jumps while at Aberdeen, he told me, and though I've forgotten how he'd acquired the training, I know I wasn't greatly surprised by his revelation.

Nor was I surprised when, later that year, he told me he'd written some poems he'd like me to look at. This was 1971. In the spring of that year I published my first pamphlet collection, *About Nottingham*, which I dedicated to him. The pamphlet, which contained some work I still think pass muster, and which earned the qualified approval of Roy Fisher and G.S. Fraser among others, was entirely made up of poems concerned with the city where I had come to live and to which I was increasingly committed. Nottingham might not be the Great Good Place – nowhere is – but it was where Pauline and I lived with our growing children in a house we loved and wanted to call home.

'How do you write poems,' Bas asked me when I gave him a signed copy of *About Nottingham*. He meant, I knew, 'how does anyone go about the task, exercise, experiment, pleasure, of making a poem.' There was no point in trying to fob him off with daft generalisations. I sat him down and, almost at random, explained to him why I'd written some of the poems in syllabics and what I hoped was to be gained by using this device, technique, call it what you will. 'It's not all tumpty-tum and words you wouldn't come across at the grocer's then,' Bas said.

'Words you overhear at the grocer's might be a good way into a poem,' I said.

'Not beautiful thoughts, then,' Bas asked.

'Definitely not beautiful thoughts,' I said.

The following week, as we were sitting in the University pavilion after the end of a drawn game against Leicester University Staff – games against that club *always* ended in a draw – Bas came across and casually dropped some pieces of paper into my cricket bag. 'Poems,' he said, 'tell me what you think. Not now, of course. When you're on your own.' I took the pieces of paper out from what seemed to be their hiding place below my cricket shirt, stuffed them into my jacket pocket and forgot about them.

But a few days later I remembered and, alone in my study, retrieved Bas's poems. There were, I think, five, written on separate pieces of lined paper that had plainly been torn from a school exercise book. As I recall, there were no titles, nor did the poems seem to be in any kind of a sequence, though they were about domestic occurrences or descriptions of how Bas himself responded to daily events. One, in particular, had what it takes: a not so comic account of the plants in the living room of the house he'd shared with his first wife. 'Spider plant will have me soon.' The shivery, funny paranoia of that line was, I told him when we next met, a show stopper.

Our conversation, which took place as we changed for another home game, was overheard by a lecturer in Education. 'Jolly good,' he said, when Bas, speaking with some diffidence, explained that he and I were talking about poetry. 'Broadening your outlook on life, eh, Basil. I'm all for it.' Standing foursquare in front of the changing room mirror, he fastened his white, silk cravat while nodding at Bas's reflected stare. 'I always think it helps a man to see life in the round.'

This man, who sent his sons to private schools, as, I'm sorry to say, did quite a few Nottingham academics, smoked a very small pipe, and once, having been bowled middle stump while effecting a model forward defensive stroke a shade outside leg, returned to the pavilion complaining that the ball had been caught in cross-air currents. Bas and I decided to defer further talk until we were on our own.

Some days later, after re-writing, Bas handed over the poems, by now typed, and I sent them to a small magazine. After the inevitable delay, three were accepted for publication. Following their appearance, Bas rather lost interest in them and I'm pretty sure he wrote no more poems. At all events, I never heard about nor was shown any. And although he sometimes came with me to poetry readings and enjoyed meeting and talking to poets he met at our house, he never mentioned that he, too, was a published poet. Like parachuting, having done it was enough.

* * *

In the summer of 1971, Bas re-married. His new wife, Judy, had been a student at Sutton Bonington, who had, as I think the phrase may have been, set her cap at him. Their marriage was one of great happiness. He asked me to be Best Man and, as we talked about the approaching wedding day, he mentioned that his future father-in-law had at some time completed an MA on the philosopher, Thomas Hobbes. 'You could quote Hobbes in your speech,' I suggested, and told him of the famous remark about the life of uncivilised man being nasty, solitary, brutish, and short. 'Why not say that now you're marrying Judy you'll be redeemed from nearly all these faults, though Judy may not be able to do much about your height.'

Bas was keen on the idea, but by the time he rose to speak on the great day itself the champagne had rather got to him. His audience was therefore bewildered by the groom assuring them that though he knew his life as a bachelor might in retrospect be considered as solitary and even brutish, marriage to Judy meant that he would no longer be short, which, miracle-worker though Judy might be, was beyond even her powers.

But it was a good marriage. Judy wanted a big family, Bas had no objections, and in the space of what seemed a few years they became parents to three sons and a daughter. Ian of the Particulars, as some of us dubbed our captain of the Reading irregulars, himself by now a married man, was visiting us one weekend when Bas dropped in. Ian and his wife, despite what Ian made clear were vigorous exercises in the marital bed, were still childless. Conversation was at first general, and continued so until the moment when Ian, impressed by Bas's polyphiloprogenitiveness, asked, 'Tell me, Basil, what are your views on foreplay?' Given that Ian's voice was one that could waken the fox from its lair in the morning, it was some time before talk could be returned to the even tenor of its way. Whether Bas's advice, whatever it was, played a part in the subsequent births of two daughters to Ian and his wife, I can't, of course, know, but I wouldn't bet against it.

The Haynes family lived in the cottage-style house Bas had bought to be near his place of work at Sutton Bonington, and after a minor heart attack persuaded him to give up his academic career, Judy and he were able to take on the work of jointly editing a well-funded Chemistry journal. Judy, a keen horse-woman, gave riding lessons, they bought a field in the village, then a horse-box, constructed a stable for the horses they'd purchased, and Bas learnt to ride. Of course he did. Impossible to imagine Bas not taking on a challenge, and not succeeding in anything he set his mind to accomplishing.

For a good many years as a married man and father of his increasing family Bas went on playing cricket, and was thrilled when his eldest son emerged as a cricketer of great promise, opening the batting for Cambridge University, where he was a student of Geology, and for some years being on Notts' books. Bas habitually took the entire family to matches in which his son featured, and with them went a dilapidated black and white mongrel called Scrub which had regularly to be rescued from nearby ponds, haystacks, back gardens, and deep bramble patches. And when at last my dear friend finally hung up his gloves, he turned to village bowls, playing regularly for Willoughby against neighbouring town and village teams.

He also took up drawing and painting in watercolours. He joined a local art group, spending occasional weekends at different venues sketching and colouring, and became increasingly adept at small landscapes, many of which featured birds, natives of the local habitat as well as more exotic visitors, because by now Bas was becoming an observant amateur ornithologist. Some of his paintings hung in their cottage, others were exhibited at local and regional art exhibitions, still others formed the basis for Christmas cards, and I have kept several of these, including one that may have been the last he finished, for Christmas 2019. On the inside page of this card is a cameo portrait of the last dog Bas owned, a small, rough-haired black-and white terrier, facing the viewer and asking, 'Will I ever get on the front page?'

No, was the answer. A few weeks after that, Bas was dead. He was found by a passing villager, lying outside his front door. He must have let the little dog out for its morning run around and then simply collapsed.

* * *

Learning of that, I inevitably thought back to those summers of cricket, a time when the only month of the summer Bas wasn't engaged in sport was when the whole family decamped for Italy, where Judy's sister lived and where they could spend each day swimming from nearby beaches. To get there, all six of the family Haynes were packed together with their luggage into the estate wagon which Bas drove from the English midlands to Paris. There they and the car transferred to a train and they completed the journey in style.

'You drove through Paris?' I asked Bas in some awe when he told me about this. 'It's more than I'd do.'

'Judy had the street map,' he said, matter-of-fact. 'She directed us so of course we got where we needed to go. No trouble.' He took her omni-competence for granted, not out of self-satisfied complacency but because he *knew* he could always rely on her.

* * *

But then in 2009 there was unavoidable trouble. Judy died, from a recurrence of the breast cancer which some years earlier had been diagnosed and of which an operation had supposedly cured her. At her funeral, held at the packed village church where she had never worshipped but where she and Bas were widely known to many in the congregation and, obviously, regarded with genuine affection, he made the best funeral oration I've ever heard. It was in praise of the wife he'd loved without stint, was entirely free of sentimentality, and it managed to be both dignified and replete with deep feeling. He told us that after Judy's successful undergraduate career and her good degree, she was offered the chance to pursue research. But she wasn't interested. There'd be no point in taking the offer up. She was going to marry and become a mother. So no thanks.

On later occasions she would, Bas said, encounter women who marvelled at, or reproved, her steady refusal of new clothes, and who were especially taken aback by her readiness to wear the same heavy-duty woollen cardigan from day to day. But why bother with new clothes? She liked what she wore. Her day-to-day wear was comfortable, practical, and, of course, was there for her each morning. She also, Bas said, enjoyed being an expert cook of wholesome meals, a gardener, a handy-woman who was able to carpenter, grout, to buy and fit new windows into the family estate car, and, of course, to groom and otherwise care for horses. And when it was discovered that she had a malign skin condition that prohibited her from riding, well, there was still plenty to do in stable work.

In addition to these accomplishments, Judy had a fine singing voice and would sometimes take part in village entertainments, singing Scottish ballads. But she was unwilling to make 'a show'. And she put an end to Bas's occasional, bachelor nights of poaching. Because, as I knew from the early days of our friendship, he was quite prepared to accompany some research students at Sutton Bonington on night trips to the grounds of a nearby grand estate where they would liberate trout from his Lordship's lake.

Bas told all of this in a manner both anecdotal and filled with wonder. His praise for Judy was untainted by any suggestion of self-reflective vanity, let alone declamation. His epithet for the wife he'd lost to death was 'incredible', and for once the word didn't seem excessive.

* * *

Getting on for thirty years earlier, in the early 1980s, Bas and I had decided we'd write a book together about the Gunns. They were a working-class Nottingham family, famous in the late nineteenth and earlier part of the twentieth centuries for their prowess as cricketers. William, the oldest, and the uncle of George – 'Rare George Gunn' – and his brother, John, also played football for Notts

County and for England. And after his retirement from sport, William made enough money by means of a sports business, Gunn and Moore, to move from his origins in a district of working-class Nottingham beside the Trent, called the Meadows, to live in some style in a grand house in The Park, the poshest part of the city.

Our book began as conversations in one or other of the pubs where Bas and I regularly met, and from these came the gradual conviction that we ought to put together what eventually became *The Trent Bridge Battery: The Lives of the Sporting Gunns*. For the first and only time in my life I contacted a London literary agent, he got us a contract with Collins, and we spent two happy years researching the book, which included interviewing old cricketers and going through newspaper cuttings of the Gunns' heydays, as well as talking to some who'd actually seen one or more of the brothers and George's younger son, also called George ('Young George' to the cognoscenti). Young George had followed his father in playing for Notts CC as a middle-order batsman, though he never came close to rivalling his father's achievements or fame.

The book was published in 1985. By then I was in Greece, where I was spending the academic year as Lord Byron Visiting Professor of English at the University of Athens (the glory, as I always say, was all in the title), and Bas was therefore on his own when it came to being interviewed by one of the BBC cricketing commentators at the appropriate Trent Bridge Test match. Sometime later, I asked Bas how the interview had gone. 'Alright,' he said.

Then, 'At least it wasn't Boycott.'

We loathed Boycott. In an act of appalling selfishness, he'd run Derek Randall out during Randall's first test at Trent Bridge. This was in 1975, after 'the Retford Ragamuffin' had scored that wondrous 174 in the centenary test at Melbourne the previous winter. Bas and I drove up to Headingly one cold spring day of the year following Boycott's unspeakable behaviour, and were compensated, even overjoyed, by being present to watch as Randall confounded Boycott by running him out, having swooped from deep cover to dislodge the bails at the end Boycott was confidently sidling toward. 'Like tickling a coiled cobra,' one cricket commentator said.

Later that day, play at Headingly having been ended by rain, we drove down to the Queen's Park, Chesterfield, where Derby were hosting Somerset. (And Botham was in the pavilion providing *The Daily Mirror* with his paid-for thoughts on the state of cricket and anything else on which he cared to offer an opinion.) The car park attendant let us in as 'Adult' (me) and 'Old-Age Pensioner' (Bas). Bas was, I should note, nothing of the sort, but by then his formerly steel-grey hair had turned to grey-white, and his back problem, not yet resolved, made for intermittent difficulties in walking.

I often thought back to that day at the cricket when, in our last years together, Bas would come hobbling out to join me from the cottage where he now lived alone. Every other Friday lunchtime I would drive from Beeston to Willoughby to collect him for a drink at a pub we favoured in the local village of Wymeswold, and there we talked of putting together another book, this one about cricketers who chose to stand out against obsequious subservience. By the time this book appeared in 2015, under the title of *The Awkward Squad: Rebels in English Cricket*, Bas had pulled out, made uncomfortable by what he saw as my relentless criticisms of the Establishment, Dexter in particular. He may have been right, though when the book appeared, I made sure to praise his research. '*Sine Qua Non*,' I said in the Preface. Without Whom Not, and it is so, I couldn't have written the book without his help, without all the research he'd taken responsibility for supplying me with. And any difference between us didn't, I'm certain, slacken let alone fray the bond that held us together. We still went for our regular lunchtime drinks, there was the same contentment of talk between us, and my loving admiration for him never faltered.

'Soldier, scholar, horseman, he,/As 'twere all life's epitome.' Yeats's aggrandising elegy for Major Robert Gregory wants us to grant Gregory a kind of Renaissance completeness, one that will seem appropriate to the son of a noble household. Bas came from working-class parents, was diffident about his various achievements and, I am sure, enjoyed turning his hand to verse-writing, painting, horse-riding, gardening (he won a good many commendations whenever he agreed to put his garden on show as part of Willoughby's village fêtes), without expecting much by way of praise for the skills he showed in all these accomplishments. Sport was perhaps a different matter, but then he was an outstandingly good cricketer and hockey-player. He was also a much-loved lecturer and someone whose research work was respected by his peers and bought him praise among the scientific community. All this may not amount to life's epitome, but it will do to be going on with. When he died, early in 2020, I felt grief at his going, but I also felt, as I feel still, a sustaining delight in our friendship.

Besides, I have seen him since then. At the beginning of 2022 I was hospitalised after several heavy, unanticipatable falls. Their cause turned out to be severe loss of sodium in my body as well as lack of essential vitamins. While these were being re-introduced to my diet I suffered a series of unpleasant, even frightening, hallucinations, chief among them the certainty that I wasn't actually in hospital in Nottingham but was immured in a prison somewhere I didn't know, where experiments were being conducted on me by a gang of rogue chemists, who pretended cordiality but were in fact determined to do me harm. As I improved, so these hallucinations faded, though I remained half-certain that my whereabouts might not be known to my family.

But early one morning I saw Bas. He was standing at the end of my bed, looking steadily at me, silent, unsmiling, but also concerned, so that I understand his presence was a reassuring sign of normality. I told my son of the visitation later that morning, when he came to see me. 'You should write about it,' Ben said, 'write about your friendship with Bas.'

So I have.

Barry

WE MET FOR THE FIRST TIME in late August, 1966. He had been recommended to me by B.S. Johnson when, earlier that year, Johnson came to give a talk at Nottingham University, where I was then a young lecturer. After an hour spent haranguing his audience for knowing nothing about contemporary literature – an ignorance he took for granted – Johnson, perhaps surprised by my being able to quote one of his own poems, unbent sufficiently to accept my suggestion that we go for a drink. It wasn't politeness alone that prompted my suggestion. With the help of another lecturer in the English Department I'd just set up The Byron Press, and it seemed likely that Johnson, who was then poetry editor for *The Transatlantic Review*, might well know of some up-and-coming poet who would benefit from a first pamphlet publication. Yes, Johnson said, over companionable drinks in a city centre pub – Johnson away from the lecture hall was a very different person from the one who'd earlier brow-beaten his audience – a friend of his called Barry Cole was looking for a publisher. 'And he's good?' 'Why else would I mention him?' Johnson said. And he gave me Barry's address.

In the days following I tracked down some of Barry's poems to such places as *The Transatlantic Review*, *Ambit*, and the Oxford-based *Nine* (edited by the then undergraduate, Peter Jay), and wrote to tell him that I liked them very much and wondered whether he might consider publishing a pamphlet with the Byron Press. A typed letter came almost by return. He was grateful for my interest but had just agreed to pamphlet publication by Bernard Stone's Turret Press. However, it would be good to meet sometime when I was in London. (I had told him I'd be teaching for three weeks during the summer at London University's Victorian Studies Summer School.) As venue for our meeting he suggested a pub called The Lord John Russell on Marchmont Street, which was, he said, midway between where I would be staying in Cavendish Square and his own flat, off King's Cross Road.

At the agreed date and time I got to the pub, a single lengthy room which opened straight off the street. It was early evening and, looking about me, I could see only a few old women sitting alone at tables, in front of them glasses of what I took to be port and lemon. I bought a beer, found a seat, and only then became aware of a man about my own age standing at the far corner of the bar. He had neatly-cropped hair, a fringe beard but with a fuller tuft on his chin, was wearing a dark-blue pinstripe suit, white shirt and tie, and could have been a smart young businessman. But what businessman rolled his own cigarettes?

I went over to where the man stood, absorbedly tamping tobacco into a cigarette paper. His movements were leisurely, expert, and only when the cigarette was lit and I had watched the man's head jerk up and back to avoid rising smoke, did I ask, 'Barry Cole?'

He stowed his tobacco tin into a jacket pocket, then, as though after a moment's thought, extended his right hand. A smile flickered and went, but what took my attention were his fingers, quite the longest I had ever seen. Very recently – I am writing this at the end of August, 2015, forty-nine years almost to the day since Barry and I met – I heard Anne Stevenson recall that at her first meeting with Lee Harwood, whose July death had brought a crowd of us together in Brighton, she had been especially struck by the length of his fingers. Her words reminded me of Barry's fingers, reminded me, too, that some twenty years ago, in Sydney, the partner of the Anglo-Australian writer Michael Wilding told me that all writers have long fingers. No, they don't. Michael's fingers aren't particularly long. But Barry's certainly were.

'John Lucas,' he said. He had a clipped, almost impersonal way of speaking, which as the evening wore on I noted was accentuated by the number of single-word sentences he used. 'Impossible'. 'Absurd'. 'Quite'. (Especially the last.) But he also spoke in sentences that rarely seemed anything other than fully shaped as they emerged from a wide-lipped mouth which sometimes, though not often, stretched still wider in an expression that acted as a kind of half-mocking approximation of a smile.

I can't possibly remember all we talked about that evening, but I know we agreed that Donald Davie's *Events and Wisdoms*, published two years previously, was a good 'un, and we were united in huge admiration for Robert Graves. Afterwards, when I thought back to my first meeting with Barry, I realised that there was a recognisable Gravesian manner in the way he himself spoke. Anyone who has heard recordings of Graves reading or talking about his work will be aware of his disconcertingly odd, clipped delivery, as though the words are being strained through clamped teeth, and how weirdly his mode of utterance seems to belie, even disown, the poems' eloquence. Graves reads his poems as though ashamed of his own linguistic and rhythmic richness, his mastery of 'the singing line', which Michael Longley, one of Graves's ablest critics, singles out for especial praise. There was nothing remotely song-like in Graves's delivery of his poems.

Neither Barry's conversational voice, nor the way in which he read his poems, were as awkwardly reticent as Graves. He seemed to be entirely at ease with how he spoke. But the command of syntax, the sense of being in control, was very noticeable. When, after our initial meeting, I was searching about for a term to characterise this manner – not mannerism – I suddenly realised that the word I needed was 'cool'. It's a quality epitomised by the title poem of his first full collection, *Moonsearch*.

> 'I am tired,' says Selene, 'of moving.
> And Endymion is a long time gone.
> Someone go and seek me out a King.'

'Tomorrow,' she says, 'I shall marry.
I'll wear Courrèges white at Caxton Hall.
I shall cross the city in a white taxi.'

II

A seeker leaves to find her a King.
'When he comes we shall marry at night.
A Queen again, a beautiful Queen!'

'Poor Endymion,' she muses, 'gone so long!'
Meanwhile, the seeker returns.
'Tell me his name,' she cries, 'tell me his name!'

'Madam,' he sighs, his old head rolling,
'There is no King. There is no King.'

The poem is managed with such insouciant panache, the rhymes so apparently casual, the break between parts so definite, that you could be forgiven for not noticing that it is a sonnet. But what are we to make of the way in which a Greek myth has been brought into contemporary London? Selene in Courrèges white at Caxton Hall. Is this belittlement or enhancement? What does the poet think about it? What does he want *us* to think? But the poem's manner, its style, is an unyielding patina. It gives nothing away. It is supremely cool.

And it is followed in the collection by a poem called 'Appearances', a tongue-in-cheek, witty tease:

You'd never know, looking at me
I had absorbed half a dozen
critiques of pure reason or had
made a list of the commas found
since nineteen hundred in poems
by Catullus; or had eaten
lychees in a town called Reading.

And you would not believe my talks
with Jack and Ho Chi Minh, and all
the subsequent correspondence;
that Marian Evans once ate
cornflakes from my daughter's dinner
plate; or the whole family lived
for a year in South Uist on tinned
rice; that my wife is the Goddess
Iduna. No – you'd never know
all this just by looking at me.

Of all the English poets who, following Thom Gunn's influential 1961 collection *My Sad Captains*, chose to write in syllabics, Barry is easily the best. In 'Appearances', for example, he handles the eight syllable line without fuss and, by constantly pushing the syntax over line-endings, avoids any suggestion that the poem, as first appearances (ha! – to use one of his stylistic gimmicks) might suggest, could be in tetrameters. But for all the poem's teasingness, it is also serious. Appearances can work both ways. As disguise and implied revelation. 'You'd never know'.

II

After a couple of pints, Barry suggested we go back to his place for coffee. This turned out to be a basement flat on Great Percy Street, up from King's Cross Road. There, I met for the first time Rita – not Iduna, the Goddess of Spring who in Norse mythology guarded the apples that kept the Gods young – but an attractive, forthright mother of three very young daughters, with, I came to realise, a sharp wit and a sceptical wariness of literary – and other – pretensions.

While we drank coffee, Barry showed me drafts of poems he was working on, and it was some hours before I left to go back to my own temporary digs in Cavendish Square. But in the following weeks we met often, sometimes at The Lord John Russell, sometimes at the flat in Great Percy Street, and by the time the Summer School came to an end we had formed a friendship that, with varying degrees of intensity, was to last until Barry's death in June, 2014.

In the early days of that friendship I found myself thinking, often, not merely about Barry's mode of speech but about his dress. Both seemed linked to the way he wrote, and at the same time both were forms of concealment. To put it differently: there were moments when I sensed that Barry's almost lapidary sentences were a deliberate acquirement. It was as though he feared he might not be as much in command as he wanted always to be. Speech and dress were forms of rehearsed control. But control over what?

He was deaf in his right ear, a condition brought about, he explained, during his National Service days, when a piece of ordnance had without warning exploded near to where he stood. Yet for all this, Barry, like most writers I have known, was a good mimic. He could, and sometimes would, do varieties of Cockney and West Indian patois, and for the latter in particular his voice seemed to drop an octave. Perhaps his way of speaking had about it an element of mimicry, a way of being a gentleman and at the same time letting you know it was all an act.

As for his laughter, it was customarily a mini-explosion of breath from pursed lips. And yet there were occasions when the laughter would become a bark, even a shout of glee, and then you realised he had deep lungs and, at a guess, was capable of projecting his voice, parade-ground style, over the squares and far, far away. I wasn't entirely surprised when I heard that in an earlier incarnation and before beginning National Service, he ran a skiffle group. Barry Cole and his Nutty Slackers, the group was called – 'Nutty slack' was the term given to cheap coal mostly made up of dust, useful for 'banking' a fire overnight – a witty enough title for a group which I've no reason to doubt was as rough and ready as most such groups were. Skiffle was the opposite of cool. It was dress-down, duffle-coat and polo-neck, do-it-yourself music.

I don't know whether the Nutty Slackers were much in demand but I doubt they had access to a p.a. system. In those days most skiffle groups were acoustic only. But the Nutty Slackers wouldn't have needed a microphone, or even the megaphone with which some groups came ready supplied. Barry's voice could reach to all corners.

As to his own, 'natural' speaking voice, I was always in doubt. The poems, however, were full of clues, suggestions that his mode of utterance was something of a put-on, formed a protective barrier he chose to erect between himself and the world. (The Man of Mode is a kind of dandy, and 'dandy' also means neat, trim, and, by implication, self-assured, self-contained.) But under the poems' almost icy calm you could glimpse a kind of anarchic energy, a dark gleam whose presence, though it rarely becomes craquelure to threaten a poem's cool surface, is there, not at all insistent, but never absent.

Barry was especially adroit at exploiting clichés. Perhaps there is a Cockney wit about this, I don't know. I do know that poems with titles such as 'Love Me, Dog My Love', 'Blind Date', and 'Skeletons', have an edge to them which is sharpened by their punning titles, although 'Skeletons' is, I regret to say, facile. 'In a large blue cupboard behind my bed/ I have stacked a collection of crockery,' it begins. And this is not all. 'And ranging one side of the closet's length/is a perfect woman's effigy,// … Once a year I perform unspeakably bestial upon the silent effigy//It is a cupboard of much interest/but I would never show it to my friends.' The ten-syllable line is managed with Barry's usual aplomb, but given that the skeletons in his cupboard *are* being shown, the poem inevitably draws attention to a gothicry that feels more Hammer Horror than is good for it, and this is true of a number of other early poems.

But this isn't the case with 'Ships That Get Pushed in the Night', which brilliantly touches on the cliché of Leviathan as the ship of state in order to voice a kind of underground protest at those who man the bridge – the ruling class, the establishment. Barry is not a political poet, but this poem has the sardonic force that goes with a disenchanted contempt for those who take entitlement for granted.

> There was this ten thousand ton ship
> leaning against the dock as if
> it were some impossible beast.
>
> We lined ourselves along the quay
> and pressed the bases of our palms
> on the iron of the starboard.
>
> The boat began to bang against
> the wharf and the captain left his
> wooden helm to investigate.
>
> 'What goes on?' (he called through the fog)
> 'Who pushes my ship, disturbs
> my landlocked equilibrium.'
>
> 'It is us!' we cried. 'We push against
> your state and wish you a hundred
> thousand fathoms deep, we wish you dead.'

Barry's last collection, *Ghosts Are People Too*, contains the characteristically understated but resonant 'Renovation'.

> Scaffolding encases the house; boards rib each floor.
> Windows, in a high summer, let in wintry light.
>
> It's a sort of armouring, a casing. Painters flit
> from floor to floor, white-suited brush monkeys.
>
> It is difficult to write, read. Move to the back,
> and they're still there; dabbing, scraping, filling.
>
> It's as if the house had been rules, is governed not by
> light and the prospect of trees, but by a Mondrian.
>
> An interruption, a once-a-decade. This time, the front
> door's been dressed in black, may well see us out.
>
> I give in, discuss the progress, discover names, offer
> tea, coffee. It won't be long, they say; it won't be long.

By the time this was written, Barry and Rita had long moved from Great Percy Street up to Myddelton Square, across from the one-time residence of B.S. Johnson. Johnson would I think have acknowledged the mordant, cool wit of the front door which, dressed in black, 'may well see us out.' 'It won't be long, they say, it won't be long.' Go back to 'Moonsearch' and see how deftly, tellingly Barry can use repetition, there, as here, in this much later poem. It was a device he'd learnt from Graves: ('Despite the snow, despite the falling snow') though turned to very different ends.

III

Graves, it may be relevant to note, was in his early years a keen sportsman. Barry may have thought to emulate Graves in this regard. He was certainly by no means alone among writers in asserting or implying a sporting prowess that invited a degree of scepticism. I think he did some boxing in National Service but I'm less sure about other of his claims. On an occasion in the 1990s, when he and the writer and publisher David Tipton were on a mini-tour of the East Midlands and staying overnight at our house, Barry announced that he always did fifty press-ups before breakfast. David, a pugnacious character and proud of his own physique, was taken aback. Fifty? *Always?* Yes, Barry said. Without removing the cigarette from his mouth, David dropped to the floor, struggled as far as thirty-five increasingly agonising press-ups and then collapsed. When he had recovered his breath he threw out the inevitable challenge. 'Now your turn.'

'What, improve on thirty five?' Barry, openly contemptuous, gave his explosive laugh. 'Not worth my while,' he said, and rolled another cigarette.

He also more than hinted that he was a better-than-average cricketer. Early on in our friendship he let it be known that he had played on a regular basis for Surrey Club and Ground. 'Bowler? Batsman?' I asked. 'Both,'

Barry said. And from then on he would allude to his all-round abilities as well as telling me that before marriage brought his cricketing days to a premature end he had turned out for some high level teams in the London area.

A pity he couldn't find time to play the occasional game, I suggested. Barry shrugged. 'Not possible,' he said. 'Family.'

Family didn't however prevent him from making frequent weekend visits to Nottingham. Sometimes Rita would be with him, but in the years when their daughters were small he more often came on his own. One weekend, which must, I think, have been during the summer of 1972, he was especially keen to visit. This was when he was still at Durham and putting together the collection of poems which would become *Pathetic Fallacies*. He wanted me to go over the poems with him. OK by me, I told him, but I was due to play cricket for the University Staff Club on Saturday, so perhaps it would be best if he travelled down in the late afternoon. But no, Barry would catch a morning train. 'You're playing in Nottingham? Fine, there'll be time for a beer or two and then I can watch you play. I'll bring a book to read if I get bored.'

Come Saturday morning, and as I was about to leave the house to collect him from Nottingham station, the club secretary phoned to say that one of our team had called in sick. 'We need an eleventh-hour replacement. Any suggestions?'

'You're in luck,' I said, and told him about Barry. 'He'll need some gear, of course, and he's bound to be rusty, but he's a good cricketer. He'll be a more than adequate replacement.'

I met Barry at the station. 'Got you a game of cricket,' I said. To my surprise, he appeared less than delighted by the news.

'I don't have the right clothes,' he said.

'No need to worry about that. There'll be some kit for you. Well, shirt and boots.' And I explained that the club kit-bag was always stuffed with a selection of different sized footwear. 'Just in case.'

After a beer at the pub behind the ground we walked across to the pavilion, Barry less conversational then usual. I introduced him to other members of the team, told them he was an experienced cricketer. Someone began rummaging around in the kit-bag but Barry said he'd be alright as he was.

We lost the toss, our opponents, Woodthorpe, chose to bat, and Barry took the field along with the rest of us, wearing the clothes he had arrived in, even his jacket.

'Where would you like to field?' I asked.

Barry shrugged, indifferent. 'Wherever,' he said.

'Mid-on then.'

Barry nodded and, having taken his tin from his jacket pocket, began to roll a cigarette.

'It's over there.'

'What is?'

'Mid-on.'

Barry wandered over to the position I'd indicated and lit up.

During the first over the ball was hit straight to him. Barry watched its approach with the mild distaste you might show for a foraging cockroach and, as it scuttled close, lifted a leg and let the ball pass underneath. Another fielder chased after the ball and lobbed it back to the bowler. Barry meanwhile concentrated on smoking his cigarette.

And so it went. If the ball came close to him he took avoiding action. If it passed either side of where he stood he simply ignored it. He was probably responsible for raising Woodthorpe's final score by some thirty or forty runs, though he appeared unaware of this, and, if aware, entirely indifferent.

After tea, which he had refused, our innings began. Recalling that on previous occasions Barry had mentioned a number of swashbuckling innings he'd played for Surrey Club and Ground, I asked him what number he would like to bat.

'Last,' he said.

'Last? Really? But in that case you might not get an innings.'

Barry shrugged. 'Give the others a chance,' he said.

As it happened, when the ninth wicket fell we were still eight runs short of overtaking Woodthorpe's total.

I had already strapped a pair of pads over Barry's cords. 'Off you go,' I said, handing him gloves and a bat.

He ignored the gloves, then, still in his jacket, walked out to the middle, bat carried over his shoulder like a gardening implement.

'Don't you want a guard?' the umpire asked him.

'Not particularly,' Barry said. He lowered the bat, bent over it in a posture reminiscent of an angle bracket, the bowler ran up, delivered a straight full toss, Barry did not move his bat, the ball broke the wickets, and Woodthorpe had won.

Later, as we were driving home, I suggested that he hadn't much enjoyed the game.

'No,' he said.

He rolled himself a cigarette, lit it, and, as usual, jerked his head up and back while expelling smoke. 'The cricket wasn't up to my standard,' he said.

I glanced across at him. He was staring straight ahead, no flicker of expression disturbing the impassivity of his gaze.

IV

You never knew with Barry. He had a habit, or maybe a style, of straight-faced tale-telling which belongs to oral culture. I came across this style during several visits I paid to Australia in the closing years of the last century. It's there in a great story called 'The Man Who Bowled Victor Trumper', in which two swagmen sit at a bar while one of them tells the other about implausible deeds he claims to be entirely true, including the one that gives the story its title. It's also there in a number of verse tales by the poet, Philip Hodgins (1959-1995), who for most of his short life farmed in rural Victoria, and whose 'The Big Goanna' is a terrific piece of tall-tale spinning, or yarning. And it's the occasion of Les Murray's poem, 'The Mitchells', where you can never be entirely sure of the truth of what either man who speaks in the poem tells the other.

> The first man, if asked, would say *I'm one of the Mitchells*.
> The other one would gaze for a while, dried leaves in his palm,
> and looking up with pain and subtle amusement,
>
> say *I'm one of the Mitchells*. Of the pair, one has been rich
> but never stopped wearing his oil-stained felt hat.
> Nearly everything
> they say is ritual. Sometimes the scene is an avenue.

Did this dead-pan style get transported with the convict ships that sailed to Australia in earlier times? I've no idea, though bearing in mind the Fat Boy in *The Pickwick Papers* and the Artful Dodger's fabrications, it seems at least possible. But then such tale-telling has always been an intrinsic part of oral or street culture.

There are poems of Barry's which hover between the truthful and the fanciful, and in which the tone is so level that you can't be sure *what* to believe. 'How I came Through' begins, 'My brain sewers broke/just after dark on Sunday', and though what follows is in some ways about experiencing and learning to cope with painful emotions, the narrative is conducted in a manner that won't countenance anything approaching self-pity, let alone a confessional form of utterance. Barry was contemptuous of the fashion for confessional verse which was all around during the 1960s, and he was especially scornful of Alvarez' claim that 'Poetry is a murderous art'. The nearest he comes to the confessional is in a poem called 'Depression', but although its last lines acknowledge that 'The grey road's endless pit suggests/we cannot recover from what we live', both the generalising insistence (not 'I' but 'we') and the replacement of 'where' by 'what' deflect attention from the merely personal.

Even in 'How I was Hated', a poem I take to be based on bullying he had to put up with during National Service, and one where, Edward Lear-like, he opposes a mindless 'they' to the loner, he ends with something closer to affirmation than dejection. 'So every night they turn my bed, not/knowing why I have to lie on it.' The bed he has made for himself is that of the poet, something of which 'they' are ignorant. The note struck, is, in its way, reminiscent of one you hear in many of Norman Cameron's poems, a kind of witty, laconic acceptance of fate, although as far as I know Barry hadn't read Cameron, a poet Graves much admired. In 'A Visit to the Dead' – a title Barry might well have envied – Cameron reports how 'Long, I was caught up in their twilit strife./Almost they got me, almost had me weaned/From all my memory of life./But laughter supervened.' You avoid whatever might be your fate by means of laughter which, at a guess, is as derisive as it is rueful. A comic grimace. The essence of the cool.

V

Fate is a portentous word, one Barry avoided. Yet it's worth saying that his entire lack of self-pity came in the face of what was sometimes a tough life. His father, who had been educated at Dulwich College but seems to have left the school under a cloud, did precious little to help any of his five children, and Barry, having failed his eleven plus exam, must have loathed having to attend secondary modern school, which he left without qualifications. From the age of fifteen until National Service claimed him he worked as a lawyer's runner, then as a runner for Columbia Pictures, and after returning to civilian life he took a variety of jobs. These included working as a clerk at St. James's Hospital, London, followed by similar work for Reuters, then for Public Ledgers, and while doing his day job he began selling books by post; and on free weekdays he helped out in an antiques shop in Camden Passage, where at weekends he ran his own antiques stall. In other words, he worked very, very hard to make a living.

It's therefore pretty remarkable that he continued and even added to the self-imposed reading programme which he had begun during National Service, or maybe earlier, as well as apprenticing himself to poetry. Most writers of his generation had a far easier start in life. They came from good schools, were university educated, and had no problem easing themselves into jobs that left them with long hours in which to practise their craft.

Barry had none of these advantages. But then, in 1963, he found employment with the Central Office of Information (COI) which guaranteed a steady income and something like financial security. He was by now four years into marriage – he and Rita had married at Finsbury Town Hall on 7th February, 1959 – and he became the father of three daughters, Celia, Becky, and Jessica. And his writing career was beginning to take shape.

Success, when it came, came quickly. Poems began to appear in magazines and national newspapers, including *The Observer*, *Tribune*, *The New Statesman*, and *The Spectator*. *Blood Ties* was published in 1967 and in November of that year he recorded some poems and an interview for the British Council. *Moonsearch* came out a year later, and at the same time his first novel, *A Run Across the Island*, was published in hardback with a paperback edition soon to follow. All of these publications were given deservedly warm reviews and his name became, as they say, 'current'. Suddenly Barry was being asked to provide regular reviews for the weeklies, and he was increasingly invited to read to poetry societies and at some then newly-fashionable festivals; he began to receive invitations to contribute to literary journals, he was even – or so I seem to remember – featured on the front cover of a fashion magazine. In 1969 he was included in Michael Horovitz' Penguin anthology *The Children of Albion*. He had, you might say, 'arrived.'

It got still better. In the spring of 1970, the year of his second collection, *The Visitors*, and a year after the appearance of his second novel, *Joseph Winter's Patronage*, he applied for and was appointed to be Northern Arts Fellow at the Universities of Durham and Newcastle, a two-year posting during which he was expected to make himself available to students seeking advice about their writing as well as getting on with his own. Something of his time in the North is recorded by other contributors to the present book and I don't therefore want to say much about it,* except that, having gladly written a letter of recommendation for Barry, and having been delighted when his application was successful, I was angered when I heard on the grapevine that others who had backed Geoffrey Hill for the Fellowship were out to cause trouble for Barry.

In the period leading up to the family's departure for Durham ('Coles to Newcastle' was a back page headline in London's *Evening News*), Barry was in ebullient mood. He resigned from the COI. After his two years at Durham had come to an end, he was, he said, quite certain that he would be able to make his way as a freelance writer. Poems would always be at the centre of his literary life, but the novels he planned to write would put food on the table.

I was less certain. Both of his novels were good, both had been well reviewed, but neither had sold especially well. They were 'literary' novels at a time when such writing was sought after or anyway tolerated by publishing houses who seemed to operate on very slender profit margins. The late 1960s was, no doubt about it, a heady time for writers.

---

* See end of this essay (p. 114)

Independent publishers were prepared to take a chance on new novelists and poets, and an abundance of independent bookshops where their books could (with luck) be sold had sprung up. But as a great friend of mine says, 'always remember 1849'. The glory years couldn't last. Nor did they. The smaller publishing houses went out of business, the independent bookshops began to close their doors.

Barry certainly took writing fiction seriously. But there was an odd disjunction between what he read and what he wrote. *A Run Across the Island* is dedicated to Stanley Middleton, a novelist Barry greatly admired. Middleton is in the realist tradition. Barry not only admired Middleton, he was a devotee of the great nineteenth-century novelists: Dickens and George Eliot were especial favourites, Elizabeth Gaskell only slightly less so, and he also read Trollope with pleasure. Arnold Bennett was another writer granted the Cole Seal of Approval and not merely because *Riceyman Steps* is set in the area of London round King's Cross Road. When in 1974 I published a study of Arnold Bennett, I dedicated it to Barry and Rita. The book picked up an appreciative review in the *TLS* although the reviewer did at one point wonder for whom it was intended. Barry wrote in to say that as it was dedicated to him and his wife he assumed the book was intended for them. This was witty but also made a serious point. Critical writing, Barry was suggesting, ought not to be reserved for an academic readership. He thought the same about novel writing. It ought not to be for a closeted elite. Hence his love for novelists of the realist tradition.

But *Joseph Winter's Patronage* apart, Barry's fiction isn't in this tradition. Far from it. The novels may be set in London, but their speculative, wide-ranging wit depends on allusion, much of it *recherché*, a clutch of near-private jokes, a stylistic range which makes much of pastiche, and a melange of narrative devices which, ingenious though they undoubtedly are, hardly guarantee a wide or even dependable readership. *The Search for Rita* was at best a *succes d'estime*, and *The Giver* wasn't even that. And with that fourth novel Barry's career as a published novelist came to an end.

VI

In the summer of 1972, Fellowship over, Barry and the family were back in London, and although they were able to resume life at Great Percy Street, Barry was now unemployed. For a while he worked for a flat-cleaning agency. (Among the flats he cleaned was that of Suzy Kendall, a minor actor and sometime girlfriend of Dudley Moore). Then he did time with the PPR Advertising Agency, after which he became editor of the short-lived *Nursing Weekly*, a more-or-less journal which lasted for as long as the *Nursing Times* was on strike, and for an issue of which I provided a detailed review of a book called *New Lamps for Old: A History of Nursing from the Crimean War to Now*. I remember that I rather took to task its author, J.S. McLelland, SRN, over perceived inadequacies in the chapter on Charcot, though I found in favour of a later discussion, 'The Home Front: Nursing in England during the Second

World War'. The book existed only in my imagination, though I doubt anybody noticed.

When *Nursing Weekly* ended, Barry took work in the sorting room of Mount Pleasant Post Office, and was even measured for the postman's suit he would be required to wear once he began life as a deliverer of the daily post. But it didn't come to that. In 1974, he was enabled to return to the COI, and he stayed there until his retirement in June, 1995.

VII

During the twenty-five years between the ending of his Fellowship and his retirement from the COI Barry published very little. His last collection with Methuen, *Pathetic Fallacies*, came out in 1973, the following year the Byron Press published a pamphlet, *Dedications*, and a few poems and pieces of prose appeared in journals. But then even these came to a halt.

Not that he had stopped writing. During this period he maintained his habit of keeping a daily journal, and he also wrote meticulous and highly entertaining accounts of the annual trips he and Rita took to Rome. At one point I was hoping to bring these together and publish them as a book to which Barry tentatively gave the title *Roman Candle*. But nothing came of it.

B.S. Johnson's death hit Barry hard. Johnson, who chose to kill himself on November 13th, Barry's birthday, also arranged for Barry to find his body. Some time later Barry wrote a very fine elegy for Johnson, 'Odds Against', which was published in the journal *Ambit* and is included in *Inside Outside*. 'Now tell the days before your death,' it begins, and does so, in a manner which very remarkably balances affection, anger, understanding and generous regard for someone to whom Barry owed much, even if he exacted more:

> You arrogant, silly, man
> you bones before your time.
>
> Awkward man! How you loved words and spoke
> of Beckett, claimed fame when broke
> and bought me crème de menthe
> in the 17th Arrondissement.
>
> You cracked old jokes at our expense
> would not admit that it made sense
> to put Austen, Eliot or Dickens
> some distance up towards the heavens.
>
> You told me: 'God's a rat and that's a fact.'
> That a poem should never be an artefact.
> You thanked me, once, for caring for your wife.
> Then ran a bath and took your life.

The separate sentences of the last four lines accentuate and intensify the previous stanzas in providing statements that cannot cohere. Johnson is presented in all his contradictorinesses. 'Odds Against' is a poem which refuses to countenance, let alone indulge, the consolations of elegy. Its strained, near-broken music implies a truthfulness beyond conventional pieties or pity.

You could, I suppose, say that this refusal to go soft is evidence of Barry as the embodiment of the cool, and indeed I think it is. But for this to feel authentic the upholder of such a stance has to be beyond self-pity, and Barry was certainly free of that vice. I never once heard him complain about the way the literary world, so quick to adopt him, had proved equally quick to blank him out. He must have hoped that the publication of *Inside Outside* in 1997 would bring him renewed – and among younger readers new – recognition. But the book went virtually unnoticed, as did the publication six years later of his final collection, the splendid *Ghosts are People Too*; nor did the re-publication of *Joseph Winter's Patronage* bring him the attention he deserved. That novel, by the way, the nearest he ever came to mainstream fiction, has as dedication, 'For BRYAN'. Barry may not have intended that as a sly joke. But I wouldn't bet on it.

It would be wrong, though, to blame Johnson's death for Barry's waning star. It was one factor among several, but, to repeat, he didn't stop writing in 1973. The two late collections contain a sizeable number of good new poems. That they were barely reviewed tells us much more about the limitations of journal editors than it does about the durability of Barry's work.

This essay first appeared in a festschrift I edited for Shoestring Press after Barry's death in 2015.

Our Cat

EARLY ONE WEEKDAY MORNING IN THE Spring of 1971 I opened our front door as usual in order to bring in the day's milk and found myself staring at a brindled cat. The cat, which I had never seen before, and which must have been asleep in our porch, roused itself to yawn and stare back at me. I like cats, and with no desire to order it off the premises or disturb it more than I already had, I reached for the milk bottles. As I did so the cat got up, shook itself, and walked past me through the open door. I turned to follow its movements and saw it was disappearing into the room on the right, where Ben and Emma sat at table, spooning up breakfast cereal.

'It's gone in there,' Ben said, pointing to the half-open door which opened onto a cupboard below the shelving where we kept our crockery and glassware. An earlier owner had chosen to make cupboarding out of the embrasures on either side of the room's fireplace, and we had taken advantage of this arrangement by fitting in our water heater to the left, to the right, domestic ware and, below, the cupboard at which my young son was pointing and which housed scraps of paper, card, torn curtains, lengths of cloth, 'any old iron', so we said, thinking of the Totter's cart which still at that time came round the neighbourhood, though it would soon be gone.

'Do you know the cat?' I asked the children. 'Does it belong to any of our neighbours, do you think?'

But they shook their heads.

'It's a witch cat,' Emma suggested.

'A witch cat is black,' Ben said. 'Always.' He spoke with the confidence that came from being an older brother.

At that moment Pauline appeared, dressed for the day in sweater and jeans, and asked what we were talking about.

The three of us tried to explain to her about the cat's mysterious appearance and its even more mysterious disappearance into the scrap cupboard, and while we talked and contradicted each other – Emma insisting the cat had magic powers while Ben suggested it could have belonged to previous occupants of the house into which we had moved less than two years before – while this was happening, Pauline had gone across to the cupboard and was now crouching, peering in at the half-open door, shifting boxes and rolls of paper in order to get a better view of the cat.

After some moments, she stood and turned to us. 'That cat is pregnant,' she said.

* * *

Instructed by Pauline, we took turns in looking after the cat. She had a saucer of milk, filled twice a day, as well as a once-a-day plate of food, and a litter tray. These were placed on a sheet of newspaper in front of the cupboard, and the newspaper was changed each day. 'Give her something different to read,' I said, though I don't remember ever seeing her emerge to lap the milk or chew the cat food, nor did she use the litter tray, not in our presence at least; but each morning both saucer and plate were empty, and the tray had been raked over.

* * *

Some three weeks after the cat had arrived, I came down to breakfast to find Pauline and the children on their knees at the narrowly open cupboard door, taking turns to squint into the semi-dark.

I went to join them and as I did so Emma said importantly, 'Tigga's got three kittens.'

It was she who had named the cat and she who now, obeying Pauline's instructions, took on the responsibility of fetching a saucer of milk which she, oh, so carefully, set down at the cupboard door. I myself took the chance to look briefly in on the scene and saw that Tigga was lying on an improvised bed of curtain material while three tiny balls of wool, so they seemed, clamped themselves to her dugs.

* * *

This is not going to be a detailed inventory of animals in the Lucas household. At different times we played host to kittens produced by one of Tigga's offspring, and we also gave house room to three rabbits, three guinea pigs, a gerbil, and a sheep. This last came courtesy of Bas (qv), though at my request because, lacking a working lawn-mower, I hoped Miss Julie, as she became called, would crop the grass for us. She did, too, but she also ate every garden flower and scrap of shrub we planted, though while she was with us I took some pleasure in watching the response of neighbours whenever Pauline took her for a walk, having first secured the sheep with washing-line in lieu of a lead before they set off down the road, Miss Julie tit-tupping contentedly along the pavement.

And then there was the summer when a family of four hedgehogs adopted us, and in the late evening Pauline and I, sitting on a bench at the back of the house, were able to follow their movements as they scrambled from the hedge at the bottom of the garden before scuttling across the lawn, pausing to snout out gobs of bread we'd scattered along their path. (Later I read that bread and milk provided wholly unsuitable food for hedgehogs. The mixture swelled their stomachs without providing the sustenance they most needed. Oh, dear.)

There were evenings of that warm summer when hedgehogs failed to appear, and we made do by watching cats slide down the slopes of a so-called 'Desert Tent' which, together with groundsheet, we bought from the local Army and Navy Store, that Ben and friends became adept at erecting on the grassy lawn, and in which they frequently slept, on all but the warmest nights making sure to enclose themselves in sleeping bags bought from the same store, though whether, as the store claimed, the equipment had actually been used by Montgomery's Eighth Army I rather doubt. More likely the claim was a form of disclaimer should you discover that neither tent nor groundsheet was waterproof. 'Well, we *did* warn you.' At all events, it wasn't unusual to go downstairs following a rainy night and find the kitchen occupied by Ben and friends, all of them spooning up bowls of cereal or making less than neat incisions into a loaf of bread. And round their feet cats might gather to hoover up crumbs or wait for the chance to lick clean the boys' abandoned cereal bowls.

* * *

Not long ago I came across an essay by that fine novelist and poet, Sylvia Townsend Warner, who throughout her long life was rarely without a cat, and who suggests that cats are 'Epochal'. Look the word up in the OED and you find: 'the beginning of a distinctive period in the history of something or someone.' And again: 'A point in time defined by the occurrence of particular events or by the existence of a particular state of affairs.'

Tigga walked into our lives in early 1971 and she died in the summer of 1992. She arrived when Ben was not yet nine years old and Emma had only recently turned six. By the summer of 1992 both were well into adulthood, and, following university studies, settling into work that would shape their future careers. In 1971 Pauline, having some ten years earlier completed undergraduate work in a University art department, was a practising artist and teacher. By 1992 she had begun to establish herself as an authority on the 20th-century English artist, Evelyn Gibbs, and would soon be involved in exhibitions of Gibbs' work as well as producing the definitive monograph, *Evelyn Gibbs, Artist & Traveller*. And in 1971 I was still a young University lecturer, whereas by 1992 I was becoming a greybeard.

These changes and/or developments in our lives would have taken place whether or no our cat belonged to the period in which they occurred. But the fact remains that she was part of them. During that epoch of twenty years she was an enduring presence. And for one year in particular, 1984-5, her presence was all-important to Pauline. That year I had been invited to be a guest of the University of Athens as Lord Byron Visiting Professor of English Literature, to give the title in full, and as I always say, the glory was all in the title. Before teaching duties began, I had a month in which, with Pauline, to explore the city and one or two of the nearby islands, and on one of these islands – Spetses – Pauline slipped and broke her right wrist. This was near the end of her time in Greece, after which she would have to return to England so as to resume her duties as a college art teacher. I saw her off from Athens airport. She was in considerable pain from her none-too-well set wrist, and understandably nervous about returning to an empty house where, both Ben and Emma being away at university, she would have to cope on her own.

* * *

That she managed as well as she did is largely due to her own resourcefulness, ingenuity, and sheer determination, but she has always said that our cat was essential to her during those first, difficult months. Tigga had the loudest purr of any cat I have known, a deep, continuous rumble which seemed the very essence of not so much contentment as reassurance. Wherever Pauline was in the house, the cat was sure to be nearby, its sound giving notice that all was and would continue to be well. And whenever Pauline sat at table to eat her evening meal, having first fed the cat, Tigga would leap up and sit beside her, purring. Or she would nuzzle the nape of Pauline's neck or, even more attentively, lean in close to flick her tongue against my wife's ear. She was the most companionable of cats.

* * *

To repeat, she was also a presence. In saying this I have especially in mind a photograph that Pauline took sometime in the early 1980s. It's a view of our galley-style kitchen, looking from the dining-room. On the right you can see the open door that leads directly into the garden, and there, sitting on the cork-tiled floor and looking intently out through the door, is Tigga. This is, so it feels, her domain.

But how did she come to be in the photograph? Neither Pauline nor I can remember her being present when

Pauline first set up and then captured the moment. In fact I'd as good as swear that there was no sign of our cat when the image was chosen, the camera pointed, and the shutter clicked. Yet there, incontrovertibly, she is. She is sitting, has been sitting, will continue to sit. The image is now unimaginable without her presence.

Presence. I go to the OED once more. 'Presence' is given much space and a good many definitions, but two will be enough. 'Presence: 1. The fact or condition of being present; the state of being with or in the same place as a person or thing … 6. Spiritual or incorporeal being or influence felt or conceived as present.' Our cat.

A Wish

Pale belly to the sun, my old cat rolls
this way and that, then stares up at a tree
whose blossom promises accustomed apples,
blinks and averts her head.
                        No memory, I hope,
of how years past she'd choose her way
among high branches hurts her this Spring day.

Letting Go

'Crooling,' I dubbed that back of throat
mew, part soft howl, 'calling her children home.'
She'd sit for hours to watch the attic stairs
though the kids were long gone, their friends' clatter,
so too her kittens and their broods.

All except one, a grandson, bloat
daft-eyed piebald: his clogged fur,
piled on the hearthrug, she'd expertly
tongue and groom to gloss as he slept on
stupefied by heat and both their dinners.

Mishap survivor, clown companion,
ok at abseiling down a garden tent
but never able to reach the plum tree's
top branches where all summer she'd flow like smoke,
he suddenly hunched round cancer's grip,
was dead in a few hours.

Now days thinned to habits:
ancient but sweet-faced still
she'd quiz the garden's silences or
sleep below her plum tree.

                        Then
Waking to one last call she lapped
water, so little, crawled to a sun-warm path

and that night, my hand cradling her head,
breathed once, twice, stopped.

It's late September and the sun
winding down. My upstairs study
looks on a garden blue with shadow,
a plum tree, her burial mound beneath it.
Blood red among abundant leaves
plums ripen and fall.

Arnold

'I THOUGHT YOU'D WANT TO SEE this,' Allan Rodway said.

'What is it?'

'A letter.'

Allan came further into my room, leaned over my desk, and, without letting go of the sheet of paper he was holding, directed my attention to a line of handwriting. At first the writing looked very like one of those on-screen graphs that alert you to irregular ups and downs of heart movements or of electrical currents, but then I saw that I could read it well enough.

The sentence which Allan was wanting me to read said, *I remember swaying about in front of John Lucas and his lovely painterly lady.*

'What's this about?'

'It's from Arnold Rattenbury,' Allan said, 'a reference to when we all met last week. In Yates's.'

I looked again, remembering, and at the same time intrigued by the penmanship of the script at which I was staring, its confident, uninsistent, angular clarity. The lettering was small but wonderfully clear, tidy, attractive:

very unlike my own unruly scrawl.

'I remember,' I said. I did, too.

Early autumn, 1971. By arrangement, Allan had brought Arnold to a city-centre pub he himself rarely used. Yates's Wine Lodge, to give the place its then full name, was at one end of Market Square, 'Slab Square', much favoured by university students as well as being a regular watering hole and meeting place for a wide variety of Nottingham's citizenry, including writers and artists, musicians, street traders, their wives and girlfriends, all of whom mingled with 'ladies of the night', and who between them created the gallimaufry that gave Yates's its uniquely raffish atmosphere.

To gain access to the Wine Lodge you had to enter through swing doors similar to those shown in Hollywood's version of a Wild West saloon, after which you headed for one of the two full-length counters that ran either side, and behind which wooden barrels were racked up almost to the high ceiling. The barrels contained whisky of dubious authenticity, red rum, and what was marketed as 'White Australian Port', though the drink that came from the barrels' spigots definitely couldn't be called white – a mucky yellow was nearer the mark – and in all probability was neither port nor Australian in origin.

Wide, curving staircases at either side of the bar's farther end led to an upper floor. There, you could sit on benches arranged along wide tables on either side of a wooden-floored aisle, and, if you chose, listen to the trio of musicians who were seated on a small raised dais at the window end and who played every evening apart from Sundays. Two ageing gents, in equally aged tuxedos, on violin and alto sax, and, at the piano, in black evening dress and with greying bun, a severe-looking lady who unaccountably put me in mind of Frankie Howerd's Madame Thea Roper. ('Poor old dear, stone deaf.') It was she who seemed to be in charge, she who, as used to be said, called the shots. The music itself never varied: medleys of light operetta and 'classics' of musical theatre and film, all the way from Gilbert and Sullivan to *Top Hat* by way of *Chu Chin Chow*, *White Horse Inn*, and Ivor Novello. I don't suppose anyone in the place ever listened to more than a few bars of a performance, though I do remember on one occasion watching a tipsy, rather too-old-for-this-kind-of-thing woman in an elaborate, satiny, pink-and-black costume attempt to serenade her beau of the evening with 'We'll Gather Lilacs', until at a moment of what she must have decided was cruel inattention she walloped him with her handbag and began to weep.

Many years after the trio had ceased to perform, I realised that the man standing beside me at the bar of another city pub was none other than the trio's violinist, and told him that I had been present at many of his performances. 'You must miss it,' I said.

He looked at me in derisive wonder. 'I bloody hated it,' he said.

* * *

In all the years I knew him, I never asked Arnold what he

thought of his first evening in Yates's. But given how invariably he welcomed, even relished, new experiences, I'm pretty certain he'd have been enthralled. At that time there were other Yates's across the Midlands and North of England. All of them, so I was told, had been set up in the earlier years of the nineteenth century as cheap lodging houses for those navvies who dug the canals and, then, railways, which connected industrial cities and for the most part led eventually to London. I have been into several of these Yates's, but none compares to Nottingham's. Yates's Wine Lodge was unique.

As for Arnold, he, too, was unique, though it took me some time to realise this. He was in the city, so he told me that evening, because he had been appointed to design an exhibition intended as the centre-piece for the first Nottingham Festival. This was due to be held the following summer, and the exhibition, which would be staged at Nottingham Castle, was to be called Young Bert, and would focus on the early years of D.H. Lawrence, before he left his home city, part outcast, part wanderer by choice.

I should perhaps say here that when I arrived in Nottingham in 1964 I was asked to represent the University in its association with Eastwood's decision to establish a D. H. Lawrence Centre in Lawrence's home town. Some years earlier, a fund had been set up, so I was told, to raise money for the proposed Centre. The fund was closed in 1968, at about the time I got back from a year in America with Pauline and our two young children. When the total amount collected was counted up it amounted to £2.6s.8d.

Lawrence was not popular in Eastwood. He was, locals said, 'a mardy-arse'. He was also too big for his boots, and he wrote 'mucky books'. The (in)famous 1960 *Lady Chatterley* trial freed the novel for public sale, and I remember being on Charing Cross Station as the court judgement came through and W.H. Smith's bookstall, which had kept copies of the Penguin unexpurgated edition under the counter, as it were, in anticipation of the outcome, put them on display. Queues formed to buy the paperback, among them many men – I don't recall seeing any women in the queues – whom you'd not readily associate with the reading of fiction. Certainly no maidservants. This, despite the fears of the QC who had defended a continuation of the ban by famously asking the book's champions, 'Would you allow your maidservant to read this book?', and who further enquired whether it was possible to have 'reverence for a man's balls.' 'Yes,' Richard Hoggart, witness for the publishers solemnly replied; but I'm not sure that publication of the unexpurgated *Lady Chatterley's Lover* did much for Lawrence's reputation in and around Eastwood. Balls to that.

All this was soon to change. I remember a wonderfully good production of his play, *The Daughter-in-Law*, at the new Nottingham Playhouse; Ken Russell's film of *Women in Love* was released a very few years later, and I mustn't forget to pay tribute to the 1961 exhibition of such of Lawrence's work as was at that time owned by the University, and which I'd travelled up from Reading to see. The exhibition was curated by the then Professor of English, Vivian da Sola Pinto, Lawrence enthusiast and an editor of the Heinemann 3-volume *Collected Poems*. I later heard that there were mutterings about the exhibition besmirching the posthumous reputation of Ernest Weekley, who had been Nottingham's Professor of German at the moment when Lawrence went off with Frieda, but the 1961 show must have helped restore and advance the writer's cause.

I have to say, though, that Arnold's *Young Bert* was in an entirely different league from the University exhibition. That showed its artefacts in museum cases with explanatory captions and a few blow-up photographs positioned on adjacent walls. *Young Bert* re-created the experience of what it must have been like to know yourself a miner's son, provided visitors to the exhibition with the feeling for a mining community, and, above all, made them aware of what he must have felt like as a youth who was both part of that community and wanting, *needing*, to get beyond it, to break away. Fifty years after encountering *Young Bert* I can still vividly recall its effect on me. For once a cliché is appropriate. Arnold's exhibition has left an indelible impression. I am still deeply affected by what I then witnessed, and took in. I had never seen anything like it. Nor, I'd swear, have I seen anything since to rival its impact (although the 1978 Louvre exhibition, *Paris-Berlin*, about the years leading up to and following the First World War, comes close); Arnold was without doubt an exhibition designer of genius and that exhibition in particular was one of unique, lasting brilliance. So: what it was like.

To get to *Young Bert* you had to climb the Castle

Museum and Art Gallery's main staircase, and as you curved upward, you became aware that you were in a sense entering an industrial, smoke-filled past: of factories and straight streets of bricky, terraced back-to-backs. Panoramic photographs of late-nineteenth century Nottingham flanked the entrance to the upper galleries.

Beyond the entrance to these galleries, which was by means of imposing wooden doors, you found yourself in a narrow, dimly-lit passage with, on either side, pictures of miners, stripped to the waist and lying at length as they hewed at coal seams.

A turn in the passage and now, unexpectedly, you were standing in a miner's kitchen, complete with kitchen range (superbly re-created by the then master carpenter at the Playhouse, Trevor Pitt.)

Another turn, and now you were in a school-room, rows of desks and more dim lighting, and beyond that the looming arch of a Congregational chapel. (Lawrence's parents belonged to the local branch.)

Through that arch and suddenly, amazingly, space opened up, artificial lighting was replaced by daylight pouring down from both overhead skylights and from high side windows, so that confined spaces were replaced by what momentarily felt limitless sky, and you realised you were now in the Art Gallery itself, Pre-Raphaelite pictures among the paintings hung on walls that embodied a new life, one created out of previously unthinkable possibilities.

Lawrence's discovery of a world of art, of imaginative wonder.

* * *

Arnold had come to Yates's Wine Lodge on the evening he and I first met because Allan had suggested that I might be able to recruit some students to help him to get the exhibition up and ready in time for the Festival opening. Soon after being appointed to curate the exhibition, Arnold, so he now told me, had made enquiries as to who in the English department at Nottingham might be interested in Lawrence, might even be 'an expert', and had been given Allan's name. He was also told that Professor James Boulton might agree to help, although Arnold later revealed that he rather discounted Boulton's worth when in casual conversation the Professor identified Sappho as a minor Greek Goddess. Allan was a likelier prospect. He had after all helped Nottingham's about-to-retire Vivian Da Sola Pinto, of whom he was fond, mount the 1961 exhibition – earlier they had collaborated on the resourceful, provocative Penguin anthology, *The Common Muse*; but he wasn't an enthusiast for Lawrence, whom he thought of as woefully lacking in the reasoned restraint which was his own yardstick for literary worth, and he was relieved when I told Arnold that not only did I passionately admire much of Lawrence's work but that I was pretty sure I could rustle up some student help.

'Payment in beer and sandwiches?' Arnold said.

'That will do,' I assured him.

It did, too. Early in 1972, when serious work on mounting the exhibition began, the students I'd volunteered found time and opportunity to get to the castle in order to take their instructions from a man they soon came to recognise as someone with an extraordinary range of skills, imaginative energy, and, always, wit. They were, I think, in awe of Arnold, as I was. They loved being in his presence, and he was always enthusiastic about and quick to praise the work they did for him. They were also taken aback by his various abilities. He was an expert paperhanger, he could turn his hand to carpentry, he painted walls, he designed and wrote the superb exhibition catalogue, and of course he was always willing to explain, compellingly, what the exhibition would look like when it was finally realised, and what it would do to make the world recognise Lawrence's own genius. 'Though,' Arnold said, 'he can be the most *appalling* bore.' Arnold enjoyed dramatic utterance, or perhaps it was that he enjoyed dramatising utterance. Either way, his words were usually accompanied by a shout of laughter.

As work progressed Arnold spent an increasing number of nights at our house, and during the evenings he and I often discussed poets and poetry. By now I had discovered that Arnold was himself a poet. As well as work in a variety of magazines and journals, all of them on the political left, a collection had been published by Chatto & Windus. Arnold was a friend of Roy Fuller and had, he revealed, given Fuller a copy of a recently published pamphlet sequence of mine, *About Nottingham*. To my surprise and, of course, pleasure, Fuller had sent him a warm note about the pamphlet, which Arnold now passed on to me. Most of the writers he knew well he had met through their being paid-up members of the Communist Party of Great Britain. These included Sylvia Townsend Warner and Edgell Rickword, both of whom he revered, Randall Swingler, Montagu Slater, and E.P. Thompson. Did I know that in his early days Thompson had written both verse and prose fiction?

'You know *Thompson*?'

Thompson was a hero of mine, his great book, *The Making of the English Working Class*, the *vade mecum* for my own early work on nineteenth-century novelists, especially Elizabeth Gaskell and, above all, Dickens. And of course his campaigning work for CND made him a hero for younger people on the left. And now I was discovering that Arnold knew him, was indeed a friend of both E.P. and 'Dottie', Dorothy, Thompson's wife, herself an historian of some distinction.

Yes, he knew Thompson. They were in fact friends from school days. Another friend from those days, Arnold added, was the great Shelley scholar, Geoffrey Matthews. As a very young man, Matthews, too, had written and published poetry, and some of the good poems he wrote during the war could be found in contemporary verse anthologies. Which school was Arnold talking about? Kingswood, he told me, a public school near Bath, an establishment especially favoured by Methodists, especially Methodist missionaries. Kingswood was the school to which many of these missionaries sent their sons. Arnold's father had spent long years, so I gathered, living and working in China, and, his first wife having died young, took for second wife the governess of his boys. She'd also, I think, then become mother to further boys; and in due course all were shipped home to England to be educated.

As he grew to man's estate, so Arnold, by then in his mid-to-late teens, together with some of his contemporaries at Kingswood, became an enthusiast for the CPGB. They somehow managed to buy and smuggle into school a number of copies of the *Daily Worker*, which they hid under their beds. Arnold's ardent commitment to the Communist cause was such that, to the headmaster's fury, he elected to play a piano piece by Bartok at a school concert. As he told me this, smoking all the time – *Senior Service* was his preferred choice and he was seldom without a packet of twenty – Arnold laughed gleefully.

'You're a pianist?'

'I *was*.' And I now learnt that in earlier years Arnold had been a performer of such promise that a career on the concert platform was dangled before him as a distinct possibility.

'What made you change your mind?'

'A little-known encounter between a tank and a bicycle in Trowbridge High Street.'

And, still laughing though now a touch ruefully, Arnold explained that after Stalin changed his mind about the worth of the Hitler-Ribbentrop Pact, or anyway had it changed for him by the Nazi invasion of the USSR, all young British communists were encouraged to fight against the Fascists who had before then been regarded as allies in the great cause of international freedom from capitalism. King Street and Harry Pollitt came calling, courtesy of the *Worker*, and as a result Arnold joined the army. Unfortunately, while undergoing training at Trowbridge he was accidentally knocked off his bike by a trainee tank driver, broke his arm in some twenty places, and that was the end of his possible career as a concert pianist.

* * *

Can you have too many talents? In the thirty or so years I knew him, I sometimes wondered whether Arnold was ever bewildered by the possibilities that must at various times have seemed open to him. He wrote plays and at least one never-to-be published novel, he wrote and published poetry, including several collections; after the war, he edited the Communist Party Journal of the Arts, *Our Time*; he loved music and but for an accident he might have become a professional musician. But then he couldn't have been an exhibition designer, could he? By the time I came to know him, he was already recognised in London for his outstanding abilities as a designer, and had, I think I'm right in saying, worked for a number of major department stores, including Heal's and Selfridge's. I've no idea how much money he got from this work. He and his wife, Simonette, known as Sim, lived in a flat in Fulham with their two children, Emma and Adam, and Sim, I learnt, was a sometime actor who had been in various productions for the CP's Unity Theatre. She was also a niece of the architect, Clough Williams Ellis, creator of Portmeirion, and she and Arnold were slowly restoring a derelict shepherd's cottage, dating back to the fifteenth century, which stood in a field on the edge of Ffestiniog, not far from Portmeirion itself.

All this information came higgledy-piggledy during the nights and occasional weekends when Arnold was our guest. He invariably rose early, ready to be off to the Castle, though before he left I would find him breakfasting with Ben and Emma in the kitchen, telling them stories, not all of them tall, and already filling the air with cigarette smoke as he drank cup after cup of the tea which he had brewed.

'Like Orwell,' I once said. But Arnold didn't approve of Orwell. Orwell had dished the dirt on various members of the CPGB and his *Animal Farm* had traduced the communist cause. 'Besides,' Arnold said, 'he writes piss-poor prose.'

Orwell? Still, I chose to keep quiet on the matter. There would be time enough.

* * *

What I hadn't reckoned on was Arnold's capacity for sudden, absolute, and unreasonable anger. This was rarely evident, but as I had cause to discover when the fit was on him conversation became impossible. Far more often, though, he was someone I identified as a man of laughter, of wit, of charm. He got on well with a wide variety of people, was a wonderful raconteur, and a gifted, semi-impromptu lecturer. I got him to talk to students at Nottingham about writers he knew, pretty sure he would have interesting and perceptive things to say (he did), as well as tales to tell about the underbelly of literary life, the rackety, hand-to-mouth unpredictability of journal publications. Again, he obliged with tales that enthralled his audience. He delighted in life's absurdities and, especially, unpredictabilities, for which reason he got on well with children, who, if our small son and even smaller daughter were anything to go by, from the first delighted in his company.

In all those months leading up to the opening of the exhibition I only once saw Arnold ill-at-ease. I had invited John Wain up to give a reading to the University's poetry society, and after the reading I arranged for several of us to share a meal at the staff club. The guests included John, of course, and also Audrey Beecham. An economist by training, Audrey was herself a published poet. Heinemann had some years earlier brought out her *Coast of Barbary*, and the fabled Tambimuttu, back in London from who knows where, was apparently promising to take another collection for his new Salamander Press. (Both publisher and press were shortly to disappear without trace: par for the course.) She and John knew each other from Oxford days, and John had arranged to stay the night at the women's hall on campus where Audrey was now a warden of fiercesome reputation. She was rumoured to carry a blunderbuss, a weapon she was ready to fire off at any importunate male student who might dare to threaten her charges' peace of mind and which she was widely reported to have carried into battle with her when she enlisted for the Republican cause during the Spanish Civil War.

I collected both visiting poet and Hall Warden at the appropriate moment, and was ordered to take charge of Audrey's voluminous, stuffed handbag, which to general bemusement – 'A *handbag*, Dr Lucas' – I carried into the room on campus where the reading was to take place. (Arnold would make his own way there.) We had a full house, to which I introduced John, and then I went back to join Audrey, intending to hand over the bag.

'Open it.'

I did so. It was full of packets of small cigars, among which she rooted before unearthing what I think she called a sufflacator, a small, metal object she claimed helped her cope with asthma. 'Wake me when he finishes,' she said, jammed the device into her mouth, shut her eyes and fell asleep.

An hour later, when John had finished his reading and answered a number of routine questions, Audrey shook herself awake, stood, gave me the handbag, and we went for our meal at the staff club. I introduced Arnold, who was waiting for us, a copy of one of John's collections under his arm, and rather hoped the three of them would find plenty to talk about. After all, Audrey and Arnold had their avowed commitment to the communist cause in common, all were poets, and Arnold and John were familiar with the literary life of London. But there was little talk. It was John who came out of the occasion best, telling some not-bad stories in the style I by then knew pretty well: bluff, self-deprecatory, edged with satiric purpose. The rest of us nodded, smiled, and occasionally laughed. But Audrey contributed little, and Arnold was silent throughout.

Why? I was puzzled by his muted presence at the table and, as I drove him back to our house – the other two would walk to the Hall where John was to be given his bed for the night – I asked him whether he had found the occasion disagreeable. No, Arnold said. He had, he insisted, enjoyed both meal and the conversation that went with it – really? – although he couldn't find much to warm to in John's poems, which he had found time earlier in the day to glance through.

Was he trying to reassure me, or was there some other explanation for his silence? Could it be that he felt himself ill at ease in the company of those who might have more social confidence than he could muster? Or was John's name, still high in the literary world, enough to stifle his own conversational wit. Such a possibility had never before occurred to me, but in later years I came to realise that Arnold wasn't necessarily the master, let alone monarch, of all he surveyed, that he needed to feel assured he was among friends or at least people he could trust before launching himself into the swirl of social occasion.

* * *

As *Young Bert* came nearer to completion, or anyway the opening date loomed closer, so the Castle's director became increasingly nervous, apprehensive as to whether all would be ready on time. I remember two moments in particular from a fraught week immediately prior to the opening. First, someone brought news that a store in Luton was being dismantled, and that a large plaster phoenix, which was part of the store's frontage, was for immediate sale. Phoenix. Lawrence's symbol. Surely we should try to buy it and hang it as part of the exhibition? Arnold was all for the suggestion.

Telephone calls were made, the cost of buying and transporting the phoenix to Nottingham declared to be 'within budget', the by now openly-twitchy Castle curator's demurrals waved away, and a flat-bed truck was hired and dispatched to fetch the bird. I happened to be in the Castle grounds when the truck arrived, and watched, both aghast and enthralled, as the vast white beast, at least five feet high and almost as round, and which looked rather more like a gigantic iced pudding than anything avian, was driven slowly up the main path to the Castle itself. There, a posse of porters, supplemented by students, somehow unmoored it, coaxed and shoved it through the Castle's front doors, staggered three abreast up the wide, curving stairs with their trophy, then with further coaxing and shoving got the entirely improbable phoenix into the entry to the exhibition, and awaited further instructions.

For once, Arnold seemed unsure where the acquisition might be placed to best advantage, but at last chose the exhibition's final room, where the phoenix, he explained, could float above flames concocted from ribbons of red satin stirred to motion by a wind machine.

'But, Arnold, we haven't *got* a wind machine.'

The curator's moan, more of a despairing whisper, was met with a disdainful smile.

'The Playhouse will lend us theirs.'

He was right. To most people's surprised relief, though not to Arnold's, a phone call to Trevor Pitt resulted in the delivery within an hour of a wind machine, brought over from the Playhouse by a couple of technicians who installed it and declared it to be in good working order. And while this was going on, some strips of ribbon, rescued from a Castle store cupboard, were being arranged in such a way as to persuade the impressionable that they constituted flames.

There was, however, a more serious problem. The phoenix would have to be hauled aloft in order to be positioned over the flames. How to manage that? Someone suggested that a system of ropes and pulleys might do the trick. There being no pulleys, we were reduced to wrapping about what we were all beginning to recognise was an increasingly dubious-looking bird lengths of rope that had been rooted out from another store cupboard, following which we had to heave the phoenix upward until it was sited approximately above the fluttering ribbons, and after we could secure the ropes to nearby wall radiators and hope that the radiators would bear the strain. Easy? A doddle, someone said.

Right, then. Heave-ho, my hearties. Five of us, including an aged porter, slowly winched the phoenix up until it was roughly in position, at which point the bird's absurd shape and colour became apparent and four of us broke into uncontrollable laughter. As laughter became hysterical we let go of our ropes and the bird began a rapid descent. The porter, however, was still clinging on to his rope, and as the bird came down so he went up. Until, that is, he realised he was on his own, at which point he let go of his rope and crashed to the floor beside the bird.

Subsequent investigation revealed that man and bird had each damaged a leg. The porter was taken to hospital, the bird, when once more hoisted aloft, left one of its legs on the floor. (And as a one-legged phoenix it would continue to preside over the exhibition's rear exit until the show was taken down.) Nevertheless, with one day to go, the phoenix was up. All was now ready.

The next day was spent in tidying, securing, last-minute titivating.

Or so we hoped. But then Arnold wanted the schoolroom to be re-figured, and once that was done some adjustments were required to the Congregational Arch. We were still at it the following morning, when the exhibition was meant to be open to the public.

There was to be a Grand Opening of the Festival that evening, at which the Festival Supremo, Richard Gregson Williams, dubbed by Arnold 'Wretched Grigson', would be in attendance, as would the Mayor and Corporation, various bits of minor royalty, and some MPs, though all day, at Arnold's insistence, *Young Bert* was meant to be accessible to anyone interested in seeing it.

Mid-morning the director, white-faced and trembling, burst in on us.

'Arnold, there's a visiting party of Americans wanting to see the exhibition.'

'Tell them to come back tomorrow,' Arnold said, surveying the re-positioned Arch.

'Arnold, they've flown over especially. They represent a Society of American Lawrentians.'

'Well, they're not coming in here,' Arnold said. 'Not yet. Talk to them. Take them for an early lunch and bring them back this afternoon. We'll be ready by then.' He was entirely at his ease.

I've forgotten the details of how that particular episode ended, but everyone who saw the exhibition, and there must have been thousands before the Festival was over, knew that they'd experienced something special, even, I want to say, wondrous. Hugely inventive, endlessly surprising, resourceful, persuasive, an eye- and even mouth-opener. And it left me, and no doubt others, certain that Arnold's ability as an exhibition designer went well beyond what could be called talent. Genius? Why not?

* * *

After *Young Bert* had been finally taken down, Arnold proposed that the season being high June and the weather settled, we should have a picnic party to celebrate and thank the many helpers who'd been recruited to offer their, usually unpaid, assistance. He would stand treat, though I suspect that his fee as designer was not enough to ensure he would finish with any money left in his pocket. I suggested that people who came should bring their own drinks. Good idea. But though he gave ground on this, Arnold insisted that he would arrange for the food.

I also suggested that an appropriate site for the party would be Dale Abbey. I had in mind a place some five or six miles into Derbyshire, where sloping fields and woods (within which were sandstone caves said to have been lived in by hermits) led down to the remains of a ruined Cistercian abbey, with a small village and public house a few strides away. Between us we had enough cars to transport all party-goers to the site, an alfresco cricket match could be arranged for anyone interested, and music would be supplied by transistor radio for those who wished to dance. A good time could be guaranteed for all. And a good time we all had. The weather was perfect, sun and blue skies, and I suspect that Arnold in particular rejoiced in the kind of occasion that was, for him, the essence of fellowship, of a sweet, even republic. Children, including our own, ran around, tumbled and rolled downhill or hid among the trees, a grotto rumoured to have once housed some of Robin Hood's outlaws (it hadn't) was a ready attraction for adults of enquiring minds, others preferred to wander about the abbey ruins, a few played a desultory game of cricket, there was some jigging and hopping to radio dance music; and when, finally, darkness began to reclaim the land, we all, surely, felt that something of lasting worth had been achieved, a time of such quality that nothing could erase or demean it. And so it proved, for one mind at least.

* * *

Later that year, Arnold was again staying with us. There were two reasons for this. The first was that Allan and I had asked if we could publish a collection of his poems under the Byron Press imprint. *Second Causes*, Arnold's Chatto book, part of the publisher's Phoenix Living Poets series, had appeared in 1969. The title came from Sir Walter Raleigh's *The History of the World*: 'To say that God was pleased to have it so, were a true but idle answer … Wherefore we may boldly look into the second causes.' And for Arnold, the committed communist, these causes had to do with how political power belongs to the ruthless, destructive force of the capitalist West. Hence, 'Nuclear Politician', a sonnet which begins: 'He seems bovine. His opinions are not that/Clear to us – though the dewlap is, the cud/ Chewing opinion.' And it ends 'butchers may make/This minister as prime as other beef.' Clever, wittily phrased, the run-on lines fracturing any hint of resolution.

In many ways the deliberate spikiness put me in mind of Arnold's calligraphy: the same elegant clarity disrupted by an almost unnerving aggression, an anger that marked moments in Arnold's life as in his art. His poems both intrigued and unsettled me, and I was keen for the Byron Press, which Allan and I had begun in 1965, to have a collection from Arnold, especially as he'd shown me a sequence called *Mozart Pieces*, which he'd had printed as a small chapbook and distributed among friends as a kind of Christmas card. I loved it, but Arnold, who never seemed short of poems, didn't want to include it. (Though it was later to make a re-appearance in *Mr Dick's Kite*, of which there will be more to say.)

The collection we published in 1972 as *Man Thinking* contains a number of Arnold's characteristically witty, excoriating poems, among them 'Reflections in a Dining Car'. In this poem, we listen in as business men chunter on while they fork up their BR dinner. 'Always "one"/ to each other, they are many: their dim validity's/That history is always with us …'. Beyond the train window are donkeys at grass, and at the moment one of the diners, by now drunk, asks, 'What's one's opinion of Inter Contillistic Ballentine Missiles?/ Damned if a donkey at Flitwick doesn't lift and bray/An immediate answer – pissed again, presumably, on thistles.' The collection's title, I should add, comes from Gorki, who is apologising to a friend for his 'sick soul', before adding that 'this, by the way, is how the soul of a thinking man should be.'

The other reason Arnold was at Beeston was that he'd come to negotiate with the Festival organisers over an exhibition on Bicycling which they wanted him to put on in 1973. Of course, he accepted the offer, of course he both designed and undertook the research for the exhibition, and of course it was a terrific piece of work, full of his exuberant wit, his take on velocipedes, tandems, penny-farthings, and all the rest of that form of transport with which Nottingham's Raleigh factory in particular was associated, which it had, you could say, made its own.

There were also two incidents to explain why I recall that visit in particular. The first was that while Arnold was with us, Ian Fletcher came to stay for a night. Known, at least in academia and its surroundings, as the university teacher without a degree, as well as a poet whose abiding passion was for the Decadence – he was an authority on Walter Pater and poets of the 1890s (the more recherché the better) – Ian was by the 1970s a senior lecturer in Reading's English department. One of the most erudite as well as one of the most unworldly men I've ever known, his possible academic career had been prevented by the Second World War, which caused him to spend years in Egypt in the army, though he was never permitted to carry a loaded gun. Not only was he chronically short-sighted, he was quite without hand-eye co-ordination, and it was feared that if required to take aim he was far more likely to damage friend than foe. He was, I think, appointed to a post in Propaganda, where he met other poets and literary men, including G.S. Fraser, who was to become a close friend when the two found themselves in post-war London. Ian's first collection, *Orisons*, was published – wouldn't you know – by Tambimuttu in 1947, and some years later, when John Wain introduced him to Reading's great, eccentric professor of English, D.J. Gordon, Gordon, encouraged by both Wain and Frank Kermode (himself a Gordon recruit from Liverpool University), appointed Ian to a lectureship in English, waving away protestations from the more conventionally minded, of whom there were many, that the new lecturer was without degree, let alone higher academic qualifications.

I had invited Ian up to Nottingham to talk to my students about the Illustrated Book in the Nineteenth Century, the subject of his belated doctoral thesis, and when Arnold, too, arrived, I hoped they might find themselves wanting to discuss what was after all a subject of great and abiding interest, especially as both were preoccupied to the point of adoration with William Morris and the Kelmscott Press.

Fat chance. Arnold mentioned that he had once come across an illustrated edition of Bunyan's *Pilgrim's Progress*.

'Fortunate to have escaped the attention of Cromwell's wreckers,' Ian said, curling a contemptuous lip, and nobody could curl such a lip more effectively than Ian.

Oh, and what was wrong with Cromwell?

'Damned philistine,' Ian said. 'No church decoration was safe while he and his minions were at large.'

Cromwell was, of course, a hero to Arnold. Cromwell, who'd opposed the brutal horrors of monarchy. He mentioned Christopher Hill's account of Cromwell the liberator.

'*Hill?*' Ian was incredulous. 'The man probably invents his sources. He certainly makes sure to suppress all the evidence that goes against him. About as trustworthy as a page of *Pravda*.'

Christopher Hill was at that time the most celebrated of English Marxist historians, though it later turned out that, as Ian claimed that evening – on what authority I don't know – Hill wasn't to be trusted with his use of sources, nor, even, the sources themselves. Arnold was outraged by Ian's claims and said so, but Ian was unrepentant. Arnold stamped off to bed.

The evening was not a success.

Fortunately, Ian had gone by the time Arnold returned the following afternoon. The thunder clouds of the previous evening had entirely blown away and he was in high good humour. Wretched Grigson had announced that the Festival Committee was delighted, excited, indeed enthralled, by Arnold's plans for the Bicycling exhibition and had offered a generous fee for all his labours, including an extra sum to cover the cost of research that would be necessary before work on the exhibition itself could begin.

We celebrated over a glass of wine. One was enough because Arnold wasn't a serious toper, and anyway a taxi would soon be arriving to take him to Nottingham station, from where he was due to return to London. He and Sim were still living most of the year in a flat in Fulham, though they were, I knew, hoping soon to take up residence in the Ffestiniog cottage.

'Oh, by the way,' he said, as we waited the cab's arrival, 'that friend of yours.'

'Ian Fletcher?'

'He's given me the idea for a chapbook and I've begun scribbling.'

Well, good. When, early next year Arnold sent to friends the short sequence, *A Minor Incident in the Civil War*, it proved to be a characteristically inventive contrivance with exuberant cover illustrations from what Arnold dubbed 'a tiny barmy comic of 1848', itself contained within 'a squib dramatisation of Macaulay's History of England called *The Groan, The Grave, and The Gallows*.'

So don't come the erudite with me, Ian Fletcher.

* * *

There would be other such sequences to greet future years, and indeed *Greetings* was what Arnold called these little chapbooks, noting the contradictory meaning of the word itself: '*to greet*: to welcome, to mourn.' We live in the best of times, we live in the worst of times.

The Greetings were identical in format: pocket book size (6x4inches), never more than 16 pp in toto, saddle-stitched, each of them with intriguing, often witty, cover designs and/or illustrations. The first and best, *Mozart Pieces*, greeted the year 1971, the last, *Seven Forms of Prayer*, was for 1975, its place of origin given as 'Ffestiniog'; and in between came *Ten Cwm Cynfal Poems*, for 1974, with illustrations by Gareth Parry. Parry was identified in a prefatory note as 'a young artist in Ffestiniog who has haunted Cwm Cynfal all his life and seems at times on almost nodding, how-do-y'do terms with every bird and twig in the place.' Arnold once again delighting in his discovery of local, unsung talent, that 'genius of the place' which goes far to explaining his rejoicing in the existence of John Clare. As for 1973's *Cold Poems in Waiting*, that was prefaced by a note identifying the illustrations as drawn by the artist

'Pauline Lucas to whom – and to … John Lucas – these poems were first sent by way of continuing the conversation.'

The conversation was taken up with the question of what, as the opening poem puts it, 'does a work of art achieve?' Answer, 'It changes me.' I remember that occasion. It was a time of cold. In the UK the Tories were back in power, elsewhere the Prague Spring of 1968 had already returned to winter, the ghastly war in Vietnam was not yet done with, while in Greece the brutal, idiotic generals had, thanks to American help, put an end to democracy. Pauline's drawings of tree forms in winter evoked gaunt shapes and spectral limbs, their greys seemingly uncompromising, deadly. But behind and even entwined with these were other shapes, thin branches asserting persistence, renewal, even the bare, as yet spectral outlines of young leaves, drawn in green. Change could, would happen.

* * *

Though the sequence of Greetings ended in 1975, Arnold wasn't by any means finished as a poet. In 1981 Harry Chambers' Peterloo Poets published *Dull Weather Dance*. The front cover of this full collection is of a detail from Sleights Tom, which a note identifies as 'probably the oldest folk costume in Britain', and is, in its higgledy-piggledy mixture of faces, costumes, animals, flower forms, and animal shapes, expressive of the kind of rich confusion in which Arnold delighted. It would never have occurred to him to condescend to folk art. I'm not at all sure that the term would have passed his lips. *All* art was eloquent, was the utterance of human desire, of yearning and attainment. And though he was dubious about jazz, wrongly identifying it as irredeemably tainted by American capitalism – the approved line followed by 30s Marxists, the worse fools they – he more readily rejoiced in both individual and community expressiveness. *Dull Weather Dance* includes more than a few poems that celebrate the history and geography of the area of North Wales where by then he and Sim lived, and which they loved.

He wanted others to love it, too. Ben told me that when as a teenager he and his mates went off on cycling tours of parts of England and Wales, he and one other, at Arnold's invitation, biked to the Rattenbury cottage, where Arnold prepared a filling midday meal, in which baked beans and potatoes featured, after which he took them on a long walk down the small, riotous river that ran at the bottom of the cottage's garden. Arnold himself provides an account of this river as a tail-note to *Ten Cwm Cynfal Poems*.

'The Cynfal,' he says, 'is a small important river which sometimes dawdles, sometimes crashes through a deep gash gouged out of the rocky bottom of its gentle Cwm. My home and other ancient places here … are named for episodes in a *Mabinogion* tale; and the Cwm is full of birds – properly, since Blodeuwydd, the story's heroine, was magicked by Merlyn out of feathers and twigs.'

'Poetry is everywhere,' Arnold adds. 'The home of sweet 17th-century Morgan Llwyd, bi-lingual poet and revolutionary, is just across the Cwm.' And he names others who once lived or at least came close to the place, including Robert Graves and Shelley. 'This is a world to surprise poems out of anyone – even an Englishman ... Christ and Zeus and Art and Time and John Clare and Revolution step in and out of mine.'

What he says in that tail-note could be said about all his collections, as reviewers, including those writing in the *London Magazine* and *TLS* readily acknowledged. They also spoke warmly of Arnold's metrical cunning, and his ability, as Brian Jones noted, to make use of – rather than be used by – traditional forms. 'Always the will to say something accurately syncopates the music we predict.' Amen to that, although Arnold remains a poet far less known and admired than he should be.

I published three of his collections for Shoestring Press: *The Frigger Makers* (1994), *Morris Papers* two years later, which was timed to coincide with the hundredth anniversary of one of Arnold's great heroes, William Morris, and then *Mr Dick's Kite*. Finally, and posthumously, Andy Croft's Smokestack Books brought out *Several Forms of Speech*, which carries the sub-title 'New, Early, Escaped and Last Poems'.

Because this present essay isn't in any sense an exhaustive account of Arnold as poet, it would be wrong to spend long on any of his collections, much though I hope someone else will want to do so. But it would be equally wrong not to point to what I especially value about the three Shoestring collections. Of them all, the one I perhaps value most is *The Frigger Makers*, and not merely because this substantial 24-page pamphlet, published in 1994 and punching far above its weight as the phrase goes, is the very first Shoestring Press publication. On the insides of the front and back card covers are images of frigger makers themselves and of the works of art, craft, objects of delight, comedy – call them what you will – that they created. These are all identified in the Key to Inside Cover Illustrations given at the back of the pamphlet, among them 'Three Cellardyke fishermen wearing knitted Ganseys (Guernseys). Scottish Fisheries Museum, Anstruther, Fife', 'Boody Dish decorated with cigar wrappers. North of England Open Air Museum, Beamish', and, three of my own favourites, 'Proggy, Cat on Mat, by Isobel Waterhouse, Bradford', 'Coronation procession for William IV. Glassworkers … bearing aloft wares and friggers … two apparently wearing glass Frigger hats. Bristol Museum and Art Gallery', and 'Slate Fan, carved and split, Blaenau Ffestiniog (private collection)'.

This last in fact hung from the mantelpiece of Arnold and Sim's cottage, an object of wonder to all who did it espy, given that it was heavy enough to have broken the wrist of anyone hoping to use it to fan the air. And this of course was the point. 'Friggers' were works created by craftsmen and women who delighted in using their skills to create articles and whimsical objects of wit, laughter, sheer devil-my-lad ingenuity. The sequence is dedicated 'to the memory of E.P. Thompson', and the opening poem, 'The

Making' and identified as 'for Edward', rejoices in all who retrieve 'artworks' from their daily toil. People not to be missed/who make such classy marvels of the heart/common – now, while history's/condescension is a privilegious Art.' That last line picks up on Thompson's own famous, scornful repudiation of history's 'enormous condescension to the poor stockinger', and *The Frigger Makers* as a whole, derived from Arnold's visits to out-of-the-way museums of curiosity and working-class history, is *of course* a poetic frigger making. Each of the sixteen poems is made up of twenty-four lines, though the lines are broken into stanzas of different lengths, sometimes snapped off mid-line, so that you could be forgiven for not noticing the ingenuity that has gone into their making. *The Frigger Makers* celebrates, rejoices in, and exemplifies the making of art as creative delight.

We launched *Morris Papers* at Morris's house in Hammersmith in 1996, to coincide with the great man's centenary. The poems of that sequence use as their starting point Morris wallpaper designs, and some of these are reproduced in the book itself, carefully and conscientiously seen through to production by Albert Haynes of Nottingham's Goater Press. A prickly man, Albert, with his own sense of what a printing press should and shouldn't do, which took some of the pleasure away from our joint enterprise. Still, the book itself was successfully seen into the world at both Hammersmith, where a sizeable number of old comrades turned up for the occasion, and Sheffield, where we presented it at the Graves Gallery, up the road from the Guild of St George, the city's Ruskin Museum. Appropriate enough, given that Ruskin, lover of craft, was one of Morris's early heroes. That Sheffield launch, in particular, I remember as an enjoyable, even festive, occasion.

I have far less happy memories of the last of Arnold's Shoestring publications, *Mr Dick's Kite*, 2005. Not because of the collection itself, which was as good as anything that went before, and which, in its title – taken from the eccentric, not-to-be-deflected dreamer of *David Copperfield* – welcomes the visions of those who refuse to be grounded by pessimism. The front cover reproduces a 1932 painting by Evan Walters which Arnold had unearthed from the basement of the Cardiff Museum and Art Gallery: a communist orator, in flaring red waistcoat, stands on a soap box, gazing toward the sky, arms flung wide as he predicts to his cloth-capped and overalled listeners a realisable future he invites them to share.

One of the most loveable, admirable, things about Arnold was his unsubduable hope. Very sadly, the launch of *Mr Dick's Kite* came near to disaster. The venue I had chosen was The Flying Goose Café in Beeston, where for some time I had been arranging monthly poetry readings, and where a sympathetic audience could be more or less guaranteed. Capacity was roughly 40, and on this occasion, as on most, we had a crammed house. Good. Not good, however, the poet I had invited to read with Arnold, a former student of mine at Nottingham and someone whose work I admired. It wasn't his work that was the problem, it was that when he arrived he turned out to be ill with some sort of bug that slurred his speech and muddied his mind. He should have been in bed, but very honourably he didn't want to let me down so forced himself to be in attendance.

Poor man, and, more especially, poor Arnold. My former student read first, a recent short story, which, he insisted, would not take long. It did. Whenever he lost his place, which seemed to be every other sentence, he would gaze blankly around at his audience as though they might be able to help, and as a result the reading seemed to go on forever. It certainly took the best part of an hour for him finally to be done. There was then an obligatory interval so that people could buy further coffees, etc. By the time I was able to introduce Arnold, who had been driven down from Sheffield by his daughter and was first eager and then increasingly impatient to read, the evening was as good as over, the majority of listeners consulting their watches, shuffling into their coats, several heading none-too-surreptitiously for the door.

When I'd invited Arnold to launch his book at the café, and told him something about the venue – 'ideal', I'd promised – I suggested he read for some half-an-hour, after which we could have a question-and-answer session. As it was, he had a bare ten minutes before the café-owner indicated that the evening, which had already overrun, was now at an end. It was a wretched conclusion to my close association with Arnold the poet.

*\ *\ *

Rather more than thirty years earlier, in 1974, Pauline and I had been to Crewe Theatre, to see Arnold's play, *A Comedy of Good Intentions*. A prefatory note in the programme for the play, which ran in repertory at Crewe from 20 February to 2 March, reports that:

'This is Arnold Rattenbury's first play to be produced – though his connection with the Theatre goes back a long way, as editor of the respected quarterly THEATRE TODAY during the '40s and '50s, and as a designer of theatre and 'happening' exhibitions then and since … his knock about, shuttlecock use of language in this play is not only very funny and very moving but something only a poet could achieve.'

A further note tells the audience that the play 'is based on an idea described to him many years ago by the American poet, Tom McGrath.'

I'd like to be able to report that the play was at least a *succès d'estime*, but for all the efforts of the cast and the young director, Charles Savage, whom Arnold at first admired but later blamed for much that went awry, it was at best a damp squib. That Arnold himself accepted this is evident not merely in his reply to a letter I sent him when we were back in Beeston, in which I did my best to find things to admire – 'What it is to have good friends, but no, the play didn't work and probably didn't deserve to' – but from a longer letter he wrote to Sylvia Townsend Warner. 'The play … went badly … But it's a good play, I think. I mean: it could work, if only because, here and there, when it was left to do so, it did.' He blames directorial interference for much of what went wrong, but also acknowledges his own errors. 'I'll clean the text up again ... I learnt a lot. You can't write plays in isolation ...' He may have re-written *A Comedy of Good Intentions*, but the play never re-surfaced in the theatre.

* * *

For all the failure of his play, Arnold was a passionate believer in the theatre, and in drama as a people's art form. It was about the time of his disappointment with the play, and perhaps because of it, when on an occasion he was with us, he became almost hysterically angry at what I thought an uncontentious remark of mine, to the effect that for many people, film and visits to the cinema had become far more popular than the theatre. Film was cheaper, you didn't have to dress up for it, it was easier to get to, and for all the glitzy commercialism of Hollywood, major creators like Sweden's Ingmar Bergman, and Billy Wilder, originally from Berlin but now within the Hollywood ambit, were able to use the medium to create major work.

Arnold wasn't having any of this. Like so many Marxists of his age, he thought of film as he did of jazz. They were both capitalist corruptions of true art, bastard products of a diseased society. I argued back. After all, in the 1950s I'd seen plenty of examples of Russian films at the National

Film Theatre, including of course *The Battleship Potemkin*, and besides, I wasn't going to allow anyone to challenge the propriety of my devotion to Louis Armstrong and the music that spread out from New Orleans. Words, as they say, were exchanged, Arnold insisting that by far the most important writer of the period of history we were living through was the dramatist John Arden; and he then stormed out.

But when he returned next evening from the work he was putting in on the then current Castle exhibition, all was well, any remaining embers of the previous evening's argument by now cold.

* * *

Always keep your friendships in good repair, Dr Johnson advised. Arnold took good care of his. As I have already noted, at least two friendships went back to his school days. E.P. Thompson and Geoffrey Matthews were friends for life. So were friends he made soon after he had joined the CPGB, among them Edgell Rickword and Sylvia Townsend Warner, both of whom he revered, as he did the less famous but estimable Montagu Slater. Slater is perhaps best known for his libretto for Britten's *Peter Grimes*. As for the poet Randall Swingler, Andy Croft, another good friend of Arnold's, rightly notes in *Comrade Heart*, his biography of Swingler, that Swingler was a man of communist principles who never abandoned his conviction that a fairer and better world, while it had to be fought for, was achievable. Arnold believed this, too, and it ran like a vein of quartz through all he did, wrote, and *was*. Hence his contempt for those fair-weather communists who abandoned the cause once the wind changed.

I think he was unfair to those who changed their minds, some of them slowly, some in a *volte-face* brought about in particular by Stalin's murderous disposal of literally millions of his fellow citizens 'We didn't know it was happening,' Arnold once said to me when I asked him about the GB Party's continuing loyalty to the smiling monster throughout the late 1930s. But I sensed that my question made him ill at ease, and he would have been even more troubled when the tanks trundled into Budapest and then, twelve years later, Prague. These events must have been sickeners for anyone as devoted to the cause as Arnold was. Better to retain faith in the inventiveness and resilience of people whose ordinary creativity shamed the prejudices of those claiming privileged status for themselves and their cliques.

* * *

At the beginning of the 1990s I was invited, courtesy of the British Council, to spend rather more than a week in Romania, reading my poems and lecturing at various cities. By then Ceausescu, 'the monster' as he was dubbed, was dead, as was his wife, the two of them assassinated in murky circumstances, and it was considered safe for me to visit Bucharest as well as some other cities. In the event, ice, fog, and snow prevented me from going beyond the capital, but while I was there, meeting and talking to writers and intellectuals, I heard enough to bewilder me out of certainty, and when I got back I set to and produced a sequence in prose and verse to which, when it was published by Sow's Ear Press, I gave the title *Flying to Romania*. I was uncertain whether to present Arnold with a copy. I knew that getting on for twenty years earlier he and a group of Party members had spent holiday time in Romania, an experience which persuaded them, not that they needed much persuading, of the superiority of communist rule to the decadence of Western capitalism. My own experience was very different. In the end I decided to give Arnold a copy of my sequence, but if he read it he made no comment.

* * *

To the end of his life, Arnold, I'm pretty sure, remained a steadfast communist. And for all I have encountered those who say that this must have damaged if not destroyed his creative impulses, I can confidently say it did no such thing. He went on rejoicing in those who opposed Authority, especially Authority's attempt to exercise the power of censorship over the voices, the imaginative energies, of ordinary people. I remember his joyous bark of laughter when I told him a story about Nottingham Forest soon after Brian Clough became manager of my local club. As with most football grounds, Forest's popular Trent End was more or less reserved for supporters with shallow pockets but deep wells of foul-mouthed abuse which they took some pleasure in pouring over visiting teams and match officials. Clough, though he himself could be and often was pretty foul-mouthed, decided on action. One Saturday, home fans were greeted by a large board at the Trent End on which the club's manager had written in chalk, *NO SWEARING PLEASE GENTLEMEN*. The appeal was signed simply *BRIAN*. After that the fans took to singing THE REFEREE'S AN ORPHAN. Arnold loved that.

Not that he was a football follower, let alone player. Beach cricket was about as far as it went. Once, when Pauline, I, and pre-teenage Ben and Emma were holidaying at Dolgellau, we joined Arnold and Sim, by then installed in their cottage, so that we all could chuffer along the old slate line's narrow gauge railway to Port Madoc. Slate mining at Ffestiniog and its surroundings had by then ceased but the line itself was kept in a state of good repair, and on Port Madoc's wide and sandy beach we played a chaotic, hilarious game of cricket, gazed down on by the wonderfully eccentric, imitation Italianate hill town of Portmeirion which had been created by Clough Williams Ellis, an architect who breathed defiance of bungaloid Britain. He was important to Arnold not merely because he was an older relative of Sim's but because Port Madoc had been the place from where in 1812 Shelley had launched fire balloons to cross the Irish sea, each of them carrying messages encouraging the Irish to rise against their English oppressors. (We did not mention the fact that contrary winds re-directed the fire balloons over Welsh thatched cottages, as a result of which some were burnt to the ground.)

But if Arnold wasn't much of a sportsman, he was without doubt an enthusiastic walker. He had what to my eyes at first looked a strange, flat-footed but straight-spined saunter, shoulders back, and with this he could cover miles without tiring. On various occasions when we were in North Wales, either staying at their cottage or going across to see them from Dolgellau or Barmouth, Pauline and I would accompany him on one of his rambles, while Sim stayed behind to tend to the lovely garden they had created and which ran down from the cottage door to the Cym.

And on the one or two occasions we were staying with our friend, Anne Stevenson and her dear husband, Peter Lucas (no relation) at the cottage not far from Bodloesgadd which Peter had inherited from his mother, we would all meet up for a meal and talk. Sometimes the poet Lee Harwood, a keen hiker, would be at Peter's cottage. Lee preferred solitary walking, but occasionally I went with him, as, once, did Arnold. They spoke of the geology of the area, about which both were knowledgeable, but never of poetry. Lee's devotion to John Ashbery was as little comprehensible to Arnold as Arnold's devotion to Edgell Rickword was to Lee.

Nor do I think Anne, all fire and air, and surely one of the finest lyric poets of our time, had anything in common with Arnold the poet. Where they came together was in music. As a girl, Anne had studied the cello, perhaps hoping for, or at least being steered toward, a career on the concert platform, though that hope remained unrealised, as did Arnold's ambition for a possible future as concert pianist. But both wrote exceptionally fine poems about music, and they were both delighted to discover that not far from where they both had their cottages, the concert pianist, Bernard Roberts, lived with his wife. Roberts supplied them with CDs of some of his recordings and concert performances, and he played at the Memorial Celebration for Arnold, an occasion arranged by Sim together with Emma and Adam, and at which Anne among others read.

* * *

Arnold had died at the end of April, 2007. The cause of death was prostate cancer probably brought on by his many years of heavy smoking; but by then he was a tired man, eighty-six years old, who throughout his life had done an enormous amount of work and, I think, sustained more than his fair share of disappointments. He made light of most of these, though the failure of the communist cause undoubtedly affected him deeply. And in late years he was bitterly angry at what he saw as the failure of Glasgow's Museum and Art Gallery to mount the exhibition of Scottish working-class artefacts – friggers and more – which they had commissioned him to design, and on which he'd spent, as he always did, much imaginative effort and ingenuity. The official reason for this rejection was that the director had come to the conclusion that there simply wasn't enough material to justify the expense involved in putting the exhibition on, but Arnold, who was I think paid a not very large refusal fee, always believed the true explanation to be that the museum authorities were running scared of the radical cause the exhibition championed.

I don't know. I do know that Arnold was someone I loved and who for more than forty years I rejoiced to call a friend. Like Brian Clough and all the others I write about in these pages, he contributed. And that, I think, is a fitting epitaph for someone of diverse talents, talents which he wanted to be of use.

Olive

'I'M A LITTLE BIT CONCERNED,' Olive said.

She was standing in the doorway of my office, dressed in her usual dark-green woollen cardigan, under it a white blouse and her grey, pleated skirt, its hem, which reached beneath her stocking-clad knees, pointing the way to dark-brown brogues that were exchanged for tan sandals during the summer months.

'I'm a little bit concerned.'

As other people might announce their presence each morning by saying, 'Well, at least the weather's good', or 'And how are *you* today?' or 'A right old time of it I had getting here, I can tell you, more traffic than ever on the M1', so Olive said, 'I'm a little bit concerned.'

'Oh?'

I could never anticipate what her concern would be over, or for. It might be that the departmental photocopier wasn't working, or that local police had been called to a campus brawl and arrested one of our students, or that a member of staff had been rushed to hospital, or that she was having difficulties deciphering her own shorthand – the shorthand which she insisted on using though rarely with complete success – or that ... But no, better not to try to guess the reason for this, or any, morning's concern. I had simply to wait for her to tell me.

By now, Olive, having shut my office door behind her as she advanced to stand beside my desk, was looking at me with her habitual smile, one that somehow combined reassurance with apprehension and revealed, whatever experience might have taught her, a determination to take the world on trust. Most people would have called it a generous smile, and I would be one of them. Olive was someone I loved, as I could not possibly love anyone who doubted her, or who indicated, whether by word or gesture or look, a measure of scepticism regarding my secretary. You had only to meet her gaze, healthy, unwavering, her eyes enlarged by her sensible spectacles, to feel the tension across your shoulder muscles begin to slacken. When Olive told you that she was a little bit concerned, you could breathe that much more easily. All would be well, all manner of things.

So, as always, I waited for her to speak again. And when she did, it was to tell me that she was worried that we – meaning that I – had not remembered to send in the order for office stationery which she had made out and which had been on my desk for the past three days. She was right. I promised to mend my ways. Olive's smile broadened. Her immediate concern was over and done with. Before the working day came to an end there would be other causes for concern, but for the moment all was well.

* * *

Olive had been appointed when in the summer of 1977 I became Professor of English at Loughborough University, and she held the post until she retired nine years later. It was only then, in 1986, that I heard she had been chosen not so much for her secretarial skills as because she was 'sensible'. And by sensible the then registrar, who oversaw the appointments of all clerical and administrative staff in the university, meant that she was unlikely to waken lustful thoughts in the breast of anyone whose secretary she became. There had been rather too much of that sort of thing going on of late, so I was told. Why, even the Professor of Mechanical Engineering, a man of some decrepitude and unprepossessing looks and personality, had left his wife of many years and was now shacked up with his secretary. Where would it end?

Well, it would end with Olive, or so the university bursar hoped. Discreet research had established that Olive was a happily married woman, and a glance at her was quite enough to establish that, as the saying went, she had 'no nonsense about her.' Though as it happened, less than a year after I took the post at Loughborough, Olive's husband died. Don Snelson had been a lecturer at the university, an electrical engineer recruited from industry, and someone much in demand for his pioneering work in making water flow uphill. But he was badly overweight and having returned from an exhausting tour of Australian universities in which he demonstrated his invention, the poor man dropped dead.

Olive was devastated. For all his irascibility, and his tendency to berate their two children, both of which flaws she acknowledged, she had loved her sometimes difficult husband, and I think took for granted that she would live out her life in their house in the town where she was a long-standing member of the WI and of the Anglican community, as well as being in charge of a Girl Guide troop. Now, she was left as widowed mother to a son and daughter, the son, Alan, whom I never met, living somewhere in the north of England, and her daughter, Pat, a dear person who in many ways closely resembled her mother, of student age and soon to go to Leeds University.

For a year after Don Snelson's death Olive kept their house going, often inviting lonely or unhappy students to Sunday meals, offering them entirely well-meant advice on their lives, listening to their worries, including inevitably love affairs that did not prosper, and, so I heard, lending them small sums of money, enough 'to tide them over', whenever they were in need. But then, the loneliness became too much to bear. She sold the house and moved into sheltered accommodation.

Here, she was nearer to the part of the university where the English department was quartered, and she soon began to join in 'out-of-hours' activities, including poetry readings and talks by visiting speakers, academic and otherwise. She also began to write poetry. It would be good to report that she discovered in herself a previously hidden talent, but no. And because I loved her and cherish her memory I don't intend to say anything about the poems she would occasionally show me, over which I think she laboured in the never-abandoned hope that one day she might begin to produce something worthwhile. The cruel truth is that she didn't, nor was there any chance she might, but a far more agreeable truth is that Olive's talent showed itself in who she was. And that talent was of inestimable worth.

'I'm a little bit concerned.' Olive really *was* concerned: for people she knew in her daily life, for the life of the department, for those she sensed needed support, a shoulder to lean or cry on (as she could but didn't say), or who needed encouragement, or who found comfort in the few minutes during which they could talk and she could listen.

Hence her concern for the secretary with whom she shared the departmental office. Jane, as I'll call this assistant secretary, was a good deal younger than Olive, unhappily married, and living with her uncaring husband some miles away, in Kegworth. Jane's secretarial skills outstripped Olive's by some distance. She was the more adroit typist, and as the first word processors began to appear and were, some of them, bought in by the university, so Jane without much difficulty adapted to them, and was, I noticed, often visited by secretarial staff from other departments, keen to learn from her how to manage their own newly-installed machines.

Jane also had a quirky, even daring sense of humour. On the morning of 1st April, 1978, a few months before Dan's unanticipated death, Olive was startled to receive a telephone call from a woman who identified herself as Secretary of the English Department at the University of Blackburn. The Department fully expected to be playing host to Professor Lucas, who had agreed to give a talk that morning on Dickens. The talk was due to commence at 11am and the time was now rapidly approaching that hour, but of Professor Lucas there was no sign. Could his secretary perhaps explain his failure to appear, because a large audience had gathered and was waiting to hear what Professor Lucas had to say on the subject on which he had been invited to lecture?

Olive was alone in the office when the call came through, but Jane soon rejoined her. Olive, who was a little bit concerned by the phone call, wondered whether she, Jane, knew anything of its purport? Had Prof Lucas perhaps told her, Jane, that he would be in Blackburn this day? She, Olive, had looked in her own departmental diary and could find no mention of a plan for Professor Lucas to be away from the university. She had, she revealed, gone so far as to knock on Professor Lucas's door, but there was no answer. Nor, when she opened his door, could she see any sign of him. She did, however, recall that he was due at a meeting of Arts and Social Science Heads of Department that morning, and she was sure that he had made no mention of this meeting coinciding with an invitation to Blackburn. 'But then he often forgets to tell me where he'll be at times I need to know. I'm always on at him to keep his diary up to date, aren't I?'

Jane, who seemed to be experiencing some difficulty in breathing and had her handkerchief over her mouth, coughed and silently nodded.

'I'd better phone the secretary at Blackburn and tell her I'm a little bit concerned. He *may* be on his way there, or, if he's gone by car, perhaps he's had an accident or a breakdown. What do *you* think I should do for the best, Jane?'

Jane's coughing fit had by now become so pronounced that speech was entirely beyond her, so at least I was later to be told.

But that was after the meeting with other Heads and when I myself was able to go into the secretarial office. I bore with me a letter I needed to dictate to Olive and was taken aback by the mixture of indignation and downright disapproval my appearance provoked. My secretary was indeed both aghast and for once more than a little bit concerned. 'Prof, why aren't you at Blackburn? They're expecting you. You shouldn't be *here*. You're meant to be *there*. If only you'd let me keep your diary up to date none of this need have happened.'

I was mystified, baffled, bewildered. 'Blackburn? But Olive, as far as I'm aware, there *is* no University of Blackburn, and even if there is, I've certainly received no invitation to give a talk at the place.'

At which point Jane became hysterical with laughter, and as we stared at her I imagine that both Olive and I took thought.

April Fool's Day.

One up to Jane.

***

For all the care we took to console her over Don Snelson's death, for all the loving attention she received from staff and students in the department, Olive took some time to recover. That was why she decided to move out of the house where she and he had brought up their children. Too many hurtful memories. But its sale and the dispersal of so many of her possessions left her lonelier than I think she could have anticipated, especially as in her new quarters, a small, ground-floor flat, she couldn't at first expect daily calls from friendly neighbours, nor from students arriving for tea and sympathy or for the kind of slap-up Sunday dinner that would set them right for the coming week, and for which so many of them would, I learnt in years to come, look back in gratitude when remembering her. And her reliance on the Church and Women's Institute, and her work for the Girl Guide troop, were never adequate compensation for the loss of her frequently ill-tempered but loving husband.

But as she began to re-make her life so she recovered both her spirits and, with them, her essential goodness. Her Christianity – and she *was* a true believer – lay in works, and a kindliness that showed itself in her genuine concern for others, once more stabilised her. From time to time, when the dailiness of lectures and tutorials were done with, I'd drop in on her for a cup of afternoon tea and we'd sit in her small lounge, chatting for an hour. Inconsequential talk for the most part, though after Jane's unhappy marriage came to an end Olive was delighted when the young woman told her that she was going to marry again, then produced the new man for inspection.

'And did you approve of him?' I asked Olive when she told me about this.

Olive smiled, that wonderful, full-on smile. 'He's a very nice man,' she said. 'Just right for Jane. He'll know how to look after her.' And then, after a moment's silence, she repeated, 'He's a very nice man.'

'Very nice.' Conventional, even glib, but when Olive spoke the words they acquired an untarnished gleam, as if new minted. She had invited the couple round for an evening meal, she told me, 'and you could see how much he cares for her. The way he listens to what Jane has to say, and doesn't ever interrupt her.'

There was a wistfulness in Olive's voice as she spoke the words, and I think that was the occasion when she told me that her own marriage hadn't always been happy. Not that she blamed her husband. 'He wasn't always well, you know, Prof. I tried to get him to see a doctor, but he wouldn't. I was quite worried about him, especially in later years when he could suddenly blow up, shout at us all. It troubled poor Pat, and, earlier, it had troubled Alan. I always think that was why Alan couldn't settle to his school work. He got out early, escaped his father's rages, married, and then went to live up North.'

Was Alan's a shotgun marriage? I didn't like to ask, and Olive didn't say. But she more than hinted that she and Don had not been at the wedding, and of Alan's wife she said nothing, or nothing I remember. She did though admit that she saw far less of her son than she would have 'chosen' [her word], and as a result wasn't able to be close to his small children, her own grandchildren.

'Admit' is the right word. It slipped out almost involuntarily, and then only because she wanted me to know how many hopes Don had invested in Pat.

This, too, was troubling. As a bright, attentive pupil at the local girls' school, Pat was already hampered by a deafness which visits to different specialists had done nothing to remedy. As a result, the girl often looked haunted by anxiety. She had her mother's ready smile, but in Pat's case it went with a desire to please, so at least it seemed to me, which was inseparable from fear of reproof. There was no doubting her academic worth. During my years at Loughborough, Pat performed well at A Levels, very well indeed, and then she went to Leeds to study Economics, where she took a good degree and was offered work with a highly successful Leicester-based business company.

She was pretty, too. Quite apart from the smile, her mother's smile, she had full lips, rounded cheeks, and there was a candid shapeliness to her body. At all events, there would have been if she hadn't so often hunched her shoulders in what seemed to me a bid for invisibility, as though not wanting to draw attention to herself. Poor girl. Looking at her you somehow knew that she felt herself destined not to walk in the light of the sun. I hope I'm wrong about this, that somewhere she is happy, fulfilled, living with someone she loves and, should she wish for them, with children to love and be loved by. And I hope this partly because I have no doubt that Olive yearned for this outcome for the daughter she so loved and at whom, when Pat visited, I would see her gaze with such absorbed attention.

* * *

Over tea one afternoon, Olive told me that at the outset of the war she had joined the Land Army. 'Life on the land,' I said, 'it must have been fun. Anyway, a great deal better than being stuck in a hosiery mill or a munitions factory. All that fresh air and choice of good things to eat.'

I was partly joking, but I was also remembering the Leicestershire village of Burbage where I spent my early years. They were years when I knew my father mostly as an absence, although I would often study the photograph of him that was propped on our mother's bedside table. In this photograph my sister, Jill, and I are sitting either side of him on our front-garden rockery. I am in grey shorts and shirt, a tie half hidden by my grey sleeveless pullover; Jill's plaits are tucked under her knitted tam-o'-shanter beret, her long white socks carefully straight, above them a woollen coat I remember as light green. As for my father: dressed in his army uniform, probably because a short period of leave has come to an end and he has soon to take a train at Hinckley Station from where to begin the long journey north to rejoin his regiment, he has an arm round each of us, and I can see the corporal's two chevrons on his right sleeve, the Tank Regiment beret tilted over his right eyebrow, while horn-rimmed spectacles and toothbrush moustache give him a disconcerting severity or look of sheer strangeness that his occasional visits on leave couldn't dispel. Who was this man?

In the early 1970s, remembering his army years and our inevitable viewing him at that time as an outsider, I wrote a poem recalling (and perhaps partly imagining) one such visit, at Easter, 1944, when Jill and I accompanied him on a long walk through lanes around the village; and what I chiefly remembered of that occasion was the sound of the wind as it howled in telegraph wires, a banshee, eldritch sound, as though he, too, was an emanation from an unfamiliar, unfriendly world, so that despite his attempts to talk to us, 'I turned from him, would not see his face'. My poor father.

* * *

Going up to my village school in Burbage I would often see Land Army women at work in the fields through which I ran. Rough-tongued women, most of them, using language I instinctively knew my mother would disapprove of; large, beefy women, some of them even frightening.

They weren't like Molly Hollis, the only Land Army girl I knew. Molly lived with her mother in the village of Earl Shilton, some five or six miles from Burbage. From time to time I would go with my grandmother by bus to visit the house where Mrs Hollis lived. It was a rather grand place, standing in its own grounds, and on occasions when Jill came with me we would spend time crawling about in the wooden dog-house where I never remember seeing a dog. It must have been shut away when visitors were expected. There was, though, always a full bowl of dog biscuits at the entrance to the kennel, and the black biscuits in particular were well worth crunching through.

Mrs Hollis wore black and had a severe, unyielding, rectangular face, in striking contrast to my grandmother's, which was soft, rounded, her mouth open in ready surprise – 'Fancy' was a favourite word, uttered in a wondering consternation – Mrs Hollis was the widow of a Commander Hollis, a close neighbour of my grandparents when they had lived in Wimbledon, though how and why she was now living in a Midlands village I don't think I ever learned. I did, though, know that her husband had been sunk 'with all hands' by a German U-boat, and that this was 'God's will.'

I enjoyed our visits to the Hollis house, though less for the place itself, intriguing though it was in its size and the comparative grandeur of its garden, than because of Mrs Hollis's daughter, Molly. Molly was what any girls' school book of the time would have called 'strapping'. 'Tall and sturdy' is what the dictionary gives for the term, though this hardly does credit to the radiant good health that is, or was, part of the word's meaning. Molly was all of those things. Perhaps 'buxom' would be a better term to account for her appearance. She had a mass of red hair, red as her cheeks, and whenever she hove in view, she could be relied on to be in Land Army uniform. Khaki brown trousers, shiny black boots, greeny-brown high-necked jersey. At all events, I never saw her dressed otherwise. On days when she wasn't working for a local farmer she joined us, her pleasure in seeing my grandmother very evident from her grin and the fact that she immediately wanted to talk to her.

Unfortunately, whatever she had to say was entirely incomprehensible. It wasn't that she had a speech impediment. She spoke, she gestured, she nodded, she laughed. But her speech was a meaningless series of vocables, ululations and gutterals, all delivered with great rapidity and varying shades of emphasis. There was no hint of distress in the sounds she made, or if there was I didn't detect any. Nor was she at all frantic. I'm sure she thought she was communicating with my grandmother. And my grandmother always smiled at the young woman in her sweet, placid way, and from time to time said 'Fancy' and told Molly how well she was looking and that life on the land, working in the open air with animals, must suit her, and how good that was to know.

And I suppose it did and it was. Many years later, I saw an exhibition at Chichester's Pallant House Gallery by WW2 women artists, including several paintings by Evelyn Dunbar of Land Army girls at work in the fields, cutting and stooking hay under blue skies, barrage balloons aloft in the sustaining air. Not a bad way to have lived through the war years, I thought. Better than being a

Canary Girl. And thinking that, brought to mind works by another woman artist, Evelyn Gibbs, on whom my wife is an expert. During the war, Gibbs made a number of large, powerful drawings of women at work in Nottingham's Raleigh Factory which in those years had been given over to war work. However exhausting work in the fields must have been, however cruel winter's frosts, or the rains and winds of spring, summer, autumn, they must have been preferable to factory labour, to serving machines that, judging from Gibbs' powerful drawings, dwarfed and oppressed the women who sat before them.

Not for Olive, though. She remembered the numbing cold of the barn where she and the other Land Army girls slept and from which they were woken early each morning to break the ice in troughs where they were expected to wash themselves – 'a bath once a week at most, and that was usually in water scummy from other bodies and hardly warm by the time you got into it', – and then having to climb into trousers and thick jerseys that scratched your skin and go out into rain in order to attend to sheep and cattle, to wade through droppings and cow pats, and the rest of it. 'Fleas, lice, in your beds, in your clothes, in your hair, trying and often failing to learn how to milk cows that wouldn't stand still so that sometimes one of the blessed things would kick over a full milk bucket, and the farmer would be shouting and swearing – every day, that was, every day we had to go out to them, those cows didn't have weekends off, so nor did we, even though some of the girls would have been out the night before, at village dances, or in the pub, and then *they'd* be ill the next morning and often you'd have to do *their* work as well as your own …'

Olive's memories came with a surprising fluency that sometimes ratcheted up to near eloquence. They also prompted an entirely understandable indignation.

'And when it was all over, most of us were let go without so much as a thank you.'

'Olive,' I said, mock severe, 'I perceive you did not enjoy doing your bit for King and Country. Did you not profit from your experience as a Land Army girl?'

'Not really. I kept in touch with a few of the other girls, though after a while we went our separate ways. Anyway, to be honest, I was glad when I could get back to sleeping in a real bed and there were fewer chilblains to pester us.'

Ah, chilblains. All children who went through the war years suffered from them. Our mothers knitted balaclavas to keep our ears warm, but still the chilblains got through, as they got through mittens and gloves and plagued our fingers. And heels, that was the worst, what happened to our heels. The poor quality material from which shoes were made – could it really have been leather? – cut at your heels until your socks developed holes in the heels that were called 'spuds', and spuds occasioned scraped skin and seepage of blood and, of course, chilblains.

But for all Olive might writhe at the memory of her outdoor life, what about life indoors? The hosiery mill at Burbage, where young women worked beside men, was rumoured to be a place of sin. In those days I had no idea what the word might mean, apart from taking the name of the Lord in vain – and I wasn't at all sure what *that* meant – but I did know that there were village dances attended by British soldiers and, in the war's later days, by GIs, American soldiers stationed in the village with whom the squaddies fought, often over women.

'Like the Wild West,' Olive suggested, sighing at her own memories of such dances. 'There's never really much peace in the world, is there, Prof? And the innocent get killed, just as much as the guilty.'

I mentioned the armaments factory at Chilwell, how the women who worked there were called 'Canary Girls'.

Olive knew about these girls, knew, too, that the explanation for the term 'Canary Girls' came from the sulphur which was a key component of the bombs made at Chilwell during the First War, and she had heard of how an explosion had killed over two hundred of the workers, women, most of them. 'It was common knowledge.'

I said, 'Well, Loughborough's not far from Chilwell, just down the line from Nottingham. I suppose it would have been local news. Or local history.'

'I don't come from round here,' Olive said. 'I was born in the Black Country.'

And of course I realised then, and not for the first time, that her accent wasn't local. The slightly sing-song pronunciation, the way she might end a sentence on a rising inflexion, no, they weren't how natives of the East Midlands spoke.

'Marlene,' I said, and Olive laughed in recognition. 'Yes,' she said, 'Marlene.'

Marlene was a character familiar to listeners to BBC radio though she never spoke, she was often referred to, in a popular, long-running radio comedy series of the 1950s called *Educating Archie*. Archie Andrews was a puppet, dressed as a public school boy in striped blazer and straw boater, whose master, Peter Brough, even though he was a much touted variety performer and usually topped any show in which he appeared, was widely recognised as so incompetent a ventriloquist that it was only on radio you couldn't see his lips move. *Educating Archie* was, therefore, well-suited to his talent, and the show featured at different times Max Bygraves and Beryl Reid, both of them comic actors. Reid's catch-phrase at a time when every well-known radio performer had to have one, was 'Marlene's my best friend and I hate her.' It was spoken in broad Brummie, of which Olive now gave a pretty good imitation.

But soon enough her smile died. 'You know, Prof,' she said, 'I sometimes thought that way about my father. I should have loved him, but I often came near to hating him. I was even glad when he died.'

I was momentarily shocked. Was Olive about to reveal some terrible secret of her childhood? But no, it was in its way sadder and more terrible than that, and it was the only occasion when I realised that for all her warm-heartedness, my dearly loved secretary and friend failed in human understanding, in sympathy, though the blame for that failure couldn't, I also realised, be pinned to her.

Her father, I knew from what she'd earlier told me of her

childhood years, had fought in the First War. Given that he was an early recruit and served most of his time in France, it might be thought that he was lucky to have survived with only minor injuries. To his body, that is. But by the time he returned to his wife he was a mental wreck. Many surviving veterans were. Others got off more lightly. They included my own paternal grandfather, though he was invalided out from Gallipoli, and could never be brought to say much of what he'd encountered during his time in the Eastern Mediterranean, so that when I came to recreate his experiences in my novel, *The Life in Us*, I had inevitably to rely at least in part on memories of what my father, who had been born in 1913, could tell me; that, and histories of 1914-18.

I don't know where exactly Olive's father was posted. I never asked and for all I know he never spoke to her of his experiences. 'He was in France', so Olive's mother informed her daughter, and that was it. My guess is that the mother herself knew precious little about what her husband had endured, nor even any details of where he had fought. Letters home were heavily censored, and for many lack-literate soldiers, written communications were restricted to the postcards issued by officialdom, and these permitted no more than the bare acknowledgement that its sender was well and in good spirits.

From time to time, Olive's father would presumably have been given a week or so at home, on leave from the army. Or would he? I have come across instances of soldiers who spent their leave time in hospital, recovering from flesh wounds, after which they were returned to front-line duties. It shouldn't have happened, but it did. And on occasions unmarried men volunteered not to take the leave due to them. (Others, of course, went home and then deserted, and who can blame them, though the price of being tracked down was that they had then to face the firing squad.) As to what happened to Olive's father, I know nothing beyond the fact that when he was returned to his family at war's end he was, in Olive's own words, 'difficult for my mother to deal with and his children daren't go near him.'

Apparently, during the post-war winter months the poor man spent his days huddled over the fire, and during warmer times went out into the garden where he sat silent from morning to night.

'Didn't he speak to you at all?' I asked Olive.

She shook her head. 'But if we came up behind him, to ask him a question or tell him his meal was ready, say, he'd shout at us. Sometimes, he'd scream, as if he'd seen a ghost. And if someone banged a door shut, he'd scream even louder.'

And then she'd repeat the words that she'd already used. 'To be honest, Prof, when he died I couldn't be sorry. I was glad. It meant my mother could at last have some peace.'

Olive, I knew, had been born after the war, in 1925. Had her father's condition, his silent alienation from his wife and children, developed some good few years after the war, or was it present from the moment he arrived back at war's end? I had read enough about the lasting horrors of shell-shock to know how soldiers returning from the 'Great War' often found it impossible to talk to those at home of their experiences. As a result, they suffered in incommunicable silence, or were driven to breakdown and, even, madness, as happened to the great poet, Ivor Gurney. Something like that must have happened to Olive's father. Poor, poor man. Poor wife. And, of course, poor Olive. No, life hadn't always been good for her.

Even the birth of her son had not been marked by the happiness she might have expected. This had nothing to do with Don, though. The man who caused her to suffer was her doctor. She was one of three women in his practice due to give birth at about the same time who simultaneously attended the doctor's surgery for pre-natal check-ups.

'It was horrible, he humiliated us,' Olive said. And diffidently, and with a hesitant stumbling very unlike her usual smiling candour, she told me that the three of them had to sit with knickers down and skirts raised so that the doctor, seated opposite, could subject them to prolonged scrutiny, and that this happened once a week for the final three months of their pregnancies. 'It should have been a happy time, but I dreaded those occasions.'

Useless to tell her that the man was plainly a pervert who enjoyed using his power over the women and that the three of them should have spoken out about his behaviour, that he should have been struck off, prosecuted, sent to prison. I doubt Olive wanted to believe in the man's wickedly perverse behaviour, her trust in authority was too great. But, I think now, may the bastard who was responsible for her suffering be rotting in some special hell.

He was gone, retired presumably, Olive said, by the time Pat was conceived, and this must, I think, go some way toward explaining Olive's uncomplicated love for her daughter.

* * *

For Olive's eightieth birthday party in 2005, a tea party was arranged at Loughborough's Gorse Covert Free Church Hall, where she worshipped, and where she was plainly a much-valued member of the community. I remember the party as a lovely, warm occasion, to which came family, friends, many of her former secretarial colleagues, Jane, now long remarried, and quite a few former students from Loughborough's English department, all of whom had good reason to be grateful to Olive for kindnesses shown, and who remembered her with love. I put together a quartet (cornet, trombone, guitar, and bass) which played what I hope was appropriate tea-time music, there was some decorous dancing, and much conversation and laughter. No speeches. Olive didn't want speeches.

* * *

Two years later, we were back at the Church once more. At the beginning of December, 2007, Olive had gone into hospital to be operated on for a previously undiagnosed 'problem', so I was told, and had died on the operating table. Her funeral, on December 21, was to be followed by a private family interment at Prestwold Natural Burial Ground. Good for her to have chosen such a burial place, and good that so many were at the service, including an increased number of those former students who had been at her birthday party. I was asked to 'say a few words', and recounted an entirely true anecdote that dated back to the time when I was lumbered with being Dean of the Faculty of Arts at Loughborough, a position I did not like and which, had it not been for Olive, I would have loathed.

April 11, 1983 was a Saturday. More importantly as far as I was concerned, it was the date of my father's seventieth birthday and I was determined to get to the family birthday party my mother had arranged to celebrate the occasion. By then my father was retired from work in London and he and my mother were living happily in the small Dartmoor village of Chagford, not far from where his family had for many years, going back into the nineteenth century, lived and worked. Unfortunately, that morning an important Deans' meeting had been arranged at Loughborough, and as it concerned the future of the Arts at the university I had no alternative but to be in attendance.

What to do? Neither train nor car could get me to Chagford in time to join the party, which was to be a celebratory late lunch. A colleague suggested that it might be possible to fly from East Midlands Airport down to Exeter. That, followed by a taxi ride, would get me up to Chagford in good time to join the family for the festive meal. Well, it was worth a try. So I asked Olive to investigate. Of course, she agreed, and an hour later was back with the news that there was indeed an early Saturday afternoon flight from East Midlands to Exeter Airport. An hour from there to Chagford by taxi, and at the very worst I'd be in time to join in the toasts.

'Brilliant,' I said. 'I'm delighted. Olive, you're a genius.'

Olive's smile was uncertain. 'But I'm a little bit concerned,' she said.

'Oh? Why?'

'It takes twenty-six hours, Prof.'

'Olive,' I said, 'a flight from East Midlands to Exeter *can't* take twenty-six hours.'

'There's an overnight stop in Amsterdam,' Olive said.

How could anybody *not* love Olive?

Cloughie

Clough: a ravine, a steep valley, usually with a torrent bed; also, a cliff, a crag, a rock. OED.

THE FIRST FOOTBALL MANAGER I TOOK as hero was Stan Cullis. He was in charge of Wolverhampton Wanderers ('Wolves') when they beat Leicester City 3-1 in the 1949 Wembley Cup Final, and at the age of thirty-three, having been appointed to the post the previous year, Cullis was widely acknowledged to be by far the youngest manager of a major English club. Most managers of that time, as of earlier decades, looked in newspaper photographs rather like bank managers on the verge of retirement or, failing that, church elders: sombre-suited, grey-haired eminences. Cullis was short-back-and-sides, but he wore a sports coat, and for all his unyielding rigidity of posture he reminded me more of a school teacher than a Man of the Establishment.

Aged eleven, I watched that 1949 Cup Final on a neighbour's television – we didn't have our own set – and remember Cullis leading his team out from the tunnel, 'like a parade-ground sergeant major' someone said. (Not a colonel, then, let alone a general.) At the time our family was living in Ashford, Middlesex, having two years previously moved from the Midlands where, during the war years and while my father was serving the nation as a tank instructor, we'd occupied a rented semi-detached house in Burbage, a village hard by the small hosiery town of

Hinckley. As Hinckley Town's football team was unknown to fame, boys at my primary school who were interested in football supported Leicester City.

But I never did. During his war years, most of them spent in the north of England, my father, who was a good enough footballer to be included in a representative army team, had mentioned to me the names of professional players he met during that time. They included Jimmy Gordon of Middlesbrough, with whom in later years he kept in contact, as well as several others, most of whom also played for Middlesbrough or other professional clubs in the North, and who, after they'd been demobbed, returned to whatever might be left of their footballing careers. And after they were let go by their clubs, which in many cases was soon, it was back to the pits or a life of unskilled labour.

Of all the footballers my father mentioned, the one who most took my boyish fancy was the Wolves' left-winger Jimmy Mullen. Apart from the fact that I, too, am left-footed, I can't now remember why Mullen's name so gripped my imagination. But I do know that it was because of what my father told me about the winger's skills, his speed, his trickery, that I chose to become a fan of Wolverhampton Wanderers. I kept quiet about this while we lived in Burbage, but once we'd moved to Ashford nobody much cared. The nearest professional club to our patch of suburbia was Brentford, and inevitably a cadre of boys loyally supported 'The Bees'. Most however who cared about football, or who anyway said they did, followed more exotic London-based clubs. (Arsenal always excepted. We were united in our hatred of the Gunners.) Chelsea was OK, Fulham was tolerated, Charlton, though further away, loved by many. This was largely because of their goalkeeper, Sam Bartram, usually referred to in the popular press by the soubriquet 'flame-haired Sam'. Bartram was revered for his ability to punt the ball on the full from one penalty area to the other. And in those days when, during rainy weather, 'the leather-panelled spheroid', as I remember one sports correspondent wrote, loaded with mud and moisture, was said to weigh more than a cannon ball, this was no mean achievement.

It was also, of course, entirely pointless, because Charlton's forwards were never far enough upfield to make use of the ball which came dropping out of the sky, 'like a doodlebug', according to one of my schoolmates, though unlike any of those high explosives that fell on London in the late days of the war, a Bartram bomb could be safely gathered in by the opposing goalkeeper and then punted or more often rolled to one of his own defenders. But for all its practical inutility, there was a time when the Bartram kick was widely agreed to be one of the wonders of the professional game.

In 1949, Wolves' goalkeeper was Bert 'The Cat' Williams, who played for England. Of Leicester City's goalkeeper, Bradley, I can recall only that he had dark hair and wasn't, so commentators agreed, to be blamed for any of Wolves' goals. The golden shirted Wanderers, with England's captain Billy Wright leading the defence, Jesse

Pye at centre forward, Johnny Hancocks on the right wing, and, of course, Jimmy Mullen on the left, were simply too good. They were riding high in the First Division, their opponents were mired somewhere in the depths of the Second Division. What else could you expect but victory for Wolves? And victory was duly delivered, though when it came it all seemed a bit anti-climactic.

As for Stan Cullis, with his buttoned-up sports coat and, despite his comparative youth, an already balding head, he seemed the epitome of the successful professional manager. Unsmiling, tight-lipped, he let his team in action do the talking for him, as the pundits, especially Raymond Glendenning of the BBC, liked to claim. I didn't then know that in the changing room Cullis could become near hysterical with rage if matters were going badly for his team: foul-mouthed, unreasonable, and, finally, and to his sad disbelief, sacked.

Nor did I know something entirely to his credit. In 1938 the England football team played an international match against Germany in Berlin. Before the game began, the teams lined up on the pitch and England's players were instructed to salute the opposition by giving the fascist stiff-armed salute. Cullis refused to do so. He was immediately substituted and sent to the dressing room.

I didn't discover this until many years later, when I was sent a pamphlet by Stephen Nicholls. Nicholls, a lecturer in German at Sussex University and himself a Jew, tells the story of that ghastly moment, and includes a photograph of the teams lined up pre-match, making the salute. You want to cringe. And so, perhaps, did those who treated Cullis's refusal to kow-tow as punishable by exclusion. At all events, my friend, the poet, publisher, and translator, Anthony Rudolf, and also a devoted follower of Wolves, tells me that Cullis was not only reinstated as an England international before the end of the year but that he was appointed to the captaincy, a remarkable honour given that he was still only 22 and therefore the youngest professional footballer ever to lead an England team. A rare instance of virtue rewarded. After that, becoming a manager at so young an age as he did, even the manager of Wolves, must have seemed a doddle.

* * *

In my teenage years cricket replaced football as the game with which I most closely identified. And seventy years later, and for all the damage done by administrators and the racist bigots who still infest the game, cricket remains an abiding passion. Trudging through wet streets in order to stand with disconsolate, beery supporters – more often detractors – at Griffin Park, or Stamford Bridge, or Craven Cottage, or the Valley, long ago lost whatever allure it might once have held. As for Elm Park, a ground I sometimes visited as a Reading University student at a time when the town's club seemed to be locked for ever in the old Third Division South – a circle of Hell Dante forgot to include in the Commedia – the opposition was guaranteed to be as near devoid of ability as the home team.

Reading's manager during at least some of that period was Roy Bentley. As centre forward at Chelsea, Bentley had become well known for gifts which, it was said, were nurtured by his unique tactical shrewdness of adopting 'a deep-lying' position. This required him not so much to lead the attack as emerge unexpectedly from behind the other forwards, having fooled the opposing centre-half required to mark him into leaving a gap through which Chelsea's inside right and left could advance on goal. That, anyway, was the announced strategy, and to prove its worth a school friend of mine insisted on one particularly soggy afternoon that I accompany him to watch Chelsea play Sunderland at 'The Bridge'.

Did Bentley's device work? If so, I have long forgotten, and though Chelsea beat the northerners 3-2, the only memory I retain of that occasion is of a Chelsea full-back, progenitor perhaps of the licensed thug, 'Chopper' Ron Harris, repeatedly fouling Sunderland's winger, Billy Bingham, until poor Bingham, a player of both skill and grace, was forced to limp off the field, at which the Chelsea supporters raised a loud cheer. After that, a day at Lord's or the Oval, even in chilly spring weather, seemed paradise enough. You could watch the game sitting down, and you could usually get a glass of lemonade, or in later, teenage years, a pint of beer, to comfort you against on-field mishaps or disasters. And with luck you could watch Denis Compton bat. And not even Bingham at his finest, nor Mullen, nor Finney, nor Matthews, nor all of them put together, could begin to compare with that experience.

* * *

In the summer of 1964, Pauline and I, together with our two small children, moved from Reading to Nottingham, where I had been appointed to a university lectureship in the English department. Several of my new colleagues were, I discovered, regular in their attendance at the City Ground. Some of them went so far as to possess season tickets, and in the early autumn of my first year at Nottingham I was invited to accompany them to watch Nottingham Forest, then in the old First Division, take on Blackburn Rovers. Forest's ground, on the far side of the Trent, wasn't in the city, while Notts County, was. County's home ground, Meadow Lane, stood on the river's city side, facing across not merely to the more modern City Ground but also to Trent Bridge, the most beautiful of all England's Test grounds, and where in the following years I would spend many summer afternoons.

But that first afternoon at the City Ground did much to revive my boyhood love of football. Forest were a class act. They won the match easily enough, by a score which was, I think, 5-2, but, more important, they played athletic, nimble, open football, fast but not furious. Their manager at the time was John Carey, who before his retirement from the professional game had been famous for the years he spent playing on the wing for Manchester United. 'Schooled by Busby,' one of my colleagues told me, 'you can't do better than that.' I think it was the same colleague from whom I learned that in his pre-match pep talks Carey always uttered the same one sentence piece of advice to his team: 'Spray it about a bit, lads', after which he would retire to the Directors' box and a well-earned glass of whisky.

Forest did as he advised. They had speedy wingers, especially 'Noddy' Hinton, from whose powerful left foot – 'thunderous' so reporters liked to say – came a ready supply of goals, they had a powerful centre-forward, Frank Wignall, and behind them was the handsome, lithe Henry Newton at right-half, plus a fine centre-half, Bob McKinlay, who was team captain, and, in goal, Peter Grummit, once described by the *Observer*'s football correspondent as 'brave and innocent', and considered by Forest die-hards to be good enough for England – until, that is, they watched Gordon Banks keeping goal for Leicester, and had to acknowledge the difference between good and great.

In the years that followed I quite often went to the City Ground, always standing in what was called 'the Enclosure', a small rectangle of open terracing below the directors' box. On one occasion I watched, amazed, as Arsenal supporters, with their backs to the pitch and ignoring what was happening on it – Forest put three goals past the Gunners that afternoon – booed and taunted poor Billy Wright, then in his last days as Arsenal's manager. (After he was replaced, Forest acquired three of Arsenal's forwards, Addison, Baker, and Barnwell, all of whom became local favourites.) On another, I was present when Tottenham Hotspur were the visitors, and Spurs' languid-seeming centre-forward, Gilzean, was urgently advised by away fans to 'get your finger out.' (Spurs lost, though I can't now remember the actual score.) And there was a wonderful game against Manchester United, marking the return of Denis Law after suspension, in which he scored with a header that required him seemingly to hang aloft for minutes on end, kestrel-like, one commentator suggested, while the ball was crossed to him by George Best, and in which game there was another transcendent moment, no doubt practised on the training ground but which looked entirely spontaneous, where Law stood in the centre circle, facing his own goal while Gregg, the keeper, punted to him on the full so that he could take the ball on his thigh, spin round and pass to the right wing where Best was already running at full speed toward the Forest goal.

And, as riposte, Forest supporters could delight in the speed that took Hinton past several defenders before he delivered the shot, from well outside United's penalty area, with which he scored the goal that ensured a two-all draw.

But the glory days at the City Ground were on the wane, though I wasn't to witness them all. In 1967 I was awarded a Fulbright scholarship to supplement the invitation to spend a year as visiting professor at the Universities of Maryland, and, in the summer, Indiana. Pauline and I packed our bags, and with Ben and Emma set out for the New World. While there I received several letters of lament from Nottingham about the steep and seemingly irreversible decline of 'the Forest'. Some of the club's best players had retired or been sold to other clubs; there was the ill-advised purchase from Sunderland of Jim Baxter (by then so addicted to the bottle he had on occasions to be substituted before a game even started); and there were other calamities, all of them itemised. I don't claim to be familiar with the chronology of events that led to Forest's all-too predictable relegation to the Second Division, but I do know that by the early seventies they had become a poor to average team thrashing about in mid-table and with precious little chance of promotion. Ichabod, Ichabod.

Ben, by then a teenager, went with his mates to home matches, but he rarely had much of an enlivening nature to report. Crowds dwindled, a kind of dank apathy took over both on and off the field. Players came, players left, as did managers. But it was the same difference. Forest seemed fated to be stamped with the mediocrity that identified so many once-distinguished clubs, Wolves included. The only quality player of that time was Duncan Mackenzie, who, so Ben tells me, would demonstrate his athleticism by leaping over a Mini parked in front of the City Ground, and who on the pitch was remarkable for outrageous dummies and long, slaloming runs through opposition defences which on one occasion led to him being largely responsible for Forest destroying Manchester City in a cup game that Forest won by 4-1. Soon after that, Mackenzie was bought by Leeds and once again mediocrity resumed its leaden sway.

And then came Brian Clough.

* * *

It was Clough, needless to say, who had signed Mackenzie for Leeds during his brief, hectic period as Leeds' manager, and it was his only signing during the 44 days he stayed there. A personal disaster for Clough, that period, though given what had been going on at Leeds, not an unforeseeable one. But the story of how, in all senses of the word, Clough managed at Forest is entirely different. What follows is not intended as a potted biography of the man familiar to so many as 'Cloughie'. There are already several such biographies, and although I've read none of them, I'm told by readers whose opinions I trust that most are of a surprisingly high quality. Not hagiographic, not dirt-digging, not dutiful, but well researched, competently written, or better, for the most part factually reliable, and between them testimony to someone truly unique.

In fact, the statue of him which stands on the edge of Nottingham's Old Market Square – still known as 'Slab Square' to locals – is no more than life-size, and shows him in his football gear. No saint, he, no puffed-up specimen of formal propriety. He is in track-suit bottoms, open-neck jersey, his hands clenched above his head in that victory salute familiar to generations of Forest fans. And round the statue people of all ages meet on a day by day basis, not so much to commemorate Cloughie as to discuss their own and others' affairs. He simply happens to be there, on his modest plinth, while round him, and often, I suspect, in unawareness of the man who is at their centre, Nottingham folk swirl, sit, laugh, talk. This is the dailiness of life. And this, I think, is how it should be. Cloughie Lives.

* * *

But I need to begin with the seeming end, his death in late September, 2004.

The day after the announcement of that death, I was driving over Trent Bridge and past the Forest ground, on my way to see an artist friend, when I noticed that a large crowd had gathered outside the ground itself, that the bridge was thronged with people, and that minute by minute more were arriving by way of the roads all about. Men for the most part, young, middle-aged, old; but also a fair sprinkling of women, and young lads, too, some no more than boys, not yet teenagers. Many stood still on the bridge, others lined the towpath beside the Trent End of City Ground, they gathered in groups, or collected in ones and twos; a few seemed to be on their own. Altogether, there must have been several thousands of them.

I drove on into the centre of West Bridgford, 'Bread and Lard Island', found a space to park the car, and walked back to see for myself what had brought so many to the spot.

Tied to a lamp post on the main road beside the bridge was a bed sheet on which had been daubed in black paint the words, *Move over God, Cloughie's Coming*. Nearby, another improvised banner read, *If there's a football XI in heaven they've now got the best manager.* There were other such banners, plus placards and scrawls of paper. Hundreds of them littered the footpath, as though the sky had been raining paper, and there were innumerable flutterings, so it seemed, of Forest scarves that had been twined round the perimeter fencing, many bearing the names of those who had played in his great teams – Shilton, Anderson, O'Neill, Gemmill, Pearce, Walker, Burns ('Kenneth', Clough always called the defender he had rescued from his thuggish days at Birmingham and so turned into a player of respect who was also respected and never sent off under his new manager.) But then I think I'm right in saying that no Forest player in Cloughie's time was ever shown the red card. No player, however sorely he might feel himself wronged, was allowed to dispute the referee's decision. Lloyd, Woodcock, Wythe, Birtles, Francis, Robertson – that 'tubby little fellow' Clough said before identifying him as the best long passer of the ball in the land – these names among others were part of the expression of rejoicing in the achievements of a football manager whose name adorned the adjacent car parks, the approach roads, and which, I discovered as I pushed further, was draped across the football pitch itself – though here the scarves and banners had to be cleared away for an entirely unimportant Coca-Cola match due to be held the following evening.

That match, against Rotherham, had been expected to draw at best two thousand spectators. In the event a crowd of more than fifteen thousand arrived, the overwhelming majority of them there to say a last farewell to a man they revered.

And yet Clough had retired from the managership some years earlier, his ending, as with so many other managers, marked by failure. He wasn't, though, sacked. Instead, as he, together with Peter Taylor, had years earlier been allowed to resign from Derby County, so at the end of the 1992-3 season, he took it upon himself to resign at the moment of Forest's relegation from 'the Top Flight'. Two seasons before that, in 1991, he had failed to 'lift' the FA Cup, the only trophy he never won. Forest lost to Spurs in that year's Cup final, although Forest supporters have never ceased to believe that had Gascoigne been sent off in the opening minutes of the game, as he deserved to be for an horrendous challenge on one of Forest's best players, the overlapping full-back, Gary Charles, the outcome would have been different. As it was, the Forest supporters' chant of 'You'll never beat Des Walker', – their wonderfully good centre-back – became more disconsolate the longer the game went on. Walker might not have been beaten, but Forest eventually were, by two goals to one.

* * *

But though the Clough era ended in 1993, the man himself was still a Nottingham hero, almost a mythical figure. Before he arrived at Forest, a taxi driver in some foreign country, having asked where you were from and having been told 'Nottingham', would say, 'Ah, Robin Hood'. But afterward, most if not all said, 'Ah, Brian Clough'.

There is of course no proof that Robin Hood, supposing he actually existed, came from Nottingham. Wakefield has often enough been identified as his place of putative birth, as have many of the exploits credited to him and his Merry Men. And the distinguished historian of medieval literature, Stephen Knight, has made a persuasive case for 'Robin of Lincoln' having originated in that county, so that Lincolnshire should be claimed as his birthplace. Well, perhaps. And perhaps England's North East – Sunderland, Middlesbrough – ought to speak up for Brian Clough as one of theirs. Which, to be fair, they occasionally do. But Nottingham is where custom fixes him and with which city he will surely continue to be identified.

And what of Derby, the city some seventeen miles from Nottingham, where Cloughie, with his partner, Peter Taylor, achieved great things for its football team, Derby County, before he fell out with Sam Longson, the portly, short-tempered chair of directors. He didn't leave in disgrace. In fact, at the home game after his going was announced, he turned up with Taylor among spectators at the popular end and was loudly and persistently cheered by thousands of the Rams' supporters.

But for all that, he was no longer a Derby man. And after his brief, contumacious spell at Leeds, he went on to Brighton, before Nottingham called him. The road leading to sustained mediocrity can seem endless for football managers, and however golden paved it once was, that road nearly always comes to a dead end of decrepitude. It did for Stan Cullis, snuffed out before his time, it was said, unable to live with the awareness of his enforced departure from Molyneux. The main road from Nottingham to Derby used to be called the Derby Road. Now it's called Brian

Clough Way. But nobody doubts that the way leads to Nottingham. Nottingham is where Cloughie was instated as not merely a great manager, but a legend. For several days after his death became public knowledge, representatives from the regional and national media camped outside the City Ground or buttonholed passers-by in the Old Market Square, interviewing whoever would agree to talk about him, and hearing again and again how much he'd meant, not merely to players and fans, but to backroom staff, to shopkeepers, to the city at large. And what they heard was that he was 'unique', that 'I loved him – we all did', that he was 'the best manager England never had', that he was 'magic'. Clichés all, but redeemed by the intensity of feeling with which they were uttered. 'He treated everyone the same,' a tea-lady at the City Ground said, and hearing her words I remembered the story of how he had made time to be interviewed by a student reporter who turned up at the ground on spec., and how Cloughie asked (ordered?) Tony Woodcock, then newly capped by England, and who happened to be within earshot, to make 'a cuppa' for the understandably nervous student whose career as a reporter of national importance began because of that interview. Looking at hard men wiping tears from their eyes as they spoke about him, hearing the unashamed declarations of love which the tears signified, it was impossible not to agree that there was a unique quality to a man I called in a poem a 'rough-tongued shaman'.

That poem, 'What Holds Them', which is dedicated to my son, was written for *Not Just A Game*, the anthology of poems about sport compiled by Andy Croft and Sue Dymoke. (Five Leaves Publications, 2006.) 'Brian Clough is gone, red-carded by cancer', it begins, before going on to identify Cloughie as the 'Rough-tongued shaman, rogue, blest necromancer', blazing new life into the teams he managed, and who ordered both them and their supporters to 'Get rid of racists!', 'We've done with fascists'. And it's true, he *did* issue such orders, just as Stan Cullis, in an earlier and, it must be said, more difficult period, wanted to be done with fascists, and, foul-mouthed though he himself could be, Cloughie *did* instruct the Trent End supporters there should be 'No swearing, gentlemen', to which the Trent End responded by chanting 'The referee's an orphan'. And after his death, the centre of Nottingham, Old Market Square, was packed with hordes of Nottinghamians as well as others who'd come from varying distances, many of whom had no love for football but who *did* love him, or felt they did, 'that cross-grained' man whose 'sending off brought them to fill/this place for one last time and holds them still'.

Hyperbole? Perhaps. And yet even as I write these words I'm aware of the stories that continue to circulate, including a recent one concerning the two young boys Cloughie met by chance on the beach at Sunderland when he was walking his dog there. He was back on home territory because Forest had been drawn against Sunderland in a Cup tie, and, realising that the boys were hungry, he bought them fish-and-chip suppers, and then invited them to come and meet the Forest team at the hotel where the players were spending the night. Not only that. On several later occasions the boys, now teenagers, stayed at the Clough family house near Derby, went on holiday with him and others, and were found work by the rough-tongued shaman. And from time to time during his Forest years Cloughie would turn up on Sunday mornings to help in the newsagent's shop his brother ran at Bramcote, a Nottingham suburb no more than a mile away from where I live in Beeston. Cloughie, man of the people. It sounds phoney but it was, it *is*, genuine.

There are, too, the tales of his instinctive generosity. Of the woman who was searching for change in a grocer's shop at West Bridgford when an arm came out from behind her and tipped the money she owed into the shop assistant's waiting hand. Cloughie's arm, of course. And when he took his car into a garage for servicing he would tell the grease monkey to take the money left in the well of the car where he always left substantial amounts of change from fill-ups at petrol pumps. He gave match-day tickets to some who couldn't afford them, he found room on the team coach for others short of the readies to get to away games, and so on.

Some of these tales should be taken with a pinch of salt, but plenty are true. He was a life-long Labour supporter who, during his time at Derby, appeared on the hustings alongside Philip Whitehead, until 1983 Labour MP for Derby North. At that time Sally Oppenheimer, junior minister of Consumer Affairs in Margaret Thatcher's Administration, took to advising all those who complained of rising prices in the shops to take their custom elsewhere. If necessary drive on to the next town. 'What a good idea,' Cloughie told a public meeting, his voice rasping with contempt. 'Really helpful, that is. You can just see her advising them to follow her example, tell their chauffeurs to try elsewhere. "No, Albert, we'll go on to Kidderminster. The shops there have unbeatable prices for baked beans." Old age pensioners living on their state pensions, mothers at home with their young children. Why don't they just get into their Jags and go in search of a bargain. That should sort it.'

At about the same time, Nottingham's daily newspaper, *The Nottingham Post*, came under the control of a consortium headed by a man called Pole-Carew, who announced his determination to de-unionise the paper. Anyone who objected could lump it. Several who did object were turfed out. They started their own newspaper, *The Nottingham News*, and Cloughie, hearing of this, gave them a substantial sum of money to help them on their way. He also announced that from then on he would give no further interviews to the *Post*, and that the *News* would be the first to hear of any important information coming out of the City Ground. Chris Arnot, the writer and journalist from whom I learnt this, and who had been instrumental in setting up the *News*, told me recently that because of Cloughie's intervention the *News* was able to print the 'exclusive' about Trevor Francis being signed for Forest, the first player to acquire the Million Pound tag. The *News*, alas, didn't survive for long. The tales of Cloughie's open-handed generosity show no signs of fading.

* * *

Some years after Cloughie's death, the Nottingham-based dramatist Stephen Lowe wrote for Nottingham Playhouse a 'Community Play' about 'Old Big 'Ead', as Clough took to calling himself following his award of the OBE. The play, a deserved success, was warts and all. It didn't shrink from presenting Cloughie's occasional fits of bullying, often whetted by his drinking habits, nor his inexcusable verbal attacks on gays, especially gay footballers. But night after night during the play's run, the Playhouse was packed out, and this unsurprisingly led to an equally well attended re-run. The last night of the re-run was, I remember, an especially festive occasion. As well as regular theatre-goers, the Playhouse was packed with Forest supporters, most of whom I'm willing to bet were attending a theatre for the first and probably last time in their lives. They wore their Forest shirts, were wrapped in red-and-white scarves, sported large rosettes and other favours, and in defiance or indifference or ignorance of the rule that no drink was to be brought into the auditorium, they clutched pints of beer and lager, which they regularly lifted in order to toast the action on stage. Many of them stood in the cross-aisles rather than bothering to sit, and when the play ended they didn't clap. Instead, they cheered and broke into chants of celebration and syncopated applause – *bam*, ba-ba *bam* – for Forest and, of course and above all, for the man himself.

It was wonderful. It was also, I'm pretty sure, unique. I can't imagine any other celebration, anywhere else in England, where such a performance could be replicated.

* * *

To repeat, these pages aren't offered as a biographical sketch. John McGovern, whom Clough brought from Derby to the City Ground and who was Forest's captain in the early period of their glory days, was once asked the secret of his manager's success, not merely on but off the field. 'I'm not sure,' he said, 'but I know that I'd run through a brick wall for him.' Just how Clough became so great a manager, became so loved, became 'Cloughie', is impossible to say, though running was certainly part of it, was integral to what his Forest teams did. They were in constant movement, switching positions, confusing defenders used to 'marking' their opposite numbers. Even the trainer ran. Jimmy Gordon, by then silver-haired, must have been one of the last, if not *the* last of football trainers to make do with bucket and sponge. As a player went down, so Gordon would be up from his bench and ready to sprint onto the pitch as soon as the referee signalled permission. The trainer's appearance on the touchline, and then his knees-up, P.E. style of running as he hastened across the pitch, was always accompanied by genially comic cheers from Forest supporters. Bucket and sponge, probably accompanied by smelling salts, was for the most part enough to revive a player, get him back on his feet, ready to resume running.

My father sometimes made the journey up from Devon where he and my mother were by then living in contented retirement. 'In order to see you all,' he insisted, though his visits occurred far more frequently during the football season. He took great pleasure in going with Ben to any of Forest's home games, because a visit to the City Ground gave him the chance to renew his acquaintance with Jimmy Gordon, that footballing friend from his wartime days. He told me that he thought Gordon was probably the fittest man he had ever known. He may well have been right. As my father's contemporary, the Forest trainer would have been in his late sixties when he made those track-suited appearances so loved by home supporters, and by then there must have been many younger trainers with more modern methods to revive players, to get them up and on their feet, than by the application of cold water to the face and back of the neck, followed by a quick swipe of smelling salts under the nose. But Jimmy Gordon of Middlesbrough was Cloughie's man, his preferred choice.

Others weren't so favourably regarded. Cloughie could be unthinkingly cruel. Gary Newbon, a sports reporter for Central TV, was a favourite butt. On an occasion when Forest had lost heavily in an away game, poor Newbon was left to enquire what had gone wrong. 'We played like bloody pansies,' Cloughie said. Then, with the camera on him, he gave the hapless Newbon an expansive kiss on the cheek, winked, and turned away.

But a few years later, when Newbon suffered a minor

heart attack, Cloughie sent him a letter of sympathy in which he promised the reporter that, once back at work, Newbon could interview him any time he wanted to do so.

* * *

In the years when Cloughie was growing up, professional footballers might become working-class heroes but their post-football lives were rarely, if ever, of much account. And their heydays could be suddenly ended by injury. Cloughie's was. Besides, players were at the mercy of directors who could sell them on as if they were of no more account than market cattle. In the morning you were registered, say, with Nottingham Forest. By evening you'd been sold to Stoke and you and your family had no alternative but to move from one city to the other. Your children were happy in their school? So what. Your wife had made friends with others in the neighbourhood? Then let her make friends elsewhere. The whole business – and it *was* business, cruel, unfeeling business – stank.

I remember reading some years ago of the death of Wilf Mannion, found dead in a ditch and, at a guess, given a pauper's funeral. I saw Mannion play in the late nineteen-forties. He was England's golden boy. Blond-haired, good-looking, he played at inside forward for Middlesbrough, and though I can recall little of that match at Highbury to which my father took me in 1947, beyond the fact that Arsenal won, walloped the visitors 7-0, and Denis Compton, the greatest of my sporting heroes, scored two goals from his position on the left wing, I do recall being taken down to the changing rooms after the game in order to meet Jimmy Gordon and other of the Middlesbrough team, and feeling an especial thrill when I was given a signed photograph of Mannion. The fact that he was part of a side that had been thrashed didn't dent my regard for him.

Mannion was then commonly agreed to be one of England's best players, quick, agile, deadly in front of goal. He had scored two of England's goals in a Festival match, presumably to celebrate victory over Hitler's Germany, which was played at Hampden Park against the Rest of Europe. Much later I learnt that on the return train from Scotland, Mannion's third-class railway ticket had required him to stand in a crowded corridor while football directors and their mates, who had gone to the game by invitation, lounged in an all but empty first-class compartment, soaking up whisky supplied by the F.A.

I can't believe that Cloughie wouldn't have heard that story. If so, it helps explain why, on an occasion when he was briefly in charge of England's youth team, he herded the players onto the team coach after a game, and ordered the driver to set off without waiting for the emergence of various F.A. officials, who had taken for granted that they could keep the players waiting until they themselves were good and ready to depart. The officials were, Cloughie said, 'clods', they were 'clowns', they were 'bloody amateurs'. He was a players' man, a players' manager. When asked what words he would choose to be remembered by, he said, 'He contributed.' Look that word up in the OED and this is what you find. 'To contribute: supply or pay along with others to a common fund ... play a part in the achievement of a result ... provide (agency or assistance) to a common result or purpose'. Modest enough. A refusal of distinction, of being set apart. But then Cloughie was a democratic socialist. He *was* special, but he was also a common man, a plain, good man. And that is much.

What Holds Them

'Move over God – Cloughie's coming.' Message written on card and left among the thousands of tributes that arrived at the City Ground after news reached Nottingham of the death of Brian Clough.

Brian Clough is gone, red-carded by cancer.
Rough-tongued shaman, rogue, blest necromancer,
who blazed new life into clubs, players, teams –
losers no more but playing out their dreams
as tricksters. 'Get rid of racists!'
Brian's order. 'We've done with fascists.
And by the way, no swearing, gentlemen.'
And the Trent End sang 'the referee's an orphan.'

He coaxed their wit, gave thumbs up to a pride
they hugged like trophies brought home by each side
he set free for the joy of it. 'The best
manager England never had,' some claim,
which may be so, although a fairer test
of worth than braggadocio sports-page fame
is that, of thousands packing the Market Square
to mourn this day, half have no love of the game
he loved, but all loved *him*, that cross-grained, rare
man whose sending off's brought them to fill
this place for one last time and holds them still.

Sunday, 3 October, 2004.

An Irregular Ode on the Retirement of Derek Randall, Cricketer

For Ben

My Batter at the Bridge, tun-voice-and-booted Randall,
who in presumptuous youth once chose to long-man-
    handle
Shuttleworth, Lever and Simmons – Lanc's gruff and
    grudging trio –
And won for Notts a match they'd hoped to draw, *con brio*.
At the non-striker's end Great Garfield Sobers stood
to grin applause at cover drives that in due season would
drive Lillee so distracted he'd steeple at your head,
though 'no use aiming there, mate, there's nowt in it,' you
    said,

'try pitching 'em up.' He did. And your Centenary
innings flowed, a two days' binge, golden, crisp and buttery.
Yet oh, what homecoming waited on that wondrous 174;
Your Trent Bridge Test, and run out by that uncallipygian
    bore
Boycott. But then a county game at his own Headingly,
he prods to cover, sets off, and the 'coiled cobra' he
had not considered zaps him with wit, speed, grace,
those Son-of-a-Gunn gifts you poured into summer's
    space.

All shirt tail, pads skew-whiff, slewed cap and Grock's
    slumped walk,
'The Sun Has Got His Hat On' you'd mourn, or scatter
    talk
wide as fielders, bat parsing each ball in optative
mood: 'I choose to cut or pull, to sweep or glance or
drive',
while stripe-tied types snuffed gin, muttering 'Crackers
in one's opinion. Chap's not one of Us.' True! And
    Packer's
Circus couldn't corral you, nor did you make bold
with Greig, Gooch and Gatting to stuff your boots with
    randgold,

but once again Down Under upped to bemused Brearley:
'Only ten minutes more it'll be fifteen to tea',
and care thus summoned dispensed with care three plush
    fours
to hoist your hundred, flay Hogg, and become fit cause
of Arlott's measured words. 'He made the method men
    look sad';
and so you did, and such sweet madness had spectators
    glad
hand you to pavilions, who knew the back-page scandal:
you were too rare a player for England, dear Derek Randall.

Lol

SOONER OR LATER, EVERYONE I MEET and get to know will remind me of a character in Dickens. Sometimes the eureka moment will take weeks, even months to arrive. But with Lol it happened almost at once. Lol is Joe Gargery. I imagine his birth name was Lawrence or Laurence, though I've never asked. To everyone he knows and to whom he's known, especially the jazzmen and women he's backed over the years, including myself, he's simply 'Lol'. Lol Ryan. A drummer whose deft skills enhance the work of any group he plays with. Not a thunder fist, never drawing attention to himself, his work on brushes especially cherishable, he's one of my favourite musicians. He's also a most loveable man, and of how many drummers can you say that?

I first came across him when, years ago now, I was asked to fill in with a Sunday lunchtime band at the Old Mill Club, Stapleford; Stapleford being a small town on the road between Nottingham and Derby. The phone call came on a Thursday evening. 'Keith here.' Keith Jordan was a trombonist with whose band I'd occasionally played, and he was phoning because he wanted to know whether, in view of the absence of his regular trumpet lead for the coming Sunday gig, I could take the vacant chair. 'Twelve-thirty until three, a tenner and two free drinks. OK?' Keith was a man of few words. Had I said no he'd have simply rung off and tried someone else.

'OK', I said. 'Black-and-white or scruff order?'

'As you are,' Keith told me. 'Not too ragged-arsed, that's all the management asks. Usual kind of repertoire. I'll handle the vocals.'

And that was that.

But in the intervening two days I remembered that on a previous occasion when I'd depped with Keith's band, I'd had to put up with a drummer who, even by the duff standards to which many drummers then aspired, came at the back end of worse than useless. From my early days as a practising and never more than average musician, I'd been amazed by the numbers of those who, presumably hoping to make up for inadequate love lives, bought themselves drum-kits and after, say, two weeks of failing to learn how to manage the hi-hat, advertised themselves as experts on the traps.

It's an old jazz joke. 'Who do drummers hang out with?' Answer: 'Musicians.' Not if the musicians have anything to do with it, they don't. Or, anyway, didn't, not in those bygone days when Trad jazz and its variants could be found in the back rooms of most pubs, village halls, and, on Saturday nights, assembly rooms the length and breadth of the land. But good drummers were hard to come by, could almost name their own price. Bad ones tipped money into the coffers of main street music shops, and their (roughly) on-beat thumps from the back of the stage created problems for the rest, including, so I was assured, heart attacks and/or hernias for dancers keen to put into practice steps they had learnt from those months of attendance at whichever local Academy of Dance they chose to favour. Quick-Step, Foxtrot, Tango, Waltz, as well as more exotic routines such as the Samba, Palais Glide, even the Scottische (never knowingly played by any band I was with, though Victor Sylvester's Ballroom Orchestra could – and did – perform it, show-offs that they were), there was no routine of steps the majority of drummers couldn't wreck.

But surely I'd been hired on this coming Sunday to play with a jazz band? Yes, indeed. But you just knew that before the session came to an end, some couple, maybe more than one, would approach the bandleader and wonder, all coyly as it might be, whether we could oblige with, say, an old-fashioned waltz. 'It's for Gran. We've brought her specially. She can't get out much nowadays, not with her knee.'

Useless to say an old-fashioned waltz wasn't in our 'book'. Pleading switched to incredulity. 'You know the Skater's Waltz, surely? No? Well, pretend you do. Drinks all round if you can give us that.'

And so more often than not we'd struggle through a few choruses of, say, 'The Blue Danube', while the dancers tried to follow the three-four time we aimed to uphold despite the drummer's unsteady four-seven beat, and the last one home was a Ninny.

But when I arrived at the Mill Club that Sunday, a drummer I didn't recognise was setting up. Keith introduced us. 'This is John,' he said to the drummer, 'John Lucas. Trumpet.' And to me, 'Lol. Lol Ryan. From Leicester.' As though this was sufficient guarantee of the drummer's ability. But I'd played with drummers as far away as Market Harborough, further than that even, and I knew better than to be fooled by Keith's attempted recommendation.

We shook hands. Lol's grip was vice-like. If he gripped the sticks that hard, heaven alone knew what damage he could inflict on the skins, let alone his cymbals.

And what to make of his smile, quick, wide-lipped, or his brief, 'Hello, mate, good to meet yer.' I'd spent early, wartime years in rural Leicestershire, and thought I could detect a little of an accent that had long ago been familiar enough; but I was far from sure, just as I was far from sure I'd be any happier with this drummer's work than I was with the band's regular thrash merchant.

A few minutes later we were 'all present and correct', in Keith's words, and he called the first number. 'Avalon, nice and light, medium tempo, OK, gentlemen?' And with his right foot, he beat the number in.

Thirty-two bars later, an odd sensation had taken hold. Surprise? Relief? Pleasure? Well, yes, but better than pleasure. Pure elation. I should say here that at the beginning of just about every session I've played in, from my seventeenth year to my eightieth, I've found pleasure in the experience of making music. Often enough, this has been less than complete. Keen anticipation dulls to acceptance of 'just another gig'. The venue turns out to be less than welcoming, one or other of the musos is having an off-night, or, it might be, year; there is disagreement about tempi or keys in which certain numbers should be played; the repertoire itself may feel wrong or unsuitable. ('Do we have to play that bloody number? Can't we do something in E♭?). Even so, as we say our goodnights, there'll be a sense of having more than survived the occasion.

But this session at the Old Mill Club was different. More. It was special. And when it came to an end I was wanting it to go on.

In the following years, whenever I played with Lol, which was often, there would be sessions where we'd experience a sense of deflation, sessions of the kind Australians call 'average': nothing out of the ordinary, even a bit of a let-down. But that first session was the real McCoy. And by the time it came to an end I was exultant, jumping. I'd had the chance to work with a wonderfully good drummer, so light, so crisp his drumming was, so swinging, so deft, so considerate of his fellow musicians. And when he switched from sticks to brushes, as he did when we played 'Rose Room', well, that seemed perfection of the kind that we were after.

As we were packing up, Lol and I fell into conversation. Did he have a group with whom he regularly played? Yes, he said, he did. But he also liked 'guesting' with other groups. 'Bit of a challenge, like. Keeps you on your toes.'

He wasn't fussy who he backed, nor what kind of music they played, provided of course that they were good company and paid him at least enough to cover his expenses. 'Don't like the ones who are all mouth and no talent. Can't be doing with them. Not my idea of a night out.'

Jazz was his preferred mode, jazz of the period 1920s to 1950s, but he often found himself backing a group of young rockers who played in and around Leicester. 'Nice lads, they are, polite enough, you know.' And there were musical evenings at a working men's club at Colville where he put in a couple of hours most Friday nights. Best of all, there was his regular group: a six-piece outfit which had a fortnightly residency at a pub in Market Bosworth. 'Zoot and his City Stompers. Heard of them?' No, I said, I hadn't.

'Zoot Morris. Used to play regular like with a dance band, but he's a jazzman at heart. You want to come over and give us a listen some time. Sit in with us, you'd fit OK.'

I was dubious. 'Don't you have a regular trumpet man?'

Lol shook his head. 'The one we use wants out. He's got plenty of other work in the Leicester area. You'd be doing him a favour.'

'And you'd be doing us a favour if you joined the little outfit I'm with,' I said.

At the time I was part of a four-piece that played Sunday evenings in the back bar of a Beeston 'hostelry', to use the term that was meant to provide us with extra cachet. Clarinet, cornet, bass, and banjo/guitar. Yes, I know, banjo is guaranteed to give any self-respecting jazz musician a dose of the squitters. But not only did ours run the outfit, he was the vocalist – a good one – and his banjo playing was way above average. Beside, Bill Cole, our bass player, was a top man, and Bill kept us in order. Look at the cover of any LP recording of a British 'trad' jazz band of the period mid nineteen-fifties to seventies and you'd be surprised by the number of times Bill features in the rhythm section. At least, I think you would. Not once you heard him play, though. He was one of the best. Bill was Colyer's first choice for several years before he – Bill, that is – married the daughter of a Nottingham professor and settled down (ha!) to a more regular life. Though, of course, he was still available for work in the area, and he'd been known to accept an engagement for a week or so elsewhere, including foreign trips: France, Holland, Belgium, Germany, Malta ... Well, you get the picture. Have bass, will travel. And because Bill was so short he was one of the few stand-up bassists who didn't suffer from a bad back.

Nor did he suffer from the prodigious amounts of beer he could put away, not at that time, anyway. True, he was sometimes pulled over by late-night traffic cops familiar with his car, a battered estate in which he occasionally slept. What alerted them to Bill's being eight and over was the fact that he was driving unusually straight and being careful to keep within the speed limit. And you couldn't very well arrest a man for doing nothing wrong. As far as any band leader was concerned, once Bill said he'd be available for a gig you could guarantee he'd be there on stand, wherever 'there' happened to be. So, yes, have bass, including brass bass, will travel.

I was confident Bill wouldn't throw a wobbly if Lol sat in with us for a night. Bill appreciated good drummers, and as I've already mentioned there weren't all that many of them about. Plenty who fancied themselves, of course, but that was a different matter. Nor, I was sure, would either our clarinettist or the main man himself, banjoist and leader, Johnny Bly, object. So I suggested that Lol join us the following Sunday. And after two numbers – maybe after one – I could see smiles and nods of approval all round. From then on, the Burgundy Street Four (stress on second syllable of Burgundy) became the Burgundy Street Five.

And meanwhile I joined Zoot and his City Stompers. To use a jazz litotes, it wasn't a bad outfit. A solid bassman, whose day job as a traffic policeman never interfered with his evening work; decent banjo/guitarist, 'El Tel', a bit of a wide boy, so I gathered, stall-holder at various local markets; and front line comprising as well as myself an above average trombonist who taught physics at a secondary school, and who combined a wide repertoire with a full tone, especially well-suited for ballads such as 'I'm Confessing' and 'Deep Purple'; plus Zoot himself on the tenor sax which he played with genuine grace and an easy swing gained through years of working with semi-pro dance bands and on which he'd learnt, as the saying goes, to give a good account of himself. The ensemble, or 'gentlemen of the orchestra' as the pub landlord tended to identify us as when handing out our earnings at the end of an evening, was of course lifted by Lol's drumming, that crisp, swinging, understated, always reassuring sound. With Lol on the traps you knew you were in good hands. Literally so.

I enjoyed those evenings. The music was above competent, we played to an appreciative audience, and we got on together. A happy band of brothers, you could say. The only duff moments came when Zoot laid aside his tenor and reached for his clarinet, an instrument on which he fancied himself as something of a maestro. How wrong can a man get? As our leader squealed and squeaked through a succession of numbers which had done him no harm but against which he seemed to have conceived a personal vendetta, we'd bite our lips and try not to look at each other while avoiding the expressions of puzzled alarm given off by those who could bear to listen. 'Ought Pest Control to be called in?' the bassist, Alan, once whispered in my ear. But then to everyone's relief Zoot would go back to his tenor and once more all manner of things would be well.

If Lol was ever concerned by Zoot's almost flawless incompetence on what the leader sometimes referred to as his 'liquorice stick', he never said so. Once or twice I fancied I saw him wince at the sounds that came from the clarinet, on other occasions he seemed to be screwing his face up in order to suppress an attack of hysterical laughter, but after all Zoot was the band's leader, Lol and he were friends, and Lol valued friendship, as he valued loyalty and love, above most other things. Lol was a man who preferred tolerance to confrontation, though cruelty to children was a vice apart. 'I'd batter any sod who hurt a little kid,' he once said, and it was the only time I saw him looking flushed and angry – at a report he'd come across of the closing down of a nearby orphanage. But he was more than willing to put up with mishaps and setbacks in the interest of preserving good relations with others. It wasn't that he feared confrontation. But life was better without it. 'Don't see the point in riling people up,' he said, 'not if it ain't needed.'

He once told me during an interval, while we stood chatting at the bar, that when he was doing his National Service on Malta he had been invited to join the Army Nursing Service. He was far too modest to say what lay behind the invitation, but I've no doubt that the relevant authorities were greatly impressed by him. In Lol they had found an ideal man for hospital duties. He had about him an unfailing cheerfulness which, coupled with those skilful hands and a concern for others that found expression when I knew him best in a determination to establish an inclusive spirit of camaraderie among musicians, made him not merely cherishable but invaluable.

'Were you tempted?' I asked, when he told me about the invitation that had come his way.

'Not half,' he said. 'I fancied it something rotten, I don't mind telling you, and I fancied life on Malta.'

'But you didn't take the offer up.'

'Couldn't. See, I'd promised Bett we'd get married soon as I was back in civvies. And Bett, she didn't want to leave England.'

I've forgotten why his wife-to-be, Betty or Bett, as he more usually referred to her, wasn't keen on foreign travel, if he ever told me, that is, which he may not have done. As far as he was concerned, it was enough for me to know that Betty was his love, that before he was called up for National Service they became engaged, that they planned to marry as soon as he was out of uniform, and that her wishes came first. End of story. Lol must have told me that story before I met Betty, but when I did I had no reason to doubt the durable quality of their marriage. By then they had been man and wife for the best part of forty years, but the bond between them was unfrayed and was kept strong by mutual respect as well as affection. 'Bett,' Lol once said to me, 'she's the reader, she gets into things, she knows more than me about the way things go.' I thought of Captain Cuttle's admiration for Bunsby, how Bunsby's sagacity 'would sink one of my tonnage soon'; and though Dickens has no doubt that the Captain's trust in his friend's boundless sagacity is misplaced, he doesn't deride it. Besides, Lol's devoted respect for his wife was well-grounded.

Betty was a Christian, an active member of their local Anglican community, though without any ostentatious show of piety. Smaller than Lol, plump where he was lean, she radiated a kind of contentment with the life she and Lol lived, which included their being devoted parents and grandparents, all without the least trace of smugness. She wasn't often at our sessions – I'm not sure she much liked jazz – but whenever she chose to appear she had a cheery word for all the musos, wanting to know how they were getting on, then, how was everything in their daily lives. Were they in good health, she meant, were their families happy – she made it her business to know who was married and who among those that were had children, how many, what were their names – and were they in steady work?

Work mattered, mattered greatly. Of course it did. Lol was a plasterer by trade. 'Mind, I could have made a bit out of using my fists, but Betty wasn't having it.' He confided this one evening while we were setting up for a gig at an athletics club annual dance where prizes and awards were laid out on a table near the bandstand.

Did he mean that he could have made a go of it as a professional boxer? 'Well, when I was a lad I went to the local club, regular like, did some scrapping and got quite good at it, and then, when we arrived on Malta, there was a sergeant with his clipboard, standing there at the bottom of the gangplank, dead keen to sign up anyone who fancied putting on the gloves. Try for the Regimental team.' At first, Lol said, he was tempted. 'Good breakfasts, you got, John, full fry-ups, and then regular gym sessions instead of all that square bashing.'

'So you signed up.'

'I asked Bett whether it would be OK. But Bett, she wasn't having any of that. She made me promise not to join the fight game.'

'She didn't want your lovely features re-arranged by

someone in leather gloves?'

'She's dead set against violence. Can't be doing with it. Her mum had to put up with some of that from her old man. Bett was forced to watch some of it when she was a girl. Mind, the bugger was dead by the time Bett and me got together. Violence against women and kids.' Lol shook his head in wonderment and, I could tell, suppressed fury. 'Makes me mad, that does. I'd have given the bastard what for, I would.'

I think he probably would have done so. Lean and still remarkably nimble in his late middle age, Lol was, as the saying goes, a man with whom you'd not want to tangle on a dark night. As a plasterer, he no doubt worked with the agile concentration that he brought to his drumming. It was a trade he enjoyed, he insisted, more than enjoyed. 'Once you know how, you never forget,' he said. 'I love it, I do. You're never out of work as a plasterer, someone always wants you. Like drumming. The phone rings and a job's on the other end of the line. Soon's you're known to be a reliable bloke, folk'll queue up for your services. And if you can do a bit else, spot of plumbing, brick-laying, then you can more or less name your price. Mind, you need your van, and you don't want to get tied down to any one company, especially not the bigger ones. Keep away from them. So much an hour, no benefits if they can avoid it, and some bloody gaffer who knows bugger all trying to tell you how to do your job. No, make sure you stay your own boss, John, that's how to do it.'

As Lol was telling me this, I was thinking of a great

friend of mine, another plasterer. This friend had been a mature student, someone I taught in the English department at Loughborough, greatly well-read, a thinker, independent minded, for whom his trade as plasterer, though he took it with absolute seriousness, caused him physical as well as mental upset. Lacking Lol's lean physique and easy grace of movement, he found his work increasingly arduous and it has left him with physical impairments which ought to cancel any sentimental nonsense about the typical health-giving properties of manual labour. He and I together wrote a book about the history of whistling, a copy of which I gave to Lol, who gave it to Betty, though whether she read it I don't know and never cared to ask.

* * *

For my seventieth birthday I arranged that The Burgundy Street Five should spend the appropriate weekend playing two gigs in North Cornwall. On the Friday night we were at Calstock, then, Saturday lunchtime, we moved a mile up the road to a pub at Gunnerslake, where we played a two-hour session in the back room of a pub. The weekend had been organised by Harry Chambers, publisher of Peterloo Poets, jazz aficionado, and good friend, whose press had published my first full collection, *Studying Grosz on the Bus*. Sometime in the 1980s, I think it was, Harry had managed to acquire a redundant Methodist chapel for his Press, which became Peterloo's headquarters, where readings were regularly held, as, less regularly, were jazz and poetry evenings. I'd performed at one of these with John Mole and a pick-up group which might more accurately have been called a non-pick-up group, given that the hired bass player from further down Cornwall had forgotten to collect the pianist who was expecting a lift from Bodmin or wherever to Calstock. Nor did the promised drummer ever arrive. That left the two of us, clarinet and cornet. We had therefore to borrow the keyboard player and drummer from a rock group which was also in session that evening. I don't like to think what kind of music we made, but the audience, stunned into torpor by beer and heat, let us off lightly. Their stupefaction must have been at least partly deepened by the fact that although Harry had made sure to get a drinks licence, he had forgotten to ask the local authorities for permission to play live music on the premises, which meant that on what was probably the hottest night of the year we had to perform to a packed house with all windows and doors tightly shut. As far as I know there were no deaths, though for several in the audience it must have been a close call.

Matters were simpler when it came to organising my birthday gigs. In the first place, although the five of us who made up the Burgundy Street group would be travelling down to Calstock separately, I made sure to arrange for us all to have places to stay. I also issued maps, provided door-to-door directions, and wrote down starting and finishing times for the two gigs. And to my amazed pleasure, we all arrived at Calstock in good time for the Friday evening, 'we' being Tony Elwell on clarinet, Ken Eatch on bass, guitarist Ian Wheatley, myself and, of course, Lol. And all, except Ken, brought wives and partners.

I had told them that they could expect to enjoy the experience of playing in the chapel, which prompted sceptically raised eyebrows, though these were lowered when they walked into the place. The chapel, built of local stone, was on the road leading down to a small village, and from the outside looked unremarkable. But enter and scepticism turned to wonderment. For where you might have expected a back wall, there was instead a vista of light over fields. The architect called in to adjust the chapel to its new, secular existence, had in a moment of pure inspiration chosen to remove the entire back wall, and in its place there was now glass, nothing but glass. And through the glass you had an uninhibited view of the banks of the Tamar river, and, beyond them, a rising stretch of lush, tussocky fields where sheep roamed or lay under full-leaved trees or stretched themselves beside green, deep bushes. There was something primal about that view, especially on a sunny evening in late June. 'Jerusalem the Golden,' someone, I think it was Ian, said. And he wasn't entirely joking.

We set up, guests and paying customers arrived, the place was soon full, there were breaks for readings by poets, a few of whom had travelled from London to be at the occasion, while others, who lived nearer, were also in attendance and, as sports writers used to say, gave good accounts of themselves, the Burgundians were on top form, so, anyway, we were assured, and the evening ended in a mood of roused contentment with an extended version of 'I'll See You In My Dreams' featuring Lol's eight-bar rimshot break – he never allowed himself more – as the outstanding contribution.

The following morning we roamed about the village where 'saft was the sunne', greeted by locals who had been at the previous evening's event and who wanted to tell us how much they'd enjoyed it – 'like real musicians,' one woman told Lol; and Betty convinced Pauline she should buy the set of coffee cups my wife had been dubitating over in the small lock-up shed which specialised, so a hand-written notice told us, in **gifts for all ocassions Gran mite like**. None of us liked to ask why Gran was being especially targeted.

After which we got into our cars and drove up the road to Gunnerslake, passing under an extraordinary slant bridge over the Tamar which had been built, we were assured, in order that Brunel's Great Western line should be enabled to continue on its route from Plymouth to Penzance.

Gunnerslake turned out to be an even smaller village than Calstock though, standing at a junction of roads, it housed three pubs to Calstock's one. So, anyway, we learned from the same man who told us about the railway bridge and who, for all any one of us knew to the contrary, had been hired by the local tourist board to provide information, misleading or otherwise, to outsiders. I was reminded of a *New Statesman Weekend Competition* which had invited entrants to provide Misleading Advice to Visitors, the competition being won by someone who told visitors to Edinburgh that in Scotland signs for men's toilets always showed a man clad in a kilt. Runner-up was the advice intended for visitors to New York. 'Do not attempt to tip a cab-driver. It offends his sturdy sense of independence.'

Harry had arranged with the largest of the three pubs for us to play in the back room, a wide space with its own bar, and where there were sufficient tables, chairs, and wall seats to accommodate up to fifty punters. By the time we'd set up, many more than that number had crowded in, a goodly number of them standing at the bar, all in receptive mood. As a result, the two-hour session we'd signed up for went on for a good three hours, though I don't think anyone minded. Anyway, as we say in the jazz world, 'If you don't like it, feel free to leave.' The Burgundy Street Five certainly didn't want to stop when time was up. Playing to a live audience is nearly always a thrill; playing to those who make no bones about shouting their applause, offering the musicians drinks, even trying out the odd two-step, is a pleasure reserved for such occasions.

But eventually the last note of 'Bourbon Street Parade' sounded as Lol used his bass drum foot pedal to signal FINIS, and slowly, slowly, the crowd began to make for the exit. We dissassembled ourselves from the musical unit we'd become over the hours of playing, packed away our instruments, declined the management's offer of a last drink, one for the road not being a recommendable possibility, and with many thanks and fond farewells to Harry, we headed for the car park.

Not, though, before we'd all said goodbye to the charming Jewish couple with whom Lol and Betty had lodged on Friday night in Tiverton, and who arrived for the Saturday gig in what I took to be Orthodox costume. At Lol and Betty's insistence, they introduced themselves to us with many shaloms, a word which we all took up, so that the air was soon thick with shaloms. 'Shalom to you, and you, and you, and you.'

And then Ken got behind the wheel of his car to start the long journey back to Nottingham – 'Shalom Kenneth' – Lol and Betty began a shorter journey to Newton Abbot, where they were eager to see and stay with their children, now living in that Devon town complete with those who Lol referred to as 'the little'uns', – 'Shalom, shalom, dear Lol, dear Betty', – and Ian, Tony and I, with our partners, headed for the South Devon village of Belstone. 'Many, many shaloms. Come again, please, and bring your music with you.'

'We will, we will. Shalom.'

* * *

We were to stay at a handsome guest house on the edge of Belstone, a village from where you could walk down to a stream and from there straight up on to the moors.

I'd stayed there before. Some years previously, after my

father's death, my widowed mother had been forced by increased lack of mobility to give up the small house in Chagford, on the edge of Dartmoor, where they'd lived for some twenty years in contented retirement, and she now had accommodation in the dull little town of Okehampton. While she was there, the family took turns to visit her, and our daughter, Emma, on one such visit, had chosen to put up in the Belstone guest house, a mile or so from Okehampton itself. Back home in New Malden, Emma phoned to tell me about her experience, her discovery. 'You'll love the house,' she told me. 'It's in its own grounds, with sheep all round, and it's run by a man called Manoel, and his wife, Geraldine. Geraldine is English and Manoel is an exile from Chile. He escaped from Pinochet. And he knows about jazz.'

'What do you mean, "knows."'

'I think he's a jazz musician. He told me he plays with some local groups. Next time you're in Okehampton you should stay at the Cleave House, that's what the place is called, then you can see for yourself.'

See? What could Emma mean? What was to see?

For my next visit to Okehampton I booked in at the Cleave House, arriving late in the evening after I'd spent much of the day with my mother.

I drove the short distance from her accommodation to Belstone, then followed directions out from the tree-lined village until I came to an open, iron-barred gate, where a gravel drive curved past thick laurel bushes to the left, and, to the right, was a spread of lawn beyond which I could see a field where sheep roamed or stood ghostly grey in the late twilight. A large, two-storied house loomed diagonally ahead. It was built of blocky granite, but its wide ground-floor windows took away any hint of grimness, let alone an attempt at imposing grandeur. It was more like the kind of nineteenth-century vicarage habituated to, and softened by, the lives of country parsons indifferent to the finer points of dogma, and who greatly preferred lepidoptery to the minatory thunderings of Leviticus.

The man who opened the door to me was tall, slim, and even in the dim, artificial light, his welcoming smile and bespectacled clean-shaven face, suggested a kind of rueful, withheld quality. But his voice, light, the words with their slightly foreign accent, were reassuringly friendly. How *was* my mother, he asked, and when I told him that she was, I feared, nearing death, he nodded in genuine concern. 'She is very old?'

'Yes,' I said, she was a very old woman, in her nineties.

'It is sad.'

Later in our acquaintanceship, when I knew more about Manoel, had heard about his narrow escape from Pinochet's police, the ruses he needed to employ as a student to get to Spain, his doubts as to whether he could ever return to Chile to see parents, relatives, friends, I became aware of sadness, a kind of fixed, gentle melancholia, far in excess of anything I had expected. But on that first evening I made small talk as though with an equal, and then, as directed, made my way upstairs to my room.

As I climbed the stairs, I noticed that on the wall to the

right of the stairs I was being accompanied by a succession of black and white photographs. Jazzmen, mostly ones I recognised, including Miles Davis, Charlie Mingus, Ella in a flowery hat that didn't suit her, others whom I was less certain of.

The following morning, seated alone at a table in the breakfast room at the back of the house which overlooked a sweep of lawn leading down to a large, reed-fringed pond, and recalling Emma's words, 'he knows about jazz', I asked Manoel as he came in with the poached egg I'd ordered, 'Who are the jazz musicians you have on the stairs? I recognised some but not all.'

'Tell me who you can identify.'

I did so and he nodded, smiling his forgiveness at my failures. 'You didn't spot Benny Carter?'

'No, sorry.'

'He's on the third stair, holding his alto; and near the top it's him again, a bit older, with trumpet. That was when he was playing at the Hot Club in Madrid.'

A pause. Then, 'I took that photo,' Manoel said.

And then it all came out. Well, not all, of course, but enough to make mine eyes dazzle. After his escape from Chile and having made his way to Spain, Manoel, who I now began to learn was as a student already a jazz guitarist of renown in his home country, and with a recommendation to the Hot Club of Madrid, found employment there and was soon installed as resident guitarist, working not merely with the house musicians but with visiting jazzmen and women, many of them with international reputations.

'After I'd been there for some months, Benny Carter brought his big band to Madrid, and he hired me to go on tour with him.' Manoel's words were uttered matter-of-fact, and how exactly Carter came to make his offer I never learnt, but clearly Manoel was no ordinary house musician. He had, he explained, been part of the Carter band when it toured Japan and other Far East countries, a tour which included a number of recording contracts, and Manoel told me that he'd play me tapes of some of the concerts, 'If you're interested.'

'I'd love to listen to whatever you choose,' I said, touched by his genuine diffidence, and I think he knew I meant it.

And so that evening, after I'd spent the day with my mother, Manoel played me tapes of the Benny Carter concerts, and I found myself listening to the guitar work of a maestro.

* * *

After my mother's death and funeral, which was held in Chagford Parish Church, the whole family stayed at the Cleave House, and during breakfast and again that evening, while he cooked us a superb dinner, Manoel played us tapes made at the time of his sessions with Benny Carter's Orchestra. The tapes weren't always of the highest quality, but there was no doubting the worth of the music. Why, I wondered, had he given all that up for life on the edge of Dartmoor and the occasional gig with local musicians. He'd previously told me about these, and of how he often gave his services for free, playing for dances and at small concerts, school fêtes, church fund-raisers. Now, he explained that marriage to Geraldine meant a kind of settling down to domestic routines, the acceptance of a need to earn a steady living, and, especially after he became a father, the requirement, to use his words, of 'putting in roots'.

But as to how he and Geraldine met, *where* they met, and *why* they settled in Belstone, I never became any the wiser. He was surely a big city boy, not a bucolic; nor, when I came to meet her and sensed her edgy dissatisfactions, did Geraldine herself strike me as being enamoured of life in this corner of rural Devon. She was intelligent, sharp, and she wanted to be elsewhere, anywhere but here. As for Manoel, there were moments when I'd come upon him sitting in the small side room where he listened to his tapes, and the deep melancholy in his eyes, his abstracted expression, indicated something of his regrets for the life not lived. He was irrecoverably separated from so much, poor man. His native land, his family and the friends of his early years, the music he loved.

* * *

I had arranged for those of us not high-tailing it back to Nottingham from Gunnerslake to stay both Saturday and Sunday nights at Manoel's, and before we began our journey to Belstone I told our guitarist, Ian, something about Manoel. 'I'll get him to play us some of his tapes,' I promised. 'Especially his sessions with the Benny Carter band. They're wonderful. He'll be delighted to meet you. Talk to him nicely and he may get his guitar out and then the two of you can give us a recital.'

But Ian looked aghast. 'Not bloody likely,' he said. 'Tell him I play the mouth organ.'

Ian was in fact a very good rhythm guitarist but I suppose he knew his limitations. I was reminded of a story I'd come across in Rex Stewart's memoirs of his years with the Ellington orchestra in the 1930s. One evening in New York, when the band had the evening free, Stewart went to a club to hear Louis Armstrong, recently recovered from the bad lip that had prevented him from playing for quite some while, though it was rumoured to have left him with impaired embouchure. Before Armstrong made his appearance with the Luis Russell Band, Hot Lips Page was on with *his* orchestra, and as he was a local hero the audience was wanting him to out-blow Armstrong, the hick from the sticks. 'Take him, Hot Lips,' Stewart reports the crowd shouting, and Page ended his set with a prolonged scatter of high notes that were received with wild applause by his numerous fans crowded together in front of the bandstand.

Then Armstrong came out, 'bounced out,' so Stewart says, dressed in a white suit, and the gleam on his trumpet from an overhead spotlight 'made it look like a magic wand.' Romantic reminiscence, no doubt,' but when he blew his first note, full in the middle, Benny Carter, who had perfect pitch and who was standing beside Stewart, whispered, awestruck, 'My god, that's high F.' And soon afterward, Hot Lip's fans crept silently away.

* * *

I reminded Ian of our weekend at Belstone when I met him not long ago, in 2022, at the funeral of Roger Keene, who had become our keyboard player for some years, now sadly ended, during which The Burgundy Street Five Plus One (Roger being the Plus) played for monthly jazz and poetry gigs at Nottingham's Hotel Deux. Ian, Ken and I were in attendance at the funeral, but Tony was poorly, and there was no sign of Lol.

But he phoned a few evenings later to apologise for his absence. 'Message never got through, John. Otherwise I'd have been there, like. I'd have wanted to pay my respects.'

I didn't doubt him. Nor did I doubt the genuine pleasure with which he told me that he still did what he called 'a bit of plastering, for neighbours, you know', and that he was still playing. 'I'm out two or three times a week. Bit of rock, like, with younger lads, some jazz, and now and then I get offered a church sing-along. Bett, she organises those.'

The glowing affability, the enthusiasm for life, were undimmed.

'Give her my regards,' I said, but when he asked, 'You still blowing?' I had to confess that I'd not picked up the horn for several years. 'The lip's gone, Lol. And I'm too old now to start all over again.'

'Ah, well,' he said. Then, brightening, 'We had some good times, though, didn't we? Remember that weekend in Cornwall. That was a bit of alright, wasn't it?'

'Among plenty of others,' I said, then, after a pause, 'Shalom, Lol.'

And laughing as he put down the phone Lol said, 'Yes, shalom, mate, shalom.'

As a Rule

'Born in Newcastle-upon-Tyne, George was brought up in children's homes in the north of England, never knowing who his real family was.' From an obituary carried in *The Beeston Express*, Friday, October 3rd, 2008

Whether they're sentinels, 'soppy-stern', or just
around to bandage hurts, whisper good night,
their smiles and hugs ones you know you can trust,
parents, the rule is, need to keep kids right.

Lacking such care a man may grow to be
a psychopath, searching out ways to injure
the best intentioned ones who try naively
to foster love: he'll storm through days of pure

self-hate, probably loathing all else, too.
But no. It seems 'Although he never married,
or had his own family', this one was true
to no such expectations. Rather, he carried

love for others like those worn, daily tools
that served him 'As gardener and handyman.'
And though he did not profit much from school
'He had an enquiring mind and his opinion

was sought on numerous issues.' What was it
that made him 'Leave his signature on walls
before papering'? Did he think it fit
way to be remembered, his bare name al-

most lost beneath pasted sheets, *George Stewart*,
then found when some new occupier peeled
old paper off, poised to re-decorate,
but briefly held by what had been concealed

so long – the name of one who hid his pride
in routine tasks that guaranteed his kids
and wife could know for sure that he'd provide
a haven for them all in all he did.

For so we'd likely think, not guessing how
some men feed well on the most meagre scraps
they warm each day by means of the heart's bellows
then swallow gratefully, perhaps. Perhaps.

Letters of Introduction: Matt and Gael

IN LATE NOVEMBER, 1987, I RECEIVED a letter from someone who signed himself Matt Simpson, and who gave his address as Boundary Drive, Liverpool. Well, well. 'Bonne chance, matey,' as was commonly said in my youth. This surely had to be the Matt Simpson whose collection of poems, *Making Arrangements*, I'd picked up by chance some years earlier while looking along the shelves of the student bookshop at Liverpool University where my son was due to begin his three years of academic study in Politics and History. At that time, Autumn, 1982, and for some years afterward, I acted as poetry reviewer for the *New Statesman*, and I was so taken by the collection I read while standing in the bookshop that I asked Derek Mahon, who was then the journal's de facto literary editor, if he would let me review *Making Arrangements*. Derek was sympathetic, but eventually said no. There were other collections on his desk he especially wanted me to notice. At that point I probably should have written to Mr Simpson, care of Bloodaxe Books, to tell him of my admiration for his poems. Now, as I opened and read his letter some five years later, I found he was telling me that he had enjoyed reading my recently-published critical study of Modern English Poetry. He had also enclosed an inscribed copy of his collection.

I wrote back, thanking him for his letter and, especially, the inscribed copy of his poems. A correspondence quickly grew between us, and late in 1988 I invited him to give a reading at Loughborough University, where I was then Professor of English. He came, we met, and one of the most enriching friendships of my life began. It lasted scarcely twenty years, and was ended by the death of my dear friend in the early summer 2009, when the post-operational effects of a quadruple heart bypass led to a massive, unstoppable loss of blood. That dire news came via an email Pauline received while we were waiting at Athens airport for our journey home after a month on Aegina, the island where we had a small flat on long-term rent, and where, first in 1996 and then again a few years later, Matt had joined us for a week on each occasion.

I'd been hoping, once we were back in England, to suggest to him that he should spend another week – longer if he chose – convalescing on Aegina, knowing that he had delighted in his two visits to what I still think of as the beloved island. But that was now impossible. Matt was dead. Sitting in the airport's departure lounge, I imagined I could hear his voice – that light baritone enriched with subtle shiftings of tone – warning me, as he had so often done, to guard against life's great expectations. 'What larks, Pip,' he would sometimes say, then, 'but remember Jaggers.' He and I often talked about Dickens, agreeing that the lawyer in Dickens's novel is about as great a fictional invention of incorruptible, pitiless knowledge as can be imagined. Though I think Matt was touched when I dedicated my Penguin study of the Inimitable's major novels to him, he said that 'either you've got me wrong, or I've got me wrong.'

I puzzled then, as I do still, the meaning of his words. Matt rarely said anything he didn't intend to be taken, at some level, seriously. He could be, and often was, very funny, and he delighted in comic anecdote. But he wasn't given to casual, let alone careless, throwaway remarks. He may have intended to imply that he was no sort of scholarly critic, which he possibly saw me as being. Early on in his professional life, after he had completed his three years as a student of Eng. Lit. at Cambridge, he became a school teacher, then a lecturer at Liverpool Hope College of F. E., and then, when the college attained university status, he was entitled to call himself a university lecturer, though I don't think he ever did.

But Matt was better read, and certainly more intelligent, perceptive, and far more critically acute, than many, if not most, university lecturers I have known, especially when talking of or writing about poetry. His natural authority, his assuredness, his acuity, are all evident in *Hugging The Shore*, a collection of his essays which I published under the Shoestring Press imprint; and for all his diffidence, he could be trusted, always, to have thought to strong purpose before he delivered himself on a literary subject. He also took for granted the democratic right to speak about the visual arts, including architecture, and music, especially music, just as he took for granted your own seriousness if you ventured to speak with him about any of these matters. As I write these words I see his face, his eyes, warming to laughter or darkening with implicit reproof, or anger. And so often I find myself wondering what Matt would think or say about any of these subjects on which I'm about to pass judgement. I once showed him a poem I'd recently finished writing about the fine Notts and England batsman, Joe Hardstaff, and of which I thought well. Matt read the poem with his customary absorbed attention which I knew better than to break, then said, as he handed the poem back, 'You probably won't believe me, but the poem starts with the second stanza. Get rid of the first one.'

I stared at my poem, puzzled and a bit offended. What was wrong with it?

As though answering my unspoken enquiry, my friend said, 'Too much explanation. Trust the reader to do the work. If readers don't want to do some work they're not worth having.'

He was right, of course he was. He wanted to share his poems with others, as he wanted to share all poems with friends and readers to whom, if necessary, he was prepared to offer explanation, justification, and, above all, pleasure. But he wasn't prepared to bother with readers who didn't take seriously the subjects he himself cared for and about. This least snobbish of men valued seriousness above all else, and he detested and despised those who trivialised what he knew to be of worth.

Music in particular was worthy of his undivided attention. He and a neighbourhood friend often spent Friday afternoons listening to records and, later, CDs of concert or studio performances by accredited if by no means always well-known composers, and it was the rule that when the performance recording came to an end the two of them would sit in silence for several minutes before either spoke. 'You need time to take in what you've been listening to,' Matt said to me. Point taken.

* * *

I have a photograph of him, no more than a casual snapshot, that's propped on the windowsill beside where I sit to eat or drink or talk with other friends. He's seated at a pub table, one of those long, wooden-slatted tables round which half-a-dozen drinkers could congregate, though he's on his own, in front of him a pint glass of ale not much more than begun. He's gazing at the spectator – me – over spectacles which he's pushed half-way down his face, his smile half-abashed, half-comic, defiant. 'Fancy,' the look says. 'Here I am, caught out, enjoying myself in Ireland.'

For that's where he is, and I know he's in the company of two younger friends, the poets Deryn Rees-Jones and Michael Murphy. Deryn and Michael had recently become engaged, and Matt, through whom I think I'm right in saying they met, and who had been a kind of mentor to both, is with them, sharing in something of their happiness. What none of them can know is that in not many years' time, after Deryn and Michael's marriage and the birth of two children, Michael will die of an incurable brain tumour. That death, like Matt's, will occur in early summer, 2009.

* * *

I have another photograph, of Matt and myself together. We are sitting at a table down by the little harbour at Faros (the word means 'lighthouse'), about to begin what will as always on the island be a leisurely meal, one that may well last the entire evening, though it took Matt almost all seven days of his first visit to Aegina to realise, let alone accept that, in Joe Gargery's words, he had no need to 'be a bolter'. 'Relax,' I would say, 'there's no hurry, we can order more wine' – that wonderful, white 'topico' which is local to the island; and Matt would do his best to lean back, or turn to look at the sea stretching beyond the harbour wall and across to the mainland not much more than a mile or so away, to wonder at the gradual emergence of those blue-grey mountains that led to Nafplion and hid from our view the open-air theatre of Epidaurus, which, to my regret, I never showed him.

But I took him round many of the sights, and sites, of the beloved island, and out of his first visit to Aegina came a long poem, 'Taking The Hexameter A Walk', which he wrote not long after he was back in England, and of which

I am the honoured dedicatee. The poem was first published in his 2001 collection, *Getting There*, which includes several good poems about his Aeginetan experiences, and is re-printed in the posthumous *Collected Poems*, which Shoestring published in 2011.

> John, there's only this half-inch of ouzo left,
> a fistful of bivalve pistachios, and half-a-dozen
> of a jar of olives. The tan's long flaked away. *Well,*
> your letter asks, *glad to be back?*

That's how the poem begins, and it then modulates into a series of vivid reminiscences of his week on the island, of people met, sights, scents, and sounds, before it ends with a verse paragraph that affects me more deeply than tears could show.

> How often we've agreed
> that there's no longer a cogent language for gratitude.
> Words turn hard in the mouth as if you've literally
> bitten your tongue and swollen it. I'm afraid, John,
> there is not enough ouzo left to make me chance
> those sort of words. Still, I raise what is to all the
> overlapping lives our easygoing friendship
> comprehends, even in a moonlit stroll round graves.

The poem that follows, 'Moonlight on Aegina', and which I think of as a continuation of the verse letter, records among other experiences an evening when I showed Matt Aegina town's cemetery, a place 'asking you to imagine/that death is not an end but a continuing', the poet muses:

> not just of atoms that disperse
> and randomly regroup, but of obstinate
> redounding memory,
> perhaps of strolling back, tipsy with talk
> from a lingered-in taverna, and walking
> among these graves with the sea –
> thalassa! thalassa! – two hundred yards away
> down a wine-dark jasmine-scented lane.

As we sauntered among the graves of Aegina's town cemetery we were, I recall, talking of Hopkins and of his ability to make poems of lasting worth out of those 'cliffs of fall' that so threatened, so oppressed him. Obstinate, redounding memory indeed, dear friend, dear Matt.

* * *

My correspondence with Gael Turnbull began in 1978. Gael was in fact writing to Christine Fell, the Icelandic/Norse scholar, at whose suggestion I had made versions of the poems contained in *Egils Saga*, one of the greatest of Norse sagas, which she translated, and for which she provided a fine Introduction and Notes. The edition was published by Dent in 1974, and then republished as an Everyman paperback the following year. This in turn became an Everyman Classic in 1996, and finally, in 2008, Redbeck Press published my stand-alone versions of the poems under the title *I, The Poet Egil*. The poems were well received, though I don't think any praise gave me more pleasure than Gael's. In his letter of 29th October, 1978, he tells Christine Fell that he is an old friend of George Johnstone, a Canadian poet and translator whom I'd met in 1974 when the Dent version of Egil had been launched in London, an event for which George had flown over; we'd got on well and I subsequently published a pamphlet of his under the Bryon Press imprint. Unfortunately, his good poems were badly printed by someone I thought I could trust and who turned out to be both incompetent and careless. I apologised to George for the look of his pamphlet, and am glad to say it didn't spoil our friendship.

In the letter to Christine in which he introduces himself, Gael, writing as a fellow Icelandic scholar as well as a poet, assures her that her version of the Saga 'is streets ahead of the Penguin one', and he also says that he has 'great admiration for what Lucas has done.' Pleased and grateful for his words, I wrote a note to thank him, and gave it to Christine to enclose with her considered reply.

There, it might have ended, but soon after Matt and I began our friendship he must have mentioned to Gael, with whom he was already on good terms, and with whom he shared an enthusiastic admiration for the work of the poet, Norman Nicholson, that he knew me and that he'd enjoyed my Everyman version of Egil; and Gael presumably told Matt that he, too, knew of my existence. Because by 1990 Gael and I were regularly exchanging letters, and soon after that we met.

As it happened, I had for some thirty years been familiar with the name of Gael Turnbull. While attached to Reading University's English department from 1956, first as an undergraduate, then postgraduate student, then an assistant lecturer, I became good friends with the wonderfully louche Ian Fletcher, poet, scholar, man of letters, and at some stage, I think while I was still an undergraduate, I became aware that Ian was the regular recipient of a roughly put-together magazine called *The Migrant Press*. This consisted of stapled sheets of paper, folio size, on which were none-too-carefully printed poems, blotchy and often badly blurred, all 'run-off', as the term went, on a Gestetner machine. The poems themselves were very much 'Redskin' as opposed to 'Paleface', terms that had become familiar through the work of the American critic Philip Rahv, who used them to distinguish between American poetry that took its bearings from the Anglo-European tradition, and that which, following the example of Whitman, looked to create work which could be adequately responsive to America's new-found land. William Carlos Williams seemed to be the hero of the Migrant Press, Ginsberg was much praised, Carl Rakosi, Robert Creeley, Cid Corman, and Charles Reznikoff among those favoured; of Hart Crane, Wallace Stevens, and, among more recent contemporaries, Robert Lowell, there was, I seem to recall, no mention.

I remember glancing through issues as they piled up on

Ian's desk, though taking little notice of the contents. I had heard Ginsberg read in London in 1958, and had been entertained – indeed, taken aback – by his performance, had even bought a copy of a copy of the City Lights' edition of *Howl and Other Poems* – but my commitments pointed elsewhere. I did, however, note that one of the editors of Migrant Press went by the name of Gael Turnbull, and that he was not, as I'd supposed, American. 'Scottish émigré,' Ian told me. 'Doctor, living in America because he refused to do National Service.'

I later found that this account needed some correction. It was Gael's father, a Scottish Baptist Minister, who at the outset of the Second World War took his family to Winnipeg, from which I assume that Turnbull Snr. was a pacifist, although entry to America must have been made possible by the fact that Gael's mother was an American of Swedish descent. This also made possible Gael's travelling back to Cambridge in 1944, where for three years he studied Natural Sciences before returning to his family in America. Three further years of study, this time at the University of Pennsylvania, led to the award of MD, which enabled him to set up in practice as a GP. I don't here need to follow the further ins and outs of his professional career, beyond saying that he himself told me that, having taken out American citizenship, he came back to England to avoid being conscripted for service in Vietnam. There was also a spell of working in general practice in a Canadian logging camp, where his experience of having been trained as an anaesthetist proved invaluable when it came to the setting of broken or partly-crushed limbs.

But once Gael returned to England in 1964, he stayed here, working in general practice, first in Worcester and the Malverns and then in Barrow, where, he once confided sadly, many of his patients, women as well as men, who came to him complaining of various forms of illness they couldn't account for or explain, were in fact suffering from prolonged depression. 'What my predecessors called low fever.' The town's shipyards had been closed down, unemployment was accordingly high, and the townspeople – especially the men – had no work, no money, and had lost their sense of self-worth.

Gael did not report this with any rancour, or an implicit protest against this state of affairs. This was how matters stood. Though I'm sure he was socialist in his sympathies, he was also a kind of stoic fatalist. Perhaps most medical men are. In this he differed from Matt, whose working class Liverpool upbringing must have had at least something to do with his detestation of the Tories, and the two also differed in that, whereas Gael took for granted his life of moving from place to place – Scotland to England to America, to England, to Canada, to England, and finally to Scotland – Matt was not merely Liverpool born and bred, he had a sense of guilt about living elsewhere. Absconding, as it were. He told me that he never felt at ease in Cambridge, a lack of ease which had much to do with the place's not merely geographical distance from the streets of Bootle; there was also his educational background as well as his Scouse accent; and when he came to visit me on

Aegina, at Easter, 1996, it was, I think I'm right in saying, only his third trip abroad. The first had been when he accompanied his wife-to-be, Monika, to meet her family in post-war Germany. The second occurred in 1994, during which year he followed me to Tasmania to spend some months as Writing Fellow to Arts Tasmania. On that occasion, he said, he had to control an urgent desire to get off the plane when, on the way out, it touched down briefly at Heathrow. He was joking, at least I think he was …

I was in Tasmania during the Australian spring of 1993, and thirty years later still treasure the gift Matt made for me to assuage any possible loneliness that might have oppressed me during my months away. It was a tape he himself had put together, of songs by Butterworth, Gurney, Howells, and Vaughan Williams, all of whose music he knew I loved. I still play that tape, though it's now badly worn, and whenever I do I imagine myself listening to Matt's own singing voice, a voice Deryn Rees-Jones tells me was, as I want to believe it to have been, warm, vibrant, and tonally true. One of the great regrets of my life is that I myself never heard my friend sing.

Gael's voice was far lighter. If you listened carefully you could detect hints of Scottish inflection, but what chiefly held you was its calm, unhurried, understated clarity. A good voice for a doctor, I suppose, a reassuring voice, even if it proved to be the bearer of less than good news; and also a good voice for a poet, at all events a poet who did without any kind of rhetorical grandeur. I was always surprised by how easily I could hear what Gael had to tell me, given that he seemed never to raise the volume with which he spoke. There was, always, the same unrufflable, even-paced, apparently restrained utterance.

I wish I could remember the first time we met. I know it was at Beeston, but I forget the date, even the year, though I think it was very early in the 1990s. He had been to see Roy Fisher, who was by then living near Buxton, to which, so my friend, the poet Jenny Swann tells me, he'd moved in 1986, and having got my address from Matt, Gael had written ahead to ask whether a brief visit would be possible. I should add that I would subsequently hear of how Gael often called on writers he wanted to meet or with whom he had matters to discuss, and would think little of either driving considerable distances to their house or taking a train for the purpose of such discussion. I told him how to get to us, and he arrived mid-morning, having driven down from Roy's place at Earl Sterndale.

The man to whom I opened the door was tall, slender, perhaps even bony-framed, and his high cheek-boned face I suppose suggested Nordic ancestry, though I was less taken by this or his candidly-watchful eyes, than by his manner of speech, so unemphatic but so modestly assured. It was the voice of a man you felt instinctively you could trust always to tell the truth, but the hint of musical laughter – a strange phrase I know – hung about it.

On this occasion Gael simply wanted to talk to me about *Egil's Saga*, as well as to enquire into my involvement with the Reading Press and, later the Byron Press, which with Allan Rodway's assistance, I had set up at Nottingham in 1965, and which ran for twelve years, until my becoming head of the new English Department at Loughborough University meant I had so much work on that I had to close the press down. I was keen that Gael should know about my friendship with Ian and my knowledge of the Migrant Press, information which he took without flinching, as it were; and he told me that the Gestetner on which copies of the magazine had been printed – 'The Monster' as it became dubbed – would be, or perhaps already was, on display at the new British Library. (It is now permanently housed at the Scottish Poetry Library.)

We talked for maybe a couple of hours, and Matt featured strongly in our conversation. We both admired his poetry, both saluted what we felt to be his unimpeachable integrity, and, in reply to a question of mine, Gael said that they'd first got into correspondence because he had sent Matt a note to let him know that he'd enjoyed something Matt had written about Norman Nicholson, and that he, Gael, having spent some early years in Jarrow before his parents emigrated to America, felt he had some sort of kinship with Nicholson's Millom. Bootle, Jarrow, Millom, we agreed, all working towns with a strong sense of identity connected to naval history and the maritime industry. But Gael reminded me that whereas Matt and Nicholson both wrote with convincing eloquence about their places of origin, he saw himself as, while by no means *déraciné*, far less compelled to define his identity in terms of locality. He was, though, so he said, fully prepared to speak of himself as a 're-adopted' Scot, having been born in Edinburgh, the city to which he had returned very recently to live out the rest of his days.

Before he left, I asked Gael whether he had any recent work he might be prepared to offer me first refusal of, because I'd love the chance to publish something of his. He had, and a few weeks later he sent me the typescript of *Transmutations*, which Shoestring published as a 24-page pamphlet in 1997. I love these 'pieces' as Gael calls them, delight in their ability to transform glimpses of people into memorable images, insights, implied histories, and narratives. As here, for example, with 'A Jazz Trumpeter', an especially concentrated exercise in observation and story.

> Heard once, price of a drink, near empty bar, half a
> lifetime away, the tunes gone, like him, but not that
>   grip
> of stained fingers, sweat on coiled veins, ballooned
>   cheeks,
> clamped mouth, tensed neck, sagged eyes
>
> which maybe saw us, maybe no, their intent not
> elsewhere but all there, on what he knew, was about,
> whether anyone heard or not, playing, as they say,
>   for all
> he was worth.

At the time of writing, Shoestring Press has published more than several hundred titles, but *Transmutations* is still among my favourites. And I hope Gael was content with what I think of as its handsome format: twenty-four pages of rough-textured paper, saddle-stitched in a flapped, brown ochre card cover. As for the poems themselves: they were printed in twelve-point liberation (I don't like sans-serif), leaded for thirteen so as to allow the eye plenty of 'breathing space' as it were (as *all* Shoestring publications are printed); and, as all the press's publications do, the front cover carries the press's colophon, centred toward the foot, of a loosely-tied shoelace, which Pauline designed for me. The edition ran to two hundred and fifty copies, priced at £2.99, (par for the course in 1997) and, again as with all pre-2000 Shoestrings, has long since sold out.

To coincide with publication, I arranged for Gael to give a launch reading. Unfortunately this couldn't be in Nottingham, because the city's independent bookshop, Mushroom, had by then virtually collapsed (brought down by the infamous Tory withdrawal of the Net Book Agreement), and the great and good Five Leaves Bookshop, set up in 2009 by the equally great and good Ross Bradshaw, who had begun Mushroom, was then no more than a distant aspiration. Fortunately I was at that time external examiner to Northampton's Higher Education College, where someone knew someone, and as a result the city's Waterstone's offered to host the occasion. Accordingly, I drove Gael down there early one evening, a fair-sized audience of some fifty or so folk gathered, and Gael did the rest. It wasn't that he gave an 'impressive' let alone 'actorly' reading. Quite the opposite. But the unemphatic clarity with which he spoke each Transmutation made its way through the ears and into the alert attention of all those present. I had taken twenty-five copies of the pamphlet with me. 'The triumph of hope over experience,' as Samuel Johnson famously remarked of second marriages. I should have taken more. Not only did I sell out, I wrote down the names and addresses of at least half-a-dozen would-be purchasers, and had I taken a further ten copies I've no reason to doubt they would all have gone.

On the way back to Beeston, I asked Gael whether he'd enjoyed the experience. Yes, he said, he had. Then, 'And I'm pleased that it was worth your while. You'll at least have covered your costs.' Not many poets, I think, would have thought of sales in those terms. But Gael's words were meant. He *was* pleased that the fifty or so mile car journey to Northampton had covered his publisher's costs.

* * *

Later that year I received a letter from Switzerland. It came from the poet, Peter McCarey, who wanted to know whether I would like to contribute to a festschrift which he planned to coincide with Gael's seventieth birthday the following year. *A Gathering for Gael Turnbull*, it was to be called, and McCarey had already secured promises from a large number of poets, British, American, and Australian, among them such luminaries as Roy Fisher, Charles Tomlinson, August Kleinzahler, Christopher Middleton, Ian Hamilton Finlay, Cid Corman, John Tranter, Robert Creeley, Edwin Morgan, Carl Rakosi, plus thirty or so others, including, of course, Matt. I assured McCarey that I was both honoured and delighted to be asked, as I was, and when in 1978 *A Gathering* appeared, among the fifty-six pages was my 'Makers: An Anecdote', which carries the dedication 'For Gael Turnbull'.

> At batlight once, thirty-six years ago,
> in the city where you now live
> I met – the how or why is gone – Robert Garioch
> and plunged with him into a Rose Street dive
> where, as hours passed, I became,
> while he seemingly did not, woefully rat-arsed.
>
> Yet at parting he forced on me
> a bag ripe with poems, confiding
> 'I could be dead by morning.
> Someone wants me out of the way.
> Aye. I've had strong warning.'
>
> Next day, after conscience opened my eyes –
> overnight some mad ostreaphile
> had been at them with a blunt knife – I lurched
> off in search of the poet who might be dead.
>
> Of course he wasn't. Encountered
> in the same Rose Street bar, he gruffed
> a mere 'ach' when I gave him his bag,
> and intimated I should buy a round.

I wasn't a publisher then but still
am pleased I guarded those poems, knowing now
they're safe in print. Garioch was a sure
'sapple' maker whose words deserve their future

as yours do. What else are publishers for?

* * *

Transmutations was the only collection of Gael's which I was privileged to publish, whereas I published several of Matt's, including his *Collected Poems* and *Hugging the Shore*, a collection of his critical essays. And I knew Matt for longer, and my friendship with him was stronger, deeper, and in ways I can't explain, more definitive. But I count myself blessed to have known them both. 'Think where man's glory both begins and ends/And say my glory was I had such friends'. Yeats's words perhaps overstate the case. Glory? Still, why not.

Paul

THE FOLLOWING WORDS ARE NOT MEANT to provide an obituary of my friend Paul McLoughlin (born 1947 - died 2021), still less a memoir. I wrote a bare-bones account of Paul's life for *PN Review*, and it will no doubt be supplemented by further, more detailed obituaries, written by one or other of the many friends who knew him from his early days. These will include his schooldays, chief among them his rebellious period at Gunnersbury Catholic Grammar School, which he loathed, and which he left after his sixteenth birthday with two O Levels to his name. Not much of an academic success, then.

After his egregious departure from full-time education, Paul found employment as a clerical assistant at Sun Life Insurance, which I can't imagine he much enjoyed. At all events, he soon became a part-time student at various London institutes of education – supporting himself by casual jobs; then, after securing 2 A Levels, followed by part-time degree work at Chiswick Poly, he became a qualified school teacher, began a teaching career, married, graduated to fatherhood, was soon earning his spurs as a jazz flautist and alto saxophonist, then – or was it coincidentally? – realised that he was a poet, and, as we all do, began to send out his poems to serious magazines and journals, and by the 1990s was ready to publish his first collection, in his case with Smith/Doorstop.

So by the time he and I met, early in the new century, I think I'm right in saying that he had retired from full-time teaching and, apart from doing supply work at various schools, was free to concentrate on poetry and jazz. Smith/Doorstop had by then already published one slim collection and I had accepted for publication another equally slim collection, *What Moves Moves*, and was looking forward to meeting its author in Newcastle, where it was to be launched together with another Shoestring collection, this one by the poet and artist, Peter Bennet.

The man who introduced himself to me on that occasion shook hands warmly but with no trace of effusiveness, and his smile, one of rueful candour, was accompanied with a slight slump of his shoulders, as if to suggest that he knew there was more to life than all this malarkey. But his cheesegrater voice came as a , shock. Louis Armstrong on speed, perhaps? (Later, I learnt it was the result of an operation for throat cancer.) Still, it didn't impede his very effective reading manner. A good-sized crowd had packed into the upper room of the central Newcastle pub that hosted the event, and after Paul and Peter's well-received readings ended there was much convivial talk and drink taken before I left to mount a train for Durham, where I was due to stay with my good friend, Anne Stevenson. Paul had been offered and had accepted a bed at Peter's house, which I seem to remember being told was on top of a hill outside the city.

I saw Paul next in London, a week later, this time at Bookmarks, the excellent socialist bookshop near the British Museum which over the years was to become Shoestring's regular London launching pad, and where *What Moves Moves* was to have its London baptism. How had he and his host got on, I wanted to know. Paul adopted his slump-shouldered stance. 'Alright,' he said, 'he was good company.' A pause. 'But blimey, he can't half talk. We didn't get to bed until 4 a.m.'

Not then knowing Paul as well as in later years I came to do, I assumed that long before the evening ended he had begun to yearn for sleep. It was only in those later years, with deepening acquaintance and new levels of understanding, that our growing friendship brought me a realisation that when it came to talk Paul was in a class of his own. 'She could talk the hind leg off a donkey,' my mother once said of a friend of hers who enjoyed nothing so much as settling in for an evening's conversation, meaning that while others listened she talked. And talked. But in Paul she would have met her match. He could have talked off all of the donkey's legs and still have been ready for more. He came from a large Irish family, and 'craic', or 'crack', is I think the word his fellow-countrymen use for good and lively talk. Dr Johnson, that adopted Londoner, put it differently. 'Let us fold our knees and have out our chat,' he commanded friends he met in coffee-house or tavern. For Johnson, while no Irishman, dearly loved conversation, especially conversation between friends, and most especially what he called 'tavern talk'.

Paul's way of opening talk, craic, chat – call it what you will – was to approach you with a kind of sidling motion, as though uncertain whether you wanted to see him, or he you, then, having made up his mind to spend a few minutes in your company, come to a halt directly in front of you, fix you with a glittering if quizzical eye, open his mouth, and begin to speak. You were seldom, if ever, allowed to interrupt.

A favourite opener was, 'Have you *heard?*', the last word uttered on a rising note and with a kind of half comic, outraged emphasis, and this was accompanied by an expression of incredulity, after which he would set you right about some unpleasant governmental pronouncement or fossick through the motives that must lie beneath some benighted critical denunciation of a favourite poet of his or a recent back page dismissal of Brentford FC's chances of promotion to football's premier league, or ... or ... Paul didn't need a pub in order to hold court, although to adapt a phrase of Byron's he had no objection to a pint of beer; what he *did* require was to find himself in the company of someone – anyone – who shared one or more of his interests. And given that these, invariably dominated by poetry and jazz though they might be, were as many and various as his friends were numerous, the opportunity for talk was seldom lacking. He was rarely, you might say, lost for a word.

An alternative button-holing method was to shake his

head in rueful despair, as though what he was thinking was beyond words, but nevertheless required him to speak. After which, he would say, "Ere, do you *know* ..." and follow up this modified Cockney opener with a remark, a revelation, that had to be brought into the open, reluctant though he might be to talk.

It was good talk: witty, always informed, and, except when it came to Brentford, plausible. Though now, as I write this in early 2024, it grieves me to be aware of the fact that the team Paul so determinedly and devotedly followed for year after year of disappointment, disillusion, and despair – was that how he came by those slumped shoulders? – as year after year they failed to win promotion to the Premier League, is now finally in that League, and, irony of sad ironies, managing without Paul waving his season ticket – that symbol of credulous loyalty – to cheer them on.

But if wild hope triumphed over realistic expectation where football was concerned, no such erratic judgement clouded his understanding of poetry. Readers of *London Grip*, among other journals, will know how good a poetry reviewer Paul was, perceptive, judicious, wide-ranging in his sympathies. And his excellent edition of Brian Jones' *New & Selected Poems*, which I was delighted to publish for Shoestring and which came out of the doctoral thesis he had written – it was examined by the distinguished poet-critic Grevel Lindop and myself – has a lengthy Introduction that is a model of its kind. Informed, deftly written, and as illuminating as it is well-balanced. It couldn't, I am certain, have been written by anyone who was not himself a first-rate poet. Helen Dunmore's praise of Paul's own verse – it possessed, she said, 'a rare clarity and exactitude' – is spot on. His talk was like that, too, as well as containing rare gobbets of out-of-the-way information or speculative wit. I can't believe that anyone meeting Paul for the first time wouldn't be eager for a second chance.

And then there is his music. Initially self-taught, as is often the way with jazz musicians, though a good reader of 'the dots', as many aren't, Paul studied music at academy level and eventually gained mastery over the flute before moving on to play both it and alto-sax with a semi-professional quartet which included his brother, Mick. They had regular gigs in the London area, including the riotous occasion when, at the end of 2004, I launched the Shoestring anthology, *Paging Doctor Jazz*. The party for this was held in the upper room of a North London pub, with musical contributions from, among others, John Mole (clarinet), plus an excellent pianist nephew of mine (Matt Lucas, piano and vocal), and Paul's quartet acted as house band for the evening. The room, large though it was, contained at least double the permitted number of attendees, evenly divided between poets and jazz aficionados, the latter of whom had sniffed out the chance of some free beer and a few of whom went so far as to pay nominal amounts for the books they all pocketed.

A few years later Paul drove himself and John Hartley Williams to Nottingham for my seventieth birthday (garden) party, held to coincide with that year's Lowdham

Summer Festival, and though John, who was no mean pianist, declined the chance to demonstrate his prowess at the keyboard, Paul sat in with my own group, The Burgundy Street Jazzmen, this time bringing his clarinet. (Our style was New Orleans to Mainstream.) When he came up to join us for a number, we chose to play the old standard, 'Indiana' – 'In the key of F,' I said, but Paul knew. 'He's alright, he is,' Lol (q.v.) our drummer said afterward, which commendation, coming from Lol, was praise indeed. But it was true.

In Paul's more recent years, I rather think that the chances to play jazz dropped away. His quartet had at one time been regularly featured in Saturday night sessions at a pub in the Richmond area, but these came to an end, why I don't know (a change of management, perhaps?) and were not replaced by other offers. And from remarks that would sometimes slide from the side of Paul's mouth, I think the group's regular drummer was making difficulties, a not unknown attribute of drummers, especially shaky timekeepers, as this one proved to be. But compensation for having fewer opportunities to make music, as I was not alone in suggesting to Paul, was that he now had more time for poetry. He didn't really need the hint, but there's no doubt that as his writing life took up more of his time so his work became more ambitiously conceived, its accomplishments more substantial, and I would certainly want to insist that what proved to be his final collection, *The Hungarian Who Beat Brazil* (2017), is a work of rare distinction. The title poem in particular, a mini-narrative, is handled without undue emphasis but with an enviably deft control; and the movement across the line-endings is quite masterly.

During these years he began the practice of sending Christmas cards to friends with, pasted into them, a poem written at, though not necessarily for, the season, and I imagine all the recipients came to treasure each year's card. It was, you could say, an ideal token of friendship.

At some time in the early to mid-teens I was able to introduce Paul to the Australian poet, Andrew Sant, whom I'd met in Tasmania some years earlier, and who for a number of years came regularly to take up teaching posts in England, courtesy of the Royal Literary Fund. The two of them got on as well as I'd predicted they would. They were roughly the same age, and Andrew, who had been taken to Australia when he was ten, was Essex born. More importantly, they both enjoyed good crack, and were appreciative of the work of Les Murray, not a poet to everyone's taste, though Paul has a lovely, witty, sympathetic poem about an occasion when Murray, on one of his frequent visits to England, stayed *chez* McLoughlin. Andrew, too, with his slant, quizzical view of the poetry of his adopted land, refused to share the view, common to contemporary Australian city poets, that Murray was of far less value than his supporters asserted. Heroes for city poets came from the New World, especially New York and West Coast America: Frank O'Hara, John Ashbery, Ginsberg, Snyder, Kleinzahler. Or they claimed to find inspiration in such nineteenth-century French poets as Baudelaire, Mallarmé, Verlaine, Rimbaud, though for the most part they rather disgracefully failed to learn any French. As far as I know the only exception to this rule of contented ignorance was the Tasmanian poet, Tim Thorne, now sadly dead.

By the time Paul and Andrew met, Pauline and I were spending part of each summer in a small rented flat on the Greek island of Aegina, which Andrew and his partner, Tina, sometimes visited as part of their European rambles. On two of these occasions Paul, too, came to the island, once with his wife, once on his own. Nina was a delight. Shorter than Paul, with a deep, gravelly voice, she had a way of making plain that she took many of his conversational openers with more than a pinch of salt. 'Oh, *Paul*,' she would say, and the emphasis left no need for the ironic lift of her shoulders at one or other of his claims. 'Oh, *Paul.*' And as she spoke, so he would look at you with a smile that as good as told you to take a sceptical response to whatever he might have happened to try on his listeners.

The smile also told you of his unabashed delight in her. They went as a couple to art exhibitions and concerts, but as far as I know she was never present at any of his readings. Poetry was an art that simply didn't interest her, unlike painting and music and, I think, architecture. There's a lovely, funny photograph of the pair of them standing side by side on a mound of rocky earth beside the Temple of Aphaia, taken after they'd spent some time examining and walking about what I think of as one of the most beautiful of all ancient Greek temples. The temple is on a wooded summit of 'our' island, and it occupies the spot where local legend reports Aphaia as having vanished from the would-be rapacious sailors from whom she'd accepted a sea voyage up the Saronic Gulf. From time to time women visiting the temple will claim that they've seen Aphaia herself emerge briefly from the pine wood and flit through the temple ruins (much of the actual temple still stands), but Nina made no such claim. The photograph, presumably taken by some willing tourist, shows her with her sun hat rammed down on her head as if she's determined to see nothing, and although Paul is trying to look at the camera, his extravagantly slumped shoulders imply a degree of exhaustion from which not even a sudden appearance of Zeus would be able to shake him into awareness.

He and Nina had taken a bus up to the temple one morning of intense heat, determined to see all they could before the sun put an end to their exploration. But the temple grounds were rarely opened up before late morning, by which time the sun was so high in the sky that even 'ruin-bibbers randy for antique', to borrow Larkin's phrase, would find themselves blurry eyed. Not that the two of them look as though they've been at the bottle. It's more that you feel their utter exhaustion. Too much sun. And, of course, an overplus of the wonderful temple, from which they could stare down past green woods to the blue, blue Aegean. Who wouldn't be drunk on such beauty?

* * *

There was a nearby taverna on the harbour front at Faros, the village where our flat is situated, and at night we'd all sit out under the stars, drinking retsina and talking, talking, talking, the wittily laconic Andrew, the volubly witty Paul: Yin and Yang, while the rest of us joined in or found other matters to discuss. And among those absent friends to whom we drank was that excellent poet and woodcut artist, Alan Dixon, who rarely left his house in Eastbourne, though, when visited there, he always made himself into a welcoming host, one who was not unnaturally especially welcoming to those who admired his work.

I'd known Alan's work as poet and artist for many years, having come across it in examples put out by Alan Tarling's Poet and Printer Press. That press had published both his woodcuts and his poetry, and at different times Andrew and Paul both made the pilgrimage to Eastbourne, where Alan took the opportunity to create superb images of them both. As a result, a sympathetic, considerate bond was woven between the four of us, perhaps best epitomised in the book of Alan's woodcuts with accompanying poems by various poets which in 2013 I published under the title *Wood & Ink*. The book contains excellent contributions by both Paul and Andrew, as well as by Wayne Burrows, Helena Nelson, Jo Shapcott, and John Hartley Williams, who by then had become a friend of mine and Paul's, and who, like Wayne and Helena, was by 2013 a Shoestring poet.

John had earlier been published by Chatto, then Bloodaxe, then Cape; but, affable and outstandingly good poet though he was, he could be a cussed difficult customer to deal with, and it sometimes took me all the tact I possess (which may not be all that much), for us to jointly agree what should and shouldn't be in his Shoestring books. Still, we managed it, and as a result I was able to see into print *Assault on the Clouds* (2012), the outrageously inventive *Golden Age of Smoking*, which came two years later, and which, apart from its intrinsic merits, testifies to how ceaselessly creative John could be, and then, finally, *Boys on a Roof* (2015), to which he gave the sub-title, *Nine Abrasions* (typically John in its cock-snookery), prose pieces which we launched at the Bookmarks bookshop in Bloomsbury when he was within weeks of death from prostate cancer.

Two summers before that, in September, 2013, he and his German partner, Elke, had spent a week with Pauline and me on Aegina, by which time the cancer was starting to affect his mobility as well as causing him great discomfort; but he maintained an insouciant indifference to its claims on him, and was as witty, argumentative, and challenging as ever in his conversation; his relish for life, and for food and drink, never seemed to desert him. John was what an earlier generation would have called a smasher, someone of outstanding merit as both man and writer. I dubbed him 'The lord of misrule, who comes to rage through the tranquil groves of English poetry', and I think – no, I'm certain – that his work deserves to be the subject of prolonged attention. As Paul said in his review of John's *Blues* (the eighth of John's more than twenty-five titles), his work always proclaims 'a fierce belief in the music of language that, like the best of jazz, is joyfully anarchic and surrealist but never free of rules', and this is so whether he is writing poetry or prose. It seems relevant to note that his daughter is the professional jazz singer, Natalie Williams, whom I once heard in session at Ronnie Scott's Jazz Club, and who sang at the memorial occasion for John that was held at the London Review of Books shop, where I wasn't greatly surprised to learn that John had himself been a pianist of some accomplishment.

But poetry was his major preoccupation. Hence, the *Teach Yourself Poetry Writing*, the primer he wrote with his friend Matthew Sweeney, and which was several times reprinted. The two also combined on a novel for which I supplied the title, *Death Comes for the Poets*, published by Muswell Hill Press. They anticipated making a good deal of money from this comic-macabre fiction, which included pastiches of variable quality of a number of contemporary poets. Sadly, having paid for its publication, they had then to cope with the book's being virtually ignored, an experience which John shrugged off more easily than did Matthew.

Shoestring published two of Matthew's collections, but he didn't contribute to *Wood & Ink*. And though for once the book wasn't seen through to publication by my typesetters, then known as Narrator, now as The Book Typesetters, and to me, always, as simply the best in the land, *Wood & Ink* is nevertheless a visual and poetic treat. Most of the contributors met for a celebratory meal at an Italian restaurant in Soho, having first toasted each other at the nearby 'French Pub'. Well, why not. That pub had been a drinking hole for writers and artists since the late nineteen thirties, and I've mentioned it in more than one of the foregoing essays.

* * *

Now, at the end of 2022, with Paul's unlooked-for death, as well as those of John and Matthew (the latter from motor neurone disease), the shades are closing in. I've not been back to the French Pub since that day in 2013, and perhaps never will. But it's good to be able to report that *The Hungarian Who Beat Brazil* has on its back cover a particularly fine, witty woodcut image of Paul's head by Alan, who at the time of writing is still alive and working – most recently for Shoestring on eight superb woodcuts he has contributed to W.D (Bill) Jackson's *Aesopean*. A new collection of Alan's poems and woodcuts will be published by Shoestring Press in 2024. And as for you, Paul, good poet and dear friend, there are no words to express my grateful thanks for having known you.

E.M. Forster: An Enabling Modesty

ON THE FIRST DAY OF 1959 E.M. Forster celebrated his eightieth birthday. Among events held to mark the occasion was an hour-long BBC television programme, the gist of which was printed in the following week's *Listener*, and articles of a more or less adulatory nature appeared in most of the quality weeklies and periodicals. There was also an interview in the *Observer* conducted by its chief book reviewer, Philip Toynbee. This is of interest, if only because it shows that Forster was keeping up his reading. William Golding is praised, as is J.D. Salinger – Forster reveals that he liked both *The Catcher in the Rye* and the story 'For Esme with Love and Squalor' – but he thinks *Dr Zhivago* overrated. 'It quite lacks the solidity of *War and Peace*. I don't think Pasternak is really very interested in people. The book seems to me most interesting for its epic quality. The political argument is quite incidental, and I don't at all feel that this was his main objective.' To this, Toynbee, who was at the time trying to advance himself as an experimental novelist, asks Forster whether he thinks that Pasternak has suffered because 'he has been isolated from the main development of the novel in the West? I believe, for example, that he has never read Proust.' Toynbee is currying favour here. He knows of Forster's often-stated admiration for Proust. But Forster nimbly side-steps. 'I don't think that's very important, do you?' he answers. 'As a matter of fact the only time I met Pasternak was in the West, in France sometime during the 30s. He was very charming and very amusing.'

Toynbee had in the 1930s been an ardent Communist, who at that time dismissed Forster as hopelessly out of touch, and by 1959 he was an equally ardent cold-war warrior as well as convert to Christianity. One of the reasons Forster's eightieth birthday was so feted – why at Reading University a third year undergraduate had even begun writing a critical monograph on him, 47 typescript pages of which survive – is that he had been neither of those things, and that during decades when it was easy to become, as he himself said, 'rattled', he tried not to panic. That this could occasionally look like willful turning away from issues of the day, is obvious. Indeed it was so obvious to intelligent and committed Marxists in the 1930s, that they not surprisingly took his refusal to appear in *Authors Take Sides* on the Spanish War as evidence of a liberalism which inevitably failed to meet the imperatives of the day. 'I do not feel that manifestos by writers carry any weight whatever,' Forster had written by way of explaining to Nancy Cunard why he wouldn't be contributing to the pamphlet of which she was chief organiser (Chisholm, 240). That Forster was not soon to be forgiven for this piece of fence-sitting, as it presumably appeared to the

Left, can be gauged from the cover illustration to the March 1948 issue of the Communist arts paper, *Our Time*, designed by James Boswell, an artist who during the previous decade had done much distinguished work for *Left Review* and the *Daily Worker*. Here, Forster, along with Aldous Huxley, Stephen Spender, Cyril Connolly and others, is shown trying to shore up the Tree of – well, of what I'm not entirely clear. Of State? Of old liberal Europe? At all events, Forster is identified with those who resist change, which, in view of the narrative he had written for Humphrey Jennings' fascinating film, *Diary for Timothy*, betrays a deep misunderstanding of Forster's desire for a different and a better world.

Or does it? Because you could say that from the start Forster had always been chary of causes. The most famous statement of his distrust, one he identifies with heroic individualism, comes in the essay 'What I Believe':

> No, I distrust Great Men. They produce a desert of uniformity around them and often a pool of blood too, and I always feel a little man's pleasure when they come a cropper. Every now and then one reads in the newspaper some such statement as: 'the coup d'etat appears to have failed, and Admiral Toma's whereabouts is at present unknown.' Admiral Toma had probably every qualification for being a Great Man – an iron will, personal magnetism, dash, flair, sexlessness – but fate was against him, so he retires to unknown whereabouts instead of parading

history with his peers. He fails with a completeness which no artist and no lover can experience, because with them the process of creation is itself an achievement, whereas with him the only possible achievement is success.

In his affectionate essay, 'Mr Forster's Good Influence', F. D. Klingopulos alludes to Forster's immediately subsequent declaration of faith in 'an aristocracy of the sensitive, the considerate, and the plucky' as 'the true human tradition, the one permanent victory of our queer race over cruelty and chaos,' as something he found valuable at the outset of the War, even though, 'They seemed frail words, even, at such a time, slightly absurd' (246). I think they are tougher than Klingopulos will allow, but this is because they seem to me *deliberately* frail. They oppose the grandiosity of public utterance, take their stand on a modesty which slyly rebukes the headier rhetoric of more insistent claims, especially those made on behalf of Great Men. And after all, the 1930s was very much the decade of the 'Great Man'. Forster's readiness to speak for the 'little man' is part of a deliberate strategy, a way of establishing himself as that despised phenomenon, the 'bourgeois liberal'.

Just how consciously he planned to make this effect can, I think, be gauged by looking at the history of the essay itself. Although in the original 1951 edition of *Two Cheers for Democracy* it is dated to 1939, it was in fact written and first published a year earlier, in the spring of 1938. The essay was prompted by an invitation to Forster to contribute to a series of articles to be called 'Living Philosophies', commissioned by the New York magazine, *The Nation*. Forster apparently worked hard on the essay, to which he gave the title, 'Two Cheers for Democracy'. But the following year, when it was broadcast by the BBC, the essay was retitled 'What I Believe'. Twenty years later, when Forster recorded the essay during June-August 1958 as one side of an Argo LP, issued in 1959, the record sleeve note tells us that, 'In an introduction to this recording Mr Forster states that some of the opinions he held when writing this essay in 1939 have been modified since, but he does not consider that a writer has the privilege of altering anything he has written.' Yet even this isn't quite right, because on the recording itself Forster prefaces his reading by noting that the essay 'was written during the last war', but that, though he has changed some of his opinions since then, 'I don't think that an author has the right to tamper with his own text.'

But he *has* tampered with it, at least to the extent of suggesting that the essay was written *after* the start of the war, when in fact it was written over a year before the war began. I don't think this can be put down to forgetfulness. My own view is that in 1958-1959 Forster was especially keen to suggest that even in wartime he had written that:

> Personal relations are despised today. They are regarded as bourgeois luxuries [...] and we are urged to get rid of them and to dedicate ourselves to

some movement or cause instead. I hate the idea of causes, and if I had to choose between betraying my country and betraying my friend, I hope I should have the guts to betray my country.

What Forster is doing, I suggest, is to signal to his audience that if he dared to say such things in wartime, they should be prepared to say them when times were easier. Here, at least, is a cause he elects to stand by, that of gay rights, as we should call them now, although in 1959, which was not long after the publication of the Wolfenden Report had been denounced by John Gordon in the *Sunday Express* as 'the Pansies' Charter', practising male homosexuality was not only still illegal, it was more or less a taboo subject. And even Forster, we may feel, has to encode his message. Still, its meaning was clear enough.

As a result, Forster's posthumous reputation had to endure the assertion by John Carey and others that he had given comfort to the 'Homintern', those left-wing intellectuals who, be it noted, had in the late 1930s denounced him as a wishy-washy liberal. Still, no man who earns the displeasure of Carey and of King Street can be all wrong, and Forster in 1958-1959 was not merely feted, he was venerated.

This veneration didn't depend on critical assessment of his fiction. I doubt that any of the growing number of critics who were writing about him thought of him as a great novelist. Lionel Trilling's 1943 study had singled him out as a supreme example of the liberal spirit in fiction, but praising *Howard's End* at the expense of *A Passage to India* was bound to seem to most a betrayal of the very cause Trilling meant to advance. And in his television interview, Forster himself went out of his way to disavow any claim to greatness. I can only write about three kinds of character, he said, those I like, those I dislike, and those I would like to be. And of course at an earlier moment, the death of D.H. Lawrence, he had famously, and, as Leavis noted, honourably, called Lawrence 'the greatest imaginative novelist of his generation' (see Coombes) – which was Forster's own generation. Besides, he was on record as remarking that his personal favourite among his own novels was *The Longest Journey*, which I imagine most readers would think the least successful of the five full-length works of fiction published during his lifetime. (Rumours of a sixth, unpublishable one were widespread but *Maurice* didn't appear until 1971, a year after Forster's death. And it was known that another, *Arctic Summer*, begun soon after the completion of *Howard's End*, had as soon been abandoned, and survived only as a fragment.)

A modest achievement, then. And modesty seems a word that attaches to Forster in a manner that is as adhesive as it may seem to be disabling. Yet if we consider his oeuvre as a whole, it is a good deal more substantial than this account would suggest. For in addition to the novels there are two collections of short stories, neither, I will admit, exceptional; there are two collections of essays, *Abinger Harvest* and *Two Cheers for Democracy*, which, though they contain some makeweights, also include a number of important pieces on which I shall draw; there is his *Aspects of the Novel*, regularly pooh-poohed by critics yet oddly memorable, even, I think, durable; two biographies, one of which, the life of his aunt, Marianne Thornton, is a first-class study that tells us much that other commentators have either ignored or said less well about nineteenth-century Evangelicalism. There is his intriguing *Guide to Alexandria*, as well as *Pharos and Pharillon*, there are two pageant plays, *The Abinger Pageant* (produced in 1934 and printed at the end of *Abinger Harvest)* and *England's Pleasant Land* (produced four years later and published in 1940 by the Hogarth Press), and there is the film script for *Diary for Timothy* (1945), as well as a mass of reviews and occasional pieces for newspapers and periodicals. In short, there is far more of Forster than you might think. There is also much more to him than those intendedly dismissive or at all events containing words 'liberal' and 'modest' can fairly suggest.

True, modesty seems Forster's stock in trade. But this can have its own proper intransigence. 'I distrust Great Men. They produce a desert of uniformity around them and often a pool of blood too' (*Two Cheers*, 82). The allusion to Shelley's 'Ozymandias' may seem to be compromised by 'a pool of blood'. Shouldn't the alternative to a desert be an ocean, or at the very least a lake? But Forster resists the rhetorical flourish that will either aggrandise or demonise. Whether he has in mind one or all of Franco, Mussolini, Hitler or Stalin, to name only the most obvious contenders, he isn't at this moment prepared to identify them as monsters. To be sure, he denounced Hitler as well as Stalin, and in a number of war broadcasts – see for example the pamphlet *Nordic Twilight* – made plain his long-standing detestation of the Nazis. Nevertheless, he refuses to raise his voice to hector his listener.

In fact, he won't raise his voice at all. In his invaluable *Red Letter Days: British Fiction in the 1930s*, Andy Croft notes that all who attended the 1935 Paris International Congress of Writers were united in their opposition to Fascism. Among the many speakers at the Congress was Forster, who made what Croft calls 'a well-received contribution' (Croft 1990, 52). Not according to others. In his biography, P.N. Furbank quotes at length from the report of the American novelist, Katherine Anne Porter, who was present on the occasion:

> I think it was just after André Malraux – then as dogmatic in communism as he is now in some other faith – had leapt to the microphone, barking like a fox to halt the applause for Julien Benda [whose sympathy with right-wing politics suggests that not all in Paris for the occasion were 'united in opposition to Fascism'], that a little slender man with a large forehead and a shy chin rose, was introduced and began to read his paper carefully prepared for the occasion. He paid no attention to the microphone, but wove back and forth, and from side to side, gently, and every time his face passed the mouth-piece I caught a high-voiced syllable or two,

never a whole word ... Then, surprisingly, once he came to a moment's pause before the instrument and there sounded into the hall clearly but wistfully a complete sentence: 'I DO believe in liberty!'

The applause at the end was barely polite, but it covered the antics of that part of the audience near me; a whole pantomime of malignant ridicule, meaning that Mr. Forster and all his kind were already as extinct as the dodo. It was a discouraging moment.

Given that this was written from McCarthyite America in 1953, we don't have to believe every one of its rhetorical flourishes in order to recognise that Forster's contribution was unlikely to have been rapturously received, and not merely because he refused to acknowledge the microphone's existence (though this is at least emblematic of his preference for the unraised voice). His talk, entitled 'Liberty in England' (it is reprinted, dated to 21 June 1935, in *Abinger Harvest*) is important because it is as unyielding a definition as anything he ever wrote of what he meant by the term, and I therefore want to spend a few moments considering what Forster says.

Freedom and Liberty are, he asserts, closely entwined, and in the past have been championed by such writers as Milton, Shelley and Dickens. This may seem an odd trinity, but I suspect that Forster is thinking of Milton less as the apologist for a God of merciless justice than as the author of *Areopagitica* (about which he was to write a sharp little essay in 1944, demanding press freedom even in, or perhaps especially during, war time), of Shelley as the author of 'Epipsychidion', lines from which, championing a kind of Fourier-like free love, form the epigraph and, of course, title of *The Longest Journey*, and Dickens as the writer who, in Orwell's words, is 'generously angry'. (And who, we should recall, was at best condescended to by the literary intelligentsia of his day gathered round the *Westminster Review* for being indifferent to the ideological orthodoxy of positivism which they espoused.) Forster then announces that he is neither fascist ('Fascism does evil that evil may come') nor communist, 'though perhaps I might be one if I was a younger and a braver man,' he adds, 'for in Communism I can see hope. It does many things which I think evil, but I know that it intends good.' As it is:

> I am actually what my age and my upbringing have made me – a bourgeois who adheres to the British constitution, adheres to it rather than supports it, and the fact that this isn't dignified doesn't worry me. I do care about the past. I do care about the preservation and the extension of freedom. And I have come to this congress mainly to listen to what is being done and suffered in other lands.

Although he repeats the word 'do' here, it is noteworthy that he doesn't capitalise it as Porter does, any more than he says that he cares about 'Liberty', which especially in the early 1950s was an American watchword.

There is a degree of mischief-making in Forster's identification of himself as a 'bourgeois', just as there will be in 'What I Believe', where he speaks of personal relationships being despised as 'bourgeois luxuries'. But this is serious mischief. Forster refuses to align himself with the determined – perhaps over-determined – anti-bourgeois stance of those attending the Paris Congress.

And this is why he modulates into an attack on what he calls the presence of 'Fabio-Fascism' in British life, which he defines as:

> [...] the dictator-spirit working quietly away behind the facade of constitutional forms, passing a little law (like the Sedition Act) here, endorsing a departmental tyranny there, emphasizing the national need for secrecy elsewhere, and whispering and cooing the so-called 'news' every evening over the wireless, until opposition is tamed and gulled.

The Sedition Act, 'passed last year by our so-called National Government', is one that strikes 'an open blow [...] against freedom of expression' and, by restoring the right of 'General Search [...] impedes the moral and political education of the soldier [...] encourages the informer, and [...] can be employed against pacifists' (64). With such an Act in existence, Forster says, it is easy to set up what he calls 'psychological censorship [...] and the human heritage is impaired' (65). And from this he moves to consider how, recently, the publishers of James Hanley's novel, *Boy*, which had appeared in 1930, were in 1934 successfully prosecuted for having 'published an obscene libel' (65).

This case, which has been written about before (Furbank has something to say on the subject, 223-4), is, I imagine, known to anyone at all interested in the 1930s. What concerns me is not the case itself but why Forster should make it central to his speech to the Congress. And to answer that question we have surely to consider what he means by 'Fabio-Fascism'. It is the spirit which, in its belief in abstract causes, considers itself justified in curbing freedoms which seem to or may be held to threaten those causes. Above all, it fears the unorthodox, which of course includes homosexuality. By 1935, Forster, who counted Isherwood among his close friends, would have known of Hitler's closing down the nightclubs of Berlin and other cities as part of a move against 'degeneracy'. He couldn't have read the following words, because they didn't appear until 1937, but the attitude they express was well entrenched by the time of the Congress:

> One sometimes gets the impression that the mere words 'Socialism' and 'Communism' draw towards them with magnetic force every fruit-juice drinker, nudist, sandal-wearer, sex-maniac, Quaker, 'Nature Cure' quack, pacifist and feminist in England.

And although Orwell, whose words these are, doesn't here use the phrase 'pansy poets', it hovers about his list of undesirables and will, of course, be produced on future occasions. As I pointed out in *The Radical Twenties* (118-25), you would be hard put to find such a list being trotted out by anyone on the Left in that decade, and this, as much as anything, might justify Forster's coinage of the term 'Fabio-Fascism'. And to sharpen this point, I will add that a month after Forster's address to the Congress in Paris, *Left Review* carried a full page cartoon by James Boswell which makes use of a comment by the Duke of Kent who had apparently said that 'there were few things in our life that gave more pleasure than flowers.' Accompanying this we get an assortment of caricatural heads of male homosexuals. Pansies, you see. Perhaps whispers about the Duke's own sexual predilections helped prompt Boswell's drawing, but this hardly excuses it. After all, the case against the Duke of Kent shouldn't have been that he was a closet gay.

The 1930s, whether to Left or Right, are undoubtedly marked by the kind of concern for 'purity' – of mind, body, political allegiance – which Orwell may pretend to despise but which he exemplifies in his snarling contempt for any show of eccentricity. Sitting beside 'an ordinary man' on a bus as two 'dreadful-looking old men got on' – both wearing shorts – he is aware that to his companion, who identifies them as socialists, 'a crank meant a Socialist and a Socialist meant a crank. Any Socialist, he probably felt, could be counted on to have *something* eccentric about him' (Orwell, 206). Lurking in the shadows of 'eccentricity' is the dread word 'degeneracy', which could be readily attached to anything thought not sufficiently pure, whether that turned out to be homosexuality or, for example, jazz. As far as I know, Forster never said anything about jazz, but such indifference or, possibly, restraint, is in itself worthy of note in a decade where by and large the orthodox reaction on the Left, quite as much as on the Right, was one of distrust deepening into downright condemnation of what the Marxist George Thomson would call 'debased commercialised music' (Thomson, 141). And his was by no means the most severe response. For Stalin, every bit as much as for Hitler, such music was anathema. It was, after all, the music of Blacks and, increasingly, Jews.

Forster's championing of James Hanley's novel isn't, then, an issue of marginal importance, even if that was how the Congress chose to see it. Censorship is the mortal enemy of freedom. In this context, it is worth pausing to consider Forster's comments on André Gide, whose novel *The Counterfeiters* he had perhaps over-praised in *Aspects of the Novel*, whom he met at the Congress, and about whom he wrote a piece in 1943, 'Gide and George' *(Two Cheers*, 233-6). There, he calls Gide a humanist, and he defines a humanist as possessing four characteristics: 'curiosity, a free mind, belief in good taste, and belief in the human race'. Furbank reports his praise of Gide's speech to the Congress, in which the French writer declared his belief that 'individuals and their peculiarities can best flourish in a communist society' (Furbank, 195). This was in line with the position of André Malraux, who had most to do with organising the Congress, and who explained that 'the Soviet Union, being frequently accused of neglecting or stifling culture, wanted a public opportunity for its writers to expound their ideas' (Furbank, 192). In view of this, it is piquant to learn that Gorki withdrew from the Soviet delegation for 'health reasons', and that Malraux, quite apart from wanting to stifle applause for Julien Benda's contribution, tried to tell delegates what they should say.

Forster's short essay on Gide is characterised by an habitual generosity of spirit the more commendable once you know that when they met in Paris in June 1935 Gide had more or less given him the cold shoulder. At all events, Forster, Gide and Malraux dined together, but at the conclusion of the meal, when Forster was anticipating conversation, the others abruptly got to their feet and left. Perhaps they feared that a threat to their communist conviction – especially new-found in Gide's case – might come from prolonged contact with the English writer. It reminds me, a little, of the later cold-shoulder turned by Sartre to Camus, and this prompts the reflection that there is a point of comparison to be made between Dr Rieux's remark in *The Plague*, to the effect that 'it's too damned silly living only for the plague', and Forster's remark towards the end of his speech to the Congress, that:

> One must behave as if one is immortal, and as if civilization is eternal. Both statements are false – I shall not survive, no more will the great globe itself – both of them must be assumed to be true if we are

> to go on eating and working and travelling, and keep open a few breathing holes for the human spirit.

These words come shortly after Forster has said that 'if nations keep on amassing armaments, they can no more help discharging their filth than an animal which keeps on eating can stop itself from excreting.' What then is a writer to do? 'We have just to go on tinkering as well as we can with our old tools until the crash comes.' After that 'if there is an after – the task of civilization will be carried on by people whose training has been different from my own' (67).

Reading those words I find coming into my head Auden's lines from 'A Summer Night' about the monsters which lie stranded among the wreckage of a post-cataclysmic world, and for whom 'sounds of riveting terrify/ Their whorled, unsubtle ears.' 'A Summer Night', which was written in June 1933, anticipates a coming collapse of the favoured and exclusive civilisation of those who shelter behind 'creepered walls' (*Look, Stranger!* Poem II, 13-16). Whether Forster had read Auden's poem is less important than his shared foreboding about a forthcoming smash. There is nothing at all unusual about this. You'd have needed to travel far and wide before finding someone who *didn't* anticipate some imminent disaster. But the point is that for Forster 'tinkering' has intrinsic value because it helps to keep open 'a few breathing holes for the human spirit'. 'A few', notice: no grand vision here. This is the essence of modesty.

Such modesty is very much to the point of the two pageants for which Forster at this time provides the working scripts. The 1934 *Abinger Pageant*, with music supplied by the socialist Vaughan Williams, is a simple enough re-telling of the history of that part of Surrey where Forster then lived, from pre-Roman times to the present. The narrator, a 'Woodman', ends up by asking his audience to consider whether it wants a future in which 'our Surrey fields and woodlands' are ruined by 'Houses and bungalows, hotels, restaurants and flats, arterial roads, by-passes, petrol pumps and pylons' *(Abinger Harvest*, 351). I am not here to defend this, although I will say that Forster's dismay over what would later be called 'planning blight' isn't as reactionary as may at first appear, and that it was and had been widely shared – by, among others, that principled man of socialist convictions, the architect Clough Williams Ellis and the equally radical poet, Ivor Gurney.

The Abinger Pageant was a parish affair. But the second pageant, *England's Pleasant Land: A Pageant Play*, written in 1938, again with music by Vaughan Williams, is rather more ambitious. Set in a slightly different part of Surrey, its historical narrative touches on the evil attending on eighteenth-century enclosures, new game laws, the mass emptying of the land as agricultural labourers move to the cities, and it ends with the arrival of the developers, the spokesman for whom is Jerry, who finds that as always the law is on his side. The pageant was written for the Dorking and Leith Hill Preservation Society, and Furbank tells us that Forster wanted to draw a parallel 'between the eighteenth-century enclosures, which had robbed the peasantry of their common land, and the twentieth-century death duties, which, in theory, returned their land to them – in theory, but not in practice.' Property developers will rob them all over again. The pageant's final episode features a kind of anti-masque 'of Horrors' in which, as Jerry and Bumble begin their dance, the direction reads:

> A procession of little bungalows […] fill the stage. Motor cars, motor bikes, motor buses, paper and empty tins. In the distance, more motor vehicles and masses of adverts. The people in the buses shriek and wave to the families in the bungalows, who shriek and wave back. Officials enter when the chaos is fully established, to plan regional development. Pedestrians are knocked down.

Forster's dislike of the motor car, which had first been voiced in *Howard's End*, here reaches what may seem to be an unintentionally comic apotheosis. Yet before we condemn it as regressive sentimentalism, we should note that Forster's pageant takes much from the Hammonds' *The Village Labourer*, and that his sympathetic inclusion of what Furbank calls the 'Labourers' Revolt of 1830' was almost certainly what led to the resignation of one of the pageant's sponsors, Lord Ferrars, who, Forster suspected, found that episode, in Forster's own words, altogether 'too bolshie' (Furbank, 238). We should also note that the following year the Communist Party of Great Britain devised a quite brilliant piece of film propaganda, intended to be shown in cinemas as part of the campaign for the General Election that the outbreak of war prevented, in which the hero is a farm labourer shown following his horse and plough over a field that can stand for England's pleasant land threatened, as ever, by rentier capitalists.

Of course it remains the case that Forster's two pageants will look to be tame, local events, and a far cry – in every sense – from the more typical public performances associated with radical activity in the 1930s: mass declamations, opera by the Clarion singers, the work of Unity Theatre and, for that matter, a huge pageant organised by the Co-operative Movement. This event, which took place in Wembley Arena on 2 July 1938, a week before *England's Pleasant Land* was presented in, so Forster says, 'surroundings of exquisite natural beauty', was to celebrate the Sixteenth Annual Co-operative Day. According to the Co-Op's souvenir programme (housed in the Co-op Library, Salford), proceedings featuring, as they say, a cast of thousands, began at 2.30, with 'Band Selections, and Clowning by Liley Bros. and Lofty', and ended with the Dagenham Girl Pipers, after which there was Ballroom Dancing until 11 pm at the Empire Stadium Ballroom. As for the pageant itself, some of which was filmed, and which was called 'Towards Tomorrow: A Pageant of Co-operation', the scenario was devised by Montagu Slater and André van Gyseghem (who also acted as pageant master – and, so I understand, demanded a considerable sum for his work), and music was composed and arranged by Alan Bush. Given that both Slater and Bush were Communist Party members, it is only to be expected that the eight 'episodes' of their pageant, which is, they tell us, about 'man and his will to cure the disease of his society and the darkness of his mind', should provide a socialist account of English history, from 'Merrie England' through to the glimpsed future, in which a Ballet of Young Workers is succeeded by an International Procession. The Programme notes that at this moment 'two decorated cars of PEACE and DEMOCRACY are drawn on by hundreds of children dressed in white'. The Co-operative Resolution is then read out:

> The Co-operators of the World [...]
>
> Renew the declaration of their unshakeable Faith in the Principles of Democracy, Freedom and Peace;
>
> Manifest their abhorrence of all interference with the Rights and Liberties of Free Peoples, and of any abrogation of their opportunities of Voluntary Association and Free Development;
>
> Proclaim their conviction that the Economic Principles and Social Ideals which lie at the basis of their World Movement constitute the best hope for the Regeneration of Society and the Surest Guarantee of Universal Peace Through Association;

Pledge Themselves, and their respective Co-operative Organisations, to redouble their efforts for the Defence of Freedom and to intensify their support of every means which afford the possibility of a Peaceful and Equitable Solution to the Present World Conflicts.

A dense white cloud of pigeons, with wings fluttering, rises up and disperses to all parts of Great Britain, carrying messages of greeting to other Co-operators.

Far more than a week seems to separate the event at Wembley from Forster's village pageant. And indeed the novelist's inherent distrust of public occasions, his preference for the small, the local, the unofficial, all come together in the Lilliputian scale of *England's Pleasant Land*. Moreover, making death duties the bogeyman which threatens England is bound to seem small beer compared to the various expressions of 'disease' which the Co-op pageant identifies as threatening people's health. It's as though, to apply to Forster the phrase by which he made C.P. Cavafy famous to Anglophone readers, he is 'standing at a slight angle' to the concern of others.

Nevertheless, there is more in common between Forster's village pageant, with its understanding of how dispossession works on individuals, and the Co-operative Day Pageant, than there is between either of them and Virginia Woolf's *Between the Acts*, the novel she began to think about in 1938 and which she eventually finished in

February, 1941, a month before she drowned herself. A pageant is at the heart of this novel, set in one country house and its estate, but it is one in which England is to be depicted from the Middle Ages to the time of Victoria, and in which the lives of the novel's characters – what happens between the acts – are remote from the social and political concerns that pageants address. In Woolf's novel the private lives of individuals are lived out in indifference to larger issues. In Forster's pageant, such lives are threatened and indeed overwhelmed by them, and even if we say that the threat seems inadequately presented, we should remember that at more or less the moment he was writing *England's Pleasant Land*, Forster was also writing 'What I Believe', in the course of which he says that force and violence are 'the ultimate reality.'

Forster arrives at this statement by means of an elaborate reading of Wagner's *Ring*, a work which had long fascinated him, as had all of Wagner's work, including *Parsifal*, whose story underpins *A Room with a View*. Force, so Forster says, 'gets out sooner or later, and then it destroys us and all the lovely things which we have made.' Fortunately, he adds, 'the strong are so stupid':

> Consider their conduct for a moment in the Nibelung's Ring. The giants there have the guns, or in other words the gold; but they do nothing with it, they do not realise that they are all-powerful, with the result that the catastrophe is delayed and the castle of Walhalla, insecure but glorious, fronts the

storms. Fafnir, coiled round his hoard, grumbles and grunts; we can hear him under Europe today; the leaves of the wood already tremble, and the Bird calls its warnings uselessly. Fafnir will destroy us, but by a blessed dispensation he is stupid and slow, and creation goes on just outside the poisonous blast of his breath. The Nietzschean would hurry the monster up, the mystic would say he did not exist, but Wotan, wiser than either, hastens to create warriors before doom declares itself. The Valkyries are symbols not only of courage but of intelligence; they represent the human spirit snatching its opportunity while the going is good, and one of them even finds time to love. Brunhilde's last song hymns the recurrence of love, and since it is the privilege of art to exaggerate, she goes even further, and proclaims the love which is eternally triumphant, and feeds upon freedom, and lives.

I suspect that these words, as much as any, prompted Auden's dedicatory sonnet to *Journey to a War*, first published early in 1939, where he writes of how learning and culture work against humankind's attraction to violence and hate, and confesses himself as among those who 'are closeted with madness', and who 'wish international evil'. Furbank reports an argument between Isherwood and Auden not long before Auden wrote the original version of this sonnet, in which Auden teased Isherwood about the latter's violent atheism, suggesting that he must be on the point of a conversion. In reply, Isherwood invoked Forster, saying that 'Morgan Forster was incapable of having truck with such "fascist filth"' (Furbank, 240).

With this in mind we can properly understand the famous remark that 'I hate the idea of causes, and if I had to choose between betraying my country and betraying my friend, I hope I should have the guts to betray my country.' The remark, which as I noted earlier has been held up for contempt by John Carey and others, is in fact – which means in context – not only defensible, it is entirely honourable. Here, then, is the passage in sufficient entirety:

> Personal relations are despised today. They are regarded as bourgeois luxuries, as products of a time of fair weather which is now past, and we are urged to get rid of them, and to dedicate ourselves to some movement or cause instead.
>
> I hate the idea of causes, and if I had to choose between betraying my country and betraying my friend, I hope I should have the guts to betray my country. Such a choice may scandalise the modern reader, and he may stretch out his patriotic hand to the telephone at once and ring up the police. It would not have shocked Dante, though. Dante places Brutus and Cassius in the lowest circle of Hell because they had chosen to betray their friend Julius Caesar rather than their country Rome […]. Love and loyalty to

an individual can run counter to the claims of the State. When they do – down with the State, say I, which means that the State would down me.

As Forster's account of the Ring would have made clear to all but the terminally stupid, the force he feared – the Strong – was Nazi Germany, even though when he sat down to write his essay, satirising Hitler was still not allowed in the British press. And here, when he speaks of the betrayal of friendship and of what was done in the name of Rome, he every bit as clearly intends to direct his readers' attention to Mussolini's increasingly brutal Fascism. This leaves those who, like Carey, deride Forster, in the position of appearing to say that dissident individuals, including homosexuals and – who knows? – Jews, should be handed over to the state and its agents, whether these happen to be the NKVD, the Hitler Youth Movement, or Mussolini's polizia. In which context, it is worth noting that in 1939 Forster wrote a short essay, 'Jew Consciousness', in which he remarked that 'A nasty side of our nation's character has been scratched up' and that:

> People who would not ill-treat Jews themselves, or even be rude to them, enjoy tittering over their misfortunes […]. The grand Nordic argument, 'He's a bloody capitalist so he must be a Jew, and as he's a Jew he must be a Red', has already taken root in our filling-stations and farms. (*Two Cheers*, 25)

Forster's unabashed admiration, in 'What I Believe', for the 'aristocracy of the sensitive, the considerate and the plucky' (*Two Cheers*, 82) gives priority to private faces in private places, as opposed to those who, in power, become 'crooked and sometimes dotty as well' (83). Forster's language, here as throughout, refuses to shift towards the rhetoric of public occasion. It remains steadfastly that of the private conversationalist. As such, it can be quietly devastating:

> The more highly public life is organised the lower does its morality sink; the nations of today behave to each other worse than they ever did in the past, they cheat, rob, bully and bluff, make war without notice, and kill as many women and children as possible; whereas primitive tribes were at all events restrained by taboos.

That was written in 1938. I don't know whether he was aware that at more or less the time he was working on his essay, Joseph Needham and a group of fellow biologists had formed the Cambridge-based Theoretical Biology Club. According to Stephen Rose, in his splendid *Lifelines: Life Beyond the Gene*, to which I owe my discovery of the Club, this was an expression among several of an 'almost underground non-reductionist tradition in biology', though 'their voices were and still are drowned out by an almost universal reductionist consensus' (78-9). Even if he did know of the Club, Forster, who as far as I know had no especial interest in the natural sciences, could have been no more than generally approving of a group which might be taken to threaten the universalist claims of, say, Lysenko or those who argued for the purity of the Aryan race or Nordic type, contempt for whose 'grand argument' we have already seen Forster expressing. But his love for those individuals who signal their continuing presence through the encroaching dark, the men and women whom he calls 'unquenchable lights of my aristocracy', and whom he imagines sending their message 'let's have a good time while we can', undoubtedly heartened Auden when, in the poem 'September 1, 1939', he, too, imagined the coming dark, where 'Defenceless under the night/Our world in stupor lies;/Yet, dotted everywhere,/Ironic points of light/Flash out wherever the Just/Exchange their messages' *(Another Time*, 112-15). I would even suggest that the voice with which Auden hopes to undo the folded lie in that poem is a Forsterian one.

By then, of course, Auden was in America. In England, Forster was asked by the BBC to broadcast talks to the nation. But not all were so lucky. With the coming of war, various performers, among them Alan Bush, found themselves blacklisted, in his case because he belonged to the 'People's Convention', a communist-run body. The blacklist was defended by Duff Cooper, Minister for Information, which suggested government-approved backing for the blacklist. The BBC Board of Governors had, Duff Cooper said, voluntarily resigned and left decision-making to him. This was news to the Governors. A mass protest meeting was held at Conway Hall on 17 March, and

Forster was one of the main speakers. Furbank describes how he read out a letter from Vaughan Williams protesting against Bush's victimisation, and he emphasised the need to be concerned for 'the smaller people. Because when important people are thrown overboard they make a big splash […]. But the smaller people don't make a splash; they vanish silently and the injustice never comes to light.' Three days after the meeting, Furbank tells us, 'Churchill promised in the House that the ban would be removed, and twelve days after that Duff Cooper announced the reconstitution of the BBC's Board of Governors', whom he had previously dismissed (Furbank, 240).

Nor was Forster done. Three years later, he gave a talk to coincide with the tercentenary of Milton's *Areopagitica*, in which he asked, would Milton have liked the wireless, and answered:

> Yes and No. He would have been enthusiastic over the possibilities of broadcasting, and endorsed much that it does, but he would not approve of the 'agreed script' from which broadcasters are obliged to read for security reasons. He believed in free expression and in punishment afterwards if the expression turned out to be illegal […]. You can argue that the present supervision of broadcasters is necessary and reasonable […]. But if you feel like that, you must modify your approval of the *Areopagitica*. […]. And do not say 'Oh it's different to-day – there's a war on.' There was equally a war on in 1644.

A year later, with the war coming to an end, Forster provided the script for Humphrey Jennings's film, *A Diary for Timothy*. The *donnée* for this is simple enough. The film opens at Christmas 1944, with the birth of a baby boy. What world will he grow up to join? Will it be one of peace, of social justice, of properly-paid work, or one in which the mistakes of the past are repeated? The film's slant is, I suppose, Labourite, redistributive. But, moving as I found it (I came upon a copy in a DVD of work for the Crown Film Unit that was part of the Paul Nash exhibition at Liverpool's Tate), I was irritated by Michael Redgrave's upper-class voice as he spoke Forster's words, and even more by the film's assumption that the infant Timothy would be from middle-class Oxford. It was therefore good to discover from Kevin Jackson's recent biography of Jennings that Forster was similarly irritated. Why shouldn't the infant have been born in working-class Liverpool, he wanted to know?

But he was dead set against social engineering, and in view of *Our Times* caricaturing him as clinging to the dying tree of, presumably, liberal England, it is equally good to know that in 1947, a year before the cartoon appeared, one of the magazine's contributors, the Communist Randall Swingler, tried to reassure him that 'Marxists share his awareness of the danger of mechanistic planning', and that Forster was right to criticise Marxists for sometimes being 'mechanistic, sectarian, philistine and dogmatic' (Croft 2003, 182). These are faults of which Forster can never be accused.

Acknowledgements

GRATEFUL THANKS TO RACHEL LUCAS FOR preparing the typescript of these essays for printing and for her unfailingly sharp editorial eye, grateful thanks also to Lawrence Sail for reviewing and suggesting corrections, to the superb Book Typesetters, to Ben and Emma, and, as always, to Pauline.

Especial thanks are due to Sue Wild of TeamWild PC Solutions, and to Sarah May and Gay Sharpe at Beeston Post Office for helpful instruction and guidance in matters relating both to word processing and the postal service.